Your Computer and the Law

ROBERT P. BIGELOW

SUSAN H. NYCUM

PRENTICE-HALL, INC., Englewood Cliffs, New Jersey

Library of Congress Cataloging in Publication Data

BIGELOW, ROBERT PRATT
    Your computer and the law.

    Includes bibliographical references and index.
    1. Computers—Law and legislation—United States.
I. Nycum, Susan H., joint author.   II. Title.
KF390.5.C6B5   340'.028'54   75-16332
ISBN 0-13-977983-3

© 1975, 1976 by Robert P. Bigelow and Susan H. Nycum

10 9 8 7 6 5 4 3

Printed in the United States of America

PRENTICE-HALL INTERNATIONAL, INC., *London*
PRENTICE-HALL OF AUSTRALIA, PTY. LTD., *Sydney*
PRENTICE-HALL OF CANADA, LTD., *Toronto*
PRENTICE-HALL OF INDIA PRIVATE LIMITED, *New Delhi*
PRENTICE-HALL OF JAPAN, INC., *Tokyo*
PRENTICE-HALL OF SOUTHEAST ASIA (PTE.) LTD., *Singapore*

CONTENTS

part one

Introduction

chapter 1

The Scope of the Book

This book is for the computer manager. More frequently than you may realize your activities as a computer manager affect your organization's legal position as well as your own. Purchases or sales of equipment or services, use of software packages, hiring and management of employees, research and development, installation security, advertising and marketing functions—all have legal implications, or even pitfalls. Some of these legal questions arise in most businesses; others, such as online security, are unique to the computer field.

This book points out the areas of activity where a lawyer should become involved and also acquaints you, the reader, with enough of the terminology and theories of law to enable you to work more effectively with counsel. It presupposes some knowledge and experience in data processing, but does not assume any training in law beyond that covered in high school.

While legal concepts must be introduced so that the reader can understand the material covered, this book is no substitute for a lawyer and his advice in particular situations. An old—and true—adage is "The man who tries to be his own lawyer has a fool for a client." This has been proven time after time in real life.

This book is designed for reference as well as for cover-to-cover reading. The individual sections and most chapters are self-contained units so that if you are interested only in contracting, for example, you can turn immediately to Chapter 9 and find the basic information necessary to understand that aspect of computer law. Cross references within that chapter note related sections in other chapters that may be of additional interest. Citations and footnotes are kept to a minimum except where necessary to explain a point.*

Subject coverage is organized by problem categories. Part I is introductory and includes an overview of the legal process and its professionals, the lawyers. Part II considers the legal aspects of primary management decisions concerning systems design. Part III discusses the knotty area of proprietary rights in computer products, particularly software. Part IV is an introduction to contract law and an application of that law to the computer environment. Part V, Computer Errors, discusses the newest concern of computer managers, computer abuses, and devotes a chapter to the implications of privacy considerations. Part VI, The EDP Manager, is directed specifically to the management problems of computer installations and to the legal aspects of day-to-day activities of that job.

---

*Attorneys can find much additional material in the *Computer Law Service,* a nine volume treatise first published in 1972 and updated frequently. Edited by Robert Bigelow and published by Callaghan and Company, Chicago, 1972.

The Service can be found in most large law libraries. The first four volumes contain articles and research materials and are cited CLSA; the remainder are case reports, cited as CLSR.

chapter 2

The Law and Lawyers

Law has been defined as a body of rules and methods, sanctioned by the state, by which society regulates the conduct of its members. The law is also used by society to define and redefine the relationships among its members and to create expectancies in them with respect to the nature and limitations of their rights, privileges, and obligations.

Because law is a set of rules and at the same time a distillation of man's constantly changing experience, it approaches—but never attains—consistency. The law is not frozen for all time or all activities, but is flexible and capable of growth and change. For example, the medieval concept of caveat emptor—let the buyer beware—has been softened by consumers' experiences in dealing with a sophisticated society. Today's buyers, using only their own caution, cannot always protect themselves. Therefore, the law, using warranties and actions for fraud, assists them in the marketplace. Buyers of computer products and services can avail themselves of both warranties explicitly made by the vendor and some that are implied by the law. (These and other aspects of buying computer products and services are discussed in Chapters 9 and 10.)

While the law is purposely flexible, matters are not left to informal decision or judicial whim. So that lawyers can to some degree predict what a court will decide, judges usually follow precedent when the same points of law arise in subsequent litigation involving different parties but substantially similar facts. This is particularly true when the point at issue is not covered by a statute enacted by the legislature. To enable their successors to understand the reasons behind these decisions, the judges write opinions which are published in a series of books called *reports*. These can be located by the *case citation*. For example the famous Benson case on software patents is reported in 409 U.S. 63, meaning that the opinion begins at page 63 of the 409th volume of the United States Reports.

When totally new fact situations are presented, for example, the unauthorized use of online programs or data, the courts may look to analagous situations in a non-computer environment to find the correct law to apply. Sometimes all historical parallels are too remote, and the matter must wait for the legislature to enact a statute specifically addressing the problem. Privacy legislation, now pending in many legislatures, is an example.

Most citizens come into contact with the law mainly through the courts in either criminal or civil matters. In criminal law a person is accused of a crime and tried—the state acting as the party suing him. The defendant is charged with committing an act against society and faces a jail sentence or a fine. In civil law, there are also two parties. The plaintiff claims injury by the defendant and sues the defendant for money damages. Automobile accidents and breaches of contract are typical civil court cases.

Generally, in civil actions, the courts award only money damages, but sometimes a plaintiff needs a court order in his favor. For example, you have in your possession an automobile which you rented from A for a month and just before you are ready to turn the car back to A, B comes along and says, "A sold me the car, give it to me." You call up A, who says, "I did not sell the car. Give it to me."

So, here you are with one car and two people claiming it. To complicate the matter, both A and B go to their lawyers and sue you for the value of the car.

To resolve this problem you make use of a branch of civil law known as *equity*. You go to court and say, "I have the car. One of these two people owns it, and I don't know which. If both their suits against me are successful, I will be out of pocket through no fault of my own." You then ask the judge to enjoin A and B from continuing their suits against you and to decide who owns the car. This *equity jurisdiction,* as it is called, is available in many situations where an order is needed to tell someone to do something or not to do something. Often you will see in the newspapers that a judge has entered an injunction. This just means that the judge is telling someone to do something, or not to do something.

The federal government and each state have a court system. The federal system provides one or more District Courts in each state; trials take place in these courts. A losing party then can appeal to one of eleven Circuit Courts of Appeal, covering different geographic areas; the case is heard by three judges. And in certain cases the party losing in a Court of Appeals can obtain further review by the United States Supreme Court; however, the Supreme Court can pick and choose its cases, and it accepts very few of them. (See Appendix A.)

At the state level, there is usually a similar arrangement of courts—trial, intermediate appeal, and state Supreme Court. The United States Supreme Court may accept an appeal from a state supreme court if the case involves the interpretation of the federal Constitution or a federal statute.

The *jurisdiction* (authority to render a decision in a case) of the federal courts is limited by the Constitution and by statute. Federal cases usually concern the enforcement of rights created by federal statute or the Constitution; the interpretation of these federal laws; or a dispute between citizens of different states. This latter jurisdiction was given to federal courts to insure that nonresident defendants (who may transfer certain cases from state to federal court) would not suffer from local prejudices.

While the courts play a major role in the law applied to computers, the computer manager is also directly affected by legislation, sometimes passed with the intention of affecting the company's business directly, sometimes touching it obliquely. Privacy laws regulating automated personal information systems have direct impact on computer managers. Tax legislation, while not directed specifically at the computer industry, is of concern particularly in deciding software and hardware procurement alternatives (see Chapter 5 for a discussion of taxes).

Statutes, the acts of the legislature, apply to all persons within the jurisdiction (nation, state, city) and therefore differ from court decisions which bind only those before the court as parties or those in *privity* with them (those in close relation to the parties such as heirs, agents, principals or assignees).

Legislative acts frequently provide for an administrative officer or an independent agency or commission to supervise compliance with the act. For example, the 1974 Koch-Goldwater bill on privacy (which was not enacted in this form) proposed a privacy board and provided for a right of appeal from the determinations of that privacy board to a designated court. Computer managers can be directly affected by administrative agency regulations. For example, the Federal Communications Commission has jurisdiction over data communications; this is discussed in Chapter 4. Appeals from most federal administrative agencies are directed to one of the eleven Courts of Appeal.

Lawyers, the professionals who work in the field of law, must be licensed in order to practice. Usually the licensing requirements include completion of law school, a passing grade on the state bar examination, and demonstration that the candidate is of sound moral character. A person meeting these requirements is sworn in as an officer of the courts of the state, and on request of a member thereof, admitted to practice in the local federal courts. Admission to the United States Supreme Court requires at least three years of local practice. All lawyers, whether or not practicing law, may lose their licenses for activities which do not meet the standards of professional responsibility of the state in which they are licensed.

What lawyers do in the actual practice of law depends on whether they are sole practitioners, or members of firms, which may have as few as two or more than two hundred members. Some lawyers specialize in litigation (the most publicized role of lawyers, thanks to television), and others are expert in patent, tax, workmen's compensation, antitrust, or probate law, or a host of other subsets of the substantive law.

Still other practitioners specialize by client and are experienced in the substantive laws that affect that client. Examples of these specialists are aeronautical lawyers, oil and gas experts, counsel for insurance companies or real estate firms, environmental protection experts, and computer lawyers. This last category is a growing group of lawyers who work on the special problems of the computer industry. They keep current in the specialty through the American Bar Association Section's of Science and Technology, The Computer Law Association, and through active membership in computer societies such as The Association for Computing Machinery (ACM), The Data Processing Management Association (DPMA), and the Computer Society of the Institute of Electrical and Electronic Engineers (IEEE/CS).

part two

Legal Considerations in Systems Design

chapter 3

Management

and the Computer

The electronic data processing (EDP) professional who reads this book is probably employed by a private company or a government agency, and has to work with all levels of management and personnel. Some of these people fear the computer, others embrace its use wholeheartedly. But the typical person has ambivalent feelings,—sometimes he'll like it, sometimes he'll hate it, and sometimes he just won't care. The computer installation with which such a reader is concerned can range from an IBM System/32 or smaller, up to a giant complex renting for hundreds of thousands of dollars per month. The smaller the equipment the less likely that management will have a sophisticated knowledge of the computer's capabilities. It will be up to you to teach management what the computer can do, and, equally important, what it cannot do. In small installations management may well expect more from the machinery than is economically feasible within the EDP budget.

Especially with the first time user, the contract may have been signed and equipment acquired before you came on board. What management remembers about the computer's capability as told by the sales representative will probably differ from what was actually said and will certainly differ from what is written in the contract.

And yet, in all but the smallest businesses, the computer has become a necessary tool for the preparation and maintenance of the records that management needs. A company that still uses hand methods for payroll, accounting, and inventory control, when all of its competitors are using data processing methods—in-house or service bureau—may well find that its overhead costs are much higher than those of the rest of the industry. And, stockholders who are not affiliated with management may become dissatisfied with the return of their investment, and file suit against management.

As EDP professionals know, the installation of a computer system does not go easily and often management must be persuaded of the truth of Murphy's Law that in any major project things will go wrong—at the worst possible time. Harvey Golub, a partner in MacKenzie & Co., Inc. refined this for computer people; in an article in *Data Management* (Sept. 1972, p. 28), he states his law: "No major computer project is ever installed on time, within budget, with the same staff that started it, nor does the project do what it is supposed to . . . it is highly unlikely that yours is going to be the first." In the same article, Golub's partner, John A. Groobey, lists three corollaries of this law:

1. The benefits will be smaller than initially estimated, if estimates were made at all.
2. The system finally installed will be installed late and won't do what it is supposed to.
3. It will cost more but it will be technically successful.

RESTRICTIONS ON THE USE OF COMPUTERS

Although a computer is primarily an office machine, it is different; it is an extraordinarily efficient machine that when properly programmed can, in effect, make decisions for the corporation. Corporations are, in the eyes of the law, run by their boards of directors, who elect officers and delegate to those officers the day-to-day execution of the company's business. The officers, in turn, hire other people to perform specified jobs with limited authority to act.

Under the law, the directors can usually delegate only those powers needed to perform the ordinary and routine jobs of the corporation. The power to inaugurate radical changes in fundamental policies and methods of conducting the business is reserved to the board of directors. Of course, in a large company officers have great authority in the day-to-day management of the corporation. But legally they are still responsible to the board of directors (who represent the stockholders) and major policy decisions must be made at the board level.

A computer can be programmed to make decisions of either a routine or nonroutine nature, but if the decisions are nonroutine, the program may inadvertently assume some of the powers of the board of directors! Such a situation might arise with an extremely advanced company-wide management information system under which the production of exception reports is determined through a complex series of programs designed by the EDP department, with limited input and review by the operating departments. Unless the parameters of those exception reports have been approved by top management, with a full understanding of what is involved, the board of directors could be held liable to dissatisfied stockholders. If the management information system produced so few reports that the board of directors did not get the information it needed to manage the company properly, the directors could likewise be held liable. Stockholder suits against directors generally occur only when the corporation has lost a lot of money; trustees in bankruptcy may also sue directors for not doing their job properly.

Of course, most report systems do not involve such serious consequences. Usually, a poorly designed report system results in firings and in adverse reaction to the data processing department.

Regulations applicable to a particular industry may, directly or indirectly, restrict computer use. Some years ago a life insurance company proposed to perform computerized record-keeping functions for its mortgage correspondents. Fortunately the question was referred to the company's lawyers, who decided that a provision of the state's insurance law prohibited such services. For a number of years there has been a continuing debate on whether banks can provide data-processing services for their customers in competition with service bureaus; the topic has been a matter of litigation, in one form or another, brought by ADAPSO against the banks, which argues that the banks can charge less because they claim to use only excess capacity. Another situation that could inhibit the "efficient" use of the computer is in an inventory control system programmed to place refill orders with suppliers based on the amount of business the suppliers had given the company doing the ordering; such a backscratching operation may well violate the antitrust laws.

CORPORATE RECORD-KEEPING REQUIREMENTS

Corporations are established under specific statutes in each of the fifty states (with similar statutes in other countries). These statutes require that certain corporate records be maintained and, sometimes, that they be maintained in specific ways. At the beginning of a new computer application involving company records, it is advisable that the corporate attorney check the proposed application, since there may be legal aspects that could affect the value of the application. For example, in Delaware a corporation may keep its records, including its stock ledger, on punch cards, magnetic tape, or microphotographs. But the statute also requires that those records "can be converted into clearly legible written form within a reasonable time. Any corporation shall convert any records so kept upon request of any person entitled to inspect the same." For the convenience of the corporation it might be very nice not ever to have to provide a clearly legible written print-out of stock records kept in machine form. After all, the mailing of dividend checks and proxy notices doesn't require a print-out. But, under the law, in certain instances any stockholder can get a copy of the stockholders' list, and Delaware law clearly requires that the system be able to provide it, at the corporation's expense.

When accounting records are kept in machine-readable form, it is sometimes necessary to produce a print-out in order to collect an unpaid bill. In general, the courts have admitted these machine print-outs as evidence that the bill was due. But not always. In 1971, a court in Texas refused to admit into evidence the computer print-out of a customer's purchase of securities when the data had been taken from hand-written order blanks, keypunched by employees of the brokerage firm, processed by a service bureau, and returned in print-out form. The court refused to admit the data since there was no proof that the person who prepared the order blanks had any personal knowledge of the data or of the information that had been keypunched (Arnold D. Kamen & Co. v. Young, 4 CLSR 444, 466 S.W. 2d 381). A point-of-sale system, with remote entry into other records, which does not produce, at the very beginning, a hard copy that can be authenticated by the customer could very easily provide insufficient authentication for the record to be considered valid in a court.

Joseph S. Elmaleh, a lawyer and computer man, has prepared "A Guide to the Perplexed" which may help readers:

> In the creation of computer systems for business, the system designer should constantly be aware of the evidentiary problems which may be raised by the use of machines. All too frequently the design is done by engineers not conversant with the problems they may create, while at the same time the potential user, having complete faith in the "thinking" machine fails to realize what is happening. It is therefore my purpose to set forth a meta-algorithm for the design of such systems.
>
> 1. A careful review must be made of all records maintained in the user's manual accounting system.
> 2. Every "bit" of information which is recorded in the manual accounting system must be recorded in the machine accounting system.
> 3. To the greatest extent possible each business transaction should be described and recorded in a single logical computer record.
> 4. No document need be retained in "hard-copy" which can be generated on an ad hoc basis from information contained in the computer record.
> 5. The system should be designed in as simple and straightforward a manner as possible so that its workings can easily be explained to court and jury if necessary.

The meta-algorithm appears simple, but its implementation is not. Computers and computer storage are expensive. On the other hand the computer offers users management information and statistics which were virtually unobtainable using conventional methods. Designers may be tempted to reduce the information necessary to establish business transactions as a trade-off for management statistics. This trade-off should not be permitted.

In the design of real-time and inter-communicating systems, it is mandatory that there be a means of identifying transmitting computers, and providing a means of establishing the computer's "authenticity" to act for its user. (J.S. Elmaleh, "Evidentiary Concepts in a Computerized Society," 3 *Computer Law Service,* Section 5-4.1, Article 1, 1972.)

In a number of industries certain procedures are required for computer records and some companies are required to keep their records in machine-readable form. These companies are usually large organizations that have their own law department and that should be familiar with these new laws as they come down (for further information see *Computer Law Service,* the introduction to Section 2-1 and Appendix 2-1a). One particular rule that applies very widely is the permission granted by the Occupational Safety and Health Administration for employers to maintain the log of occupational injuries in machine-readable form under certain conditions. (See 29 CFR 1904.2, CLS Appendix 2-1a, No. 3.)

An actual example of improper reliance on computer records, and possibly improper delegation, arose when the Columbia Gas Company of Ohio used a computer to generate notices to allegedly delinquent customers that the gas would be shut off; many of these notices were inaccurate; those that were accurate were frequently not followed by an actual shutoff; and sometimes the notice arrived after the gas had been shut off. The court noted that while the highly computerized collection and termination practices of the company had been governed by a need for efficiency in the protection of its assets, the United States Constitution recognized higher values than speed and efficiency. The Court held that the procedures used by the gas company did not satisfy the due process clause of the Fourteenth Amendment (Palmer v. Columbia Gas Co. of Ohio, Inc., 4 CLSR 705, 342 F. Supp. 241, aff'd 4 CLSR 761, 479 F. 2d 153).

TAX RECORDS

Compliance with Internal Revenue Service requirements in the maintenance of records is vitally important to any business using computerized techniques. Though the story may be apocryphal, one of the authors was once told by an official of the Internal Revenue Service that a company listed on the New York Stock Exchange failed to comply with these requirements when it designed its computer system. The Internal Revenue agents would not accept any records produced by this system, and the entire project had to be redone at great expense.

In 1964, the Internal Revenue Service issued a set of guidelines for the basic record requirements for the records it felt essential when the taxpayer maintained its records on a computerized system. These required primarily that the general ledger and certain subsidiary ledgers be printed out with appropriate references at certain times; that the audit trail be designed so that the hard copy underlying the summary accounting data could be identified and examined; that the records provide an opportunity to trace any transaction back to its original source or forward to final total; and that the programs be documented in sufficient detail to indicate the application, the procedures involved therein, the controls used to insure accuracy, and the chronological record of changes. Finally "adequate record retention facilities must be available for storing tapes and printouts as well as all applicable supporting documents" (Revenue Procedure 64-12, CLS Appendix 2-3.1a No. 2).

In 1971 the Internal Revenue Service defined in more detail what records had to be kept. In essence, the government requires that practically every machine-readable record be retained until tax liabilities have been terminated. However, the IRS will reach agreement with individual companies to reduce the number of records that need to be so retained; experience during the first few years of this procedure indicates that the Internal Revenue Service has been quite accommodating in limiting the number of records required. Without such an agreement and without the "punched cards, magnetic tapes, discs, and other machine-sensible data media used for recording, consolidating and summarizing accounting transactions and records with a taxpayer's automatic data processing system," the company could be required to prepare complete hard-copy records from invoices and vouchers. (See Revenue Procedure 71-20, reproduced as Appendix B).

Since 1967 the Internal Revenue Service has permitted the filing of certain tax returns on magnetic tape. These include forms W-2, 1099, 1087, 941, and 1042F. Detailed specifications for filing such returns are set forth in Revenue Procedures issued by the Internal Revenue Service. In many cases, these specifications change slightly from year to year, and what is proper one year may not be proper the next. A computer manager must maintain close liaison with the accounting or the tax department.

STANDARDS

There are problems of standards and compatibility throughout the computer industry. For example, a USA standard COBOL has been adopted by the federal government and all COBOL compilers delivered to the Department of Defense since the beginning of 1970 have had to meet this standard. The American Standard Code for Information Interchanges (ASCII) has likewise been adopted by presidential order pursuant to the Brooks Bill, and is required on federally procured equipment since July 1, 1969. The federal government's emphasis on standards will reduce complaints such as that of the Air Force, which reported difficulties with the interconnection of the variety of systems that is has purchased over the years. Joseph F. Cunningham,* while Director of the ADP Management Staff, Bureau of the Budget (and later Executive Director of ACM) has called for standardization in application packages, data element definitions, code representations, recording media, and programming languages "to eliminate or at least minimize conversion costs, thereby achieving optimum flexibility with greater economy." Dr. Grace Hopper** has warned management to:

*J.F. Cunningham, "The Need for ADP Standard in the Federal Community." *Datamation,* Vol. 15, Feb. 1969, p. 26.
**Grace M. Hopper, "Standardization and the Future of Computers." Data Management, Vol. 8, April, 1970, p. 32-33.

. . . be aware (1) that not only do they have a computer "in the house" to be programmed, but, further, that it will ultimately be replaced by one or more different computers, (2) that not only must programs be written, debugged and maintained but also transferred to another computer, probably of the next generation and possibly built by a different manufacturer, (3) that programmers may be assigned to continue the work of another programmer, they may be transferred, they may be promoted.

Federal government efforts at enforcing standards and improving compatibility will help prevent wasteful duplication of effort and equipment.

The competing interests of the various industries on compatibility and standards were well expressed by Walter M. Carlson, former president of the Association for Computing Machinery, when he said,

> Each manufacturer wants to preserve uniqueness and exclusivity to gain the rewards of a special position in the marketplace. Each user wants to have a wide choice among standards, compatible options to increase competitive pressures and to reduce costs, while obtaining no loss of efficiency. Each long-established industry (communications, electrical manufacturing, banking, transportation, to name a few) wants to prevent the newly emerging computer technologies from disrupting or bypassing conventions and national standards promulgated by that industry. Each professional wants freedom to explore innovative solutions to his tasks without being forced to use standards that are based upon what he considers obsolescent technology. Each manager wants to reduce or eliminate the risk of unnecessary experimentation when tried and proven approaches are available. (Communications of the ACM, February 1970.)

The American National Standards Institute in New York, a private organization which acts as a clearing house for standardized procedures in the United States, has issued a number of standards in the computer field ranging from the meaning of words to such staples as the American Standard Code for Information Interchange (ASCII). Some of these standards have been adopted by the federal government and are frequently included as part of the contract terms for government procurements.

Data-processing trade and technical associations such as the Data-Processing Management Association (DPMA) and the Association for Computing Machinery (ACM) have adopted standards of conduct for their members that they call guidelines. Similarly, standards may be adopted by particular industry groups that use computers (MICR coding on checks is one example) and an individual company may establish standards of documentation and procedure for use by its own personnel.

The data-processing department must be aware of these standards and be prepared to explain not only to management, but possibly also in court, why it has chosen not to follow a particular standard in a particular situation. The fact that the manager was unaware that the standard existed is no excuse. Neither management nor a jury is persuaded by the "expert" who has to say "Gee, I never heard of it."

chapter *4*

Data Communications

This chapter discusses some of the regulatory forces at work in the computer and communications industries and some of the current legal problems of interest to developers and users of computer networks and utilities. Topics considered include the computer-communications interface, wire communications, CATV, microwave, and satellites, tariffs, multiple suppliers, network regulation, and antitrust considerations.

THE REGULATORY FORCES

To provide a framework for these legal problems, it may be helpful first for us to outline the various forces which in one way or another

*This chapter is abridged from a paper ("Some Legal and Regulatory Problems of Multiple Access Computer Networks.") first prepared for the Interdisciplinary Conference on Multiple Access Computer Networks, and published in that form in *Jurimetrics Journal,* Vol. 11, p. 47, December 1970. © 1970, 1972, 1974, 1975, 1976 by Robert P. Bigelow.

have an impact on the development of the industry. When we first studied the political organization of the United States, we were taught that there are three levels of government—federal, state, and local—and that the federal government has three branches:— the executive, the legislative, and the judicial. In the federal government the three branches are designed to act as checks and balances on each other so that no one branch becomes overly powerful. However, as our federal government has developed it seems to have acquired a fourth branch: the so-called independent agencies. When we deal with the question of communications and computers, we become involved with all four branches, the executive, the Congress, the courts, and the aforementioned independent agencies.

The basic source of regulation in the computer and communications industries is, of course, congressional legislation. Two acts have particular relevance here: the Communications Act of 1934, and the Communications Satellite Act of 1962.

Agencies

The Communications Act of 1934 established the Federal Communications Commission and gave it, as a general matter, control of all "interstate and foreign communications by wire or radio and all interstate and foreign transmission of energy by radio." It did not give the Commission control of intrastate communication service; this was reserved to the states. So far as computers have been concerned, state authority has not been much of a problem until recently; however, federal-state relationships have created some problems in the interconnection, specialized-common-carrier, and CATV fields. Within the FCC our prime interest is with the work of the Common Carrier Bureau, and secondarily, with the CATV Bureau. A common carrier is defined as "any person engaged as a common carrier for hire, in interstate or foreign communication by wire or radio, or in interstate or foreign transmission of energy (except radio broadcasters)". Common carriers must "furnish such communication service upon reasonable request therefor" (47 USC§201a) and all their "charges, practices, classifications, and regulations for and in connection with such communication service, shall be just and reasonable, and any such charge, practice, classification, or regulation that is unjust or unreasonable is declared to be unlawful" (47 USC § 201b). The common carriers must file their rates, and hearings can be held on such rate filings either after complaints by a third party or upon the commission's own notice. The Common Carrier Bureau has been in charge of telephone filings, specialized microwave common carriers, and domestic satellites, as well as interconnect problems and new developments such as multipoint distribution service. That bureau originally handled cable television, but a new bureau to handle this specific area was established by the commission in 1970.

Somewhat analogous to an independent agency is INTELSAT, the International Telecommunications Satellite Consortium. This was created in 1964 with the express purpose of establishing and developing a planetwide commercial satellite system. Over 60 nations are members of this consortium which owns and operates the international satellites; the United States, which has made the major investment, is represented by COMSAT.*

Executive Branch

Several offices in the executive branch are concerned with computers and communications. Directly under the President is the Office of Management and Budget which is charged with fiscal and policy control of the government's automatic data processing equipment and review of the General Services Administration's decisions.

Another office directly under the President is the Office of Telecommunications Policy (which has assumed the functions of the former Director of Telecommunications Management). The director of this office serves as the President's principal advisor on federal telecommunications policy in both the domestic and international spheres, manages radio spectrum resources for the federal

---

*For a discussion of INTELSAT, see Chapter 3 of the *Final Report of the President's Task Force on Communications Policy,* December 7, 1968 (often called the Rostow Report).

government, makes recommendations to the FCC on civilian spectrum management, presents the position of the executive branch on policy issues to Congress and the FCC, administers national communications resources in the event of war (under HUD), and coordinates federal assistance in telecommunications matters to state and local governments. The Office of Telecommunications Policy is responsible for the planning and operation of the federal government's communications systems, including the development of governmental standards for equipment and procedures; evaluation of the various national communications resources for security and emergency requirements; recommendations to the Budget Bureau for funding communications systems and research and development programs; and preparation of guidelines for economical procurement of federal communications services. Research assistance for the Office is provided by the Commerce Department.

The Department of Commerce controls several organizations that have taken a considerable interest in computers. Among these are the Office of Telecommunications, which provides support for the Office of Telecommunications Policy and performs research functions, and the National Bureau of Standards with its Center for Computer Sciences Technology.

Other examples of executive involvement in the regulation of communications are the various federal communications networks, the largest of which is administered by the Defense Communications Agency in the Department of Defense. In mid-1972, the General Services Administration designated the National Communications System (NCS) to represent the government as a user in the development of telecommunications standards in computer-communications interface. Communications research and development is currently being done by the Departments of Defense and Commerce and NASA; the latter also provides launch services for satellites. Even the State Department has communications responsibilities pursuant to the Communications Satellite Act and the Cable Landing Act.

Congress

The General Accounting Office, under the Comptroller General (an official appointed by Congress), has issued decisions on procurement of computer communications and services. The major impact of Congress, however, is in the legislation it passes and in the hearings it holds.

Judiciary

The judiciary serves as a regulator of communications and computers through court decisions interpreting both federal law (including many knotty communications problems) and as an arbitrator between private litigants, particularly in the interconnect field. If the federal government's antitrust suit against the American Telephone and Telegraph Company reaches trial, the court's decision could have a major effect upon data communications.

Other Regulatory Forces

The state governments, by their procurement policies and legislative and licensing policies, and local utilities commissions, which determine the propriety of intrastate telephone rates and competition, can have considerable effect upon the form that multiaccess computer networks will take. As noted below, there are major state efforts in the interconnect field at the present time.

We should not forget the regulatory influences within the computer and communications industries themselves. The activities of American National Standards Institute and its counterparts in other countries, should also be considered. There are many organizations within the computer industry that have taken positions or expressed opinions with respect to legal and regulatory matters: these include the Association of Data Processing Service Organizations (ADAPSO), with its two subsections, one concerned with Computer Time-Sharing (CTSS), the other with software (formerly the Association of Independent Software Companies); the Computer and Business Equipment Manufacturers Association (CBEMA); the Computer Industry Association (CIA); the Electronic Industries Association (EIA); the Data Processing Management Association (DPMA); the Association for Computing Machinery (ACM); the American Federation of Information Processing Societies (AFIPS); the Computer Society of the Institute of Electrical and Electronic Enginerrs (CSIEEE); The Society of Certified Data Processors (SCDP); the Computer Peripheral

Manufacturers Association; and the Computer Lessors Association. In the communications industry there are organizations such as the United States Independent Telephone Association (USITA), the North American Telephone Association (NATA), and the Independent Data Communications Manufacturers Association.

Finally there are user organizations, many of which filed responses to the FCC inquiry into the interrelationship between computers and communications (1966-1973). These included such organizations as the American Bankers Association, American Truckers Association, Association of American Railroads, National Association of Manufacturers, Federal Reserve Board, and Inter-University Communications Council (EDUCOM). Each of these organizations, by developing a position with respect to regulation, affects the legal and the regulatory attitudes of those who legislate or administer. By adopting positions, these organizations also determine, to some degree, how their constituent members will conduct themselves. In so doing, such an association treads a narrow line between improving the conduct of its members and coercing their conduct in violation of the antitrust laws.

LEGAL AND REGULATORY PROBLEMS IN COMMUNICATIONS MANAGEMENT

Having reviewed the regulatory forces, let us now examine some of the areas where legal and regulatory problems have arisen and where they may arise.

Foreign Attachments and Interconnect

For many years, the telephone companies took the position that all equipment which connected directly or indirectly to the dial network had to be supplied by the telephone company. The major challenge to this position was made by Thomas F. Carter, the inventor of the so-called Carterfone, which acts as an interconnecting device between the telephone network and a mobile radio system. When the telephone caller speaks, the voice control circuit in the Carterfone switches on the radio transmitter; the circuit returns the radio transmitter to a receiving condition when the telephone caller stops talking. The crucial decision in the Carterfone case came from the Federal Communications Commission on June 26, 1968 (Carterfone, 1 CLSR 1019, 13 FCC 2d 420 and 1 CLSR 1030, 14 FCC 2d 149,), when the Commission held that the tariff filed by the Bell system which provided that "no equipment, apparatus, circuit or device not furnished by the Telephone Company shall be attached to or connected with the facilities furnished by the Telephone Company, whether physically, by induction or otherwise. . . ." was unreasonable and discriminatory. The Commission said that a ". . . customer desiring to use an interconnecting device to improve the utility to him of both the telephone system and the private radio system should be able to do so, so long as the interconnection does not adversely affect the Telephone Company's operations or the telephone system's utility for others" (1 CLSR at 1025); the Commission did hold that the Telephone Company could prevent use of devices which would cause actual harm to the network, and could set up reasonable standards for interconnecting devices.

The Bell System was obviously not pleased with the Commission's ruling, and has based its continued opposition on arguments about safety of the network. The FCC requested the Computer Science and Engineering Board of the National Academy of Science to study the question in more detail. The NAS report, delivered in June 1970, found that uncontrolled access would be harmful and that technical requirements for interconnection should be established. The NAS study was limited to technical considerations; these and the economic considerations were studies by Dittberner Associates who rendered a report to the FCC in September 1970. Dittberner recommended:

> . . . that customer-provided equipment be allowed to interconnect directly to common carrier networks without the necessity of common-carrier-provided interconnecting arrangements as long as such equipment meets common carrier developed and FCC approved standards for network protection capability and is installed and maintained by an FCC certified installation/maintenance organization or individual

contractor. [The summary of the report] is printed in 4CLS, App. 6-5a, No. 2.]

Since the Dittberner report, there has been some interconnection. Some state public utility commissions have permitted interconnection, while others, notably Nebraska, Oklahoma and North Carolina have taken the position that equipment supplied by noncommon carriers cannot be connected to the intrastate network. So far the Federal Courts have generally supported the FCC.

In the fall of 1975 the Commission ruled that registered customer owned terminal equipment with protective circuitry could be hard wired to the telephone network without modems. This ruling was scheduled to go into operation on May 1, 1976, but was delayed by court order. A number of bills have been filed in Congress to prohibit interconnection.

To further complicate the matter, some interconnect companies have commenced antitrust cases against the common carriers; the courts customarily have referred the technical questions to the FCC. In at least one case, the court requested and got very prompt action by the Commission (Chastain, 4 CLSR 586, 4 CLSR 1225, 43 FCC 2d 1079).

Any company considering the interconnection of communications equipment to the common carrier network should consider the particular problems that will be encountered with two suppliers. A number of these are considered, primarily in the light of voice communications, in the Interconnect Contract Checklist, Appendix C. The discussion of the general subject of multiple suppliers later in this chapter and in Chapter 10 may also be helpful.

Data Paths

Determining the rules under which various kinds of data paths are to be established and maintained is another area of communications management which has given birth to many regulatory problems. Regulatory problems have already arisen in data transmission by wire, microwave, cable television, and satellite. A very informal ruling has held that the transmission of data by laser is subject to FCC jurisdiction. Infrared data transmission is now feasible over short distances, but we have been told that at the present time the FCC considers that the low frequencies used by infrared are beyond the spectrum subject to regulation. The Bell system is experimenting with waveguide transmission and expects to have this operable by 1979.

Wire

When we look at the data paths by wire we find an analog system designed to carry voice, not data, and requiring multiple conversion and reconversion of electronic signals to and from audible signals through use of modems. We find a plant in which the telephone companies have invested millions of dollars in cable and switching equipment. We find in many places a system which cannot now handle the traffic it has, much less the requirements of multiple-access computer networks. Some frustrated users even sue because of poor service. One response by the telephone companies appears to have been to raise intrastate rates for Information System Access Lines; this has been, so far, successfully fought by the time-sharing services. The effect of such rate changes, especially on regional networks, might provide a reason for the FCC to get into the regulation of intrastate rates, at least in the time-sharing area. This will depend on whether the courts will sustain a possible FCC holding that the entire communications path is interstate or whether past decisions that the terminal equipment is intrastate will be followed.

Another hot area in wire communications is the multiple channel offerings, originally Telpak. The history of Telpak is rather long and involved; it has been the subject of numerous hearings before the FCC and even a major court case in which the Telpak A and B rates were held discriminatory. One problem in the Telpak area is the reasonableness of Bell's tariff providing for higher rates for both Telpak C and D and the series 11,000. Another Telpak problem relates to the provision in the Telpak tariff that allowed regulated users, such as airlines and utilities, to split up Telpak channels between themselves, but prohibited nonregulated entities from doing the same thing. This became the subject of an FCC inquiry. On June 10, 1970, the Commission held that AT&T and Western Union were engaged in unlawful discrimination by distinguishing between regulated and nonregulated companies in permitting sharing of Telpak lines. The FCC's decision on discrimination was sustained, but its order was reversed on technical grounds. The FCC ordered Bell to eliminate discrimination; to which Bell responded by dropping the Telpak tariff completely. Despite the pleas of users, the Commission refused to prescribe shared rates, and its action was sustained on appeal. Recently, other provisions allowing certain customers to share facilities have come under attack, and the FCC has begun a further investigation of this approach.

Additional wire communications are now the subject of investigation, such as Message Toll Telephone Service (MTS) and Wide Area Telephone Service (WATS), packet-type transmission based on the Advanced Research Projects Agency (ARPA) network studies and Multipoint Distribution Services (MDS).

The Bell system has proposed the establishment of additional data services, the first step of which is its Digital-Under-Voice (DUV) technology. In June 1973, the commission approved the building of the first stage of this network, but postponed other policy questions, such as the reasonableness of the tariff and resale rights, for further consideration. In early 1975, the Bell system received the Commission's approval, but the decision was then appealed to the courts.

CATV

Another type of wire communication, but one which should be considered separately, is community antenna television systems. These are high-capacity cables which can be converted to broadband uses; when the CATV Bureau was created by the FCC in February 1970, there were over 2,000 systems serving about 12 million viewers. The potential for data transfer by cable television networks is immense. One editorial writer predicted, "but a few short steps before each home and commercial office is linked by a wired network similar to the phone system supplying 20 TV channels of programming, pay TV, motion pictures, data communications, microfilm versions of library books, facsimile versions of newspapers, computerized banking, computer assisted instruction, retail merchandise display, direct stock exchange quotations, and almost anything else the mind can conceive."*

The relationship between the cable television industry, the broadcasting industry, the FCC, and the local regulatory agencies has been stormy to say the least. In 1968 the FCC ruled that under section 214 of the Communications Act, cable television systems were interstate service and telephone companies could not construct such systems without FCC approval. This was upheld by the court of appeals in Washington. The Supreme Court ruled in 1970 that the FCC has authority to regulate CATV systems, and later affirmed a decision permitting a state to regulate CATV to the extent it is not regulated by the FCC. As a result of these decisions, and another by the Sixth Circuit Court, the FCC instituted an inquiry into the method of resolving the federal-state relationship.

Challenges to the FCC continue, primarily involving rules relevant to data communications. In a series of cases the courts have backed the Commission, though sometimes by narrow margins.

The Federal Communications Commission has also issued a rule prohibiting telephone companies from entering the CATV business in areas where they offer voice service and giving those who are already in it four years to get out. As might be expected, the ruling was appealed; the Commission's decision was affirmed. One part of the ruling in this case is of particular interest because of its possible implications for the data-processing industry. The Commission noted that the telephone companies have a monopoly position in the community through control of the pole lines required for the construction and operation of the system, and further noted that this gave the telephone company an opportunity to favor itself in providing service. In August 1973 the Commission asserted jurisdiction over pole-line attachment rates.

New rules governing CATV transmission were issued in February 1972. As the Commission put it:

---

*Martin Nussbaum, "The Cable." *Data Processing Magazine* **12,** 10 (Jan. 1970).

. . . the rules we are adopting are the result of a number of interwoven proceedings. The program is designed as a single package because each part has impact on all the others. Our concerns may generally be divided into four main areas:

television broadcast signal carriage;
access to, and use of nonbroadcast cable channels, in-
    cluding minimum channel capacity;
technical standards;
the appropriate division of regulatory jurisdiction be-
    tween the federal and state-local levels of govern-
    ment. [Cable Television Report and Order, 36 FCC
    2nd 141, 147, 3 CLSR 425, 431 (1972).]

Most of the new rules deal with broadcasting requirements; however, data communications received particular impetus from the requirement of two-way communications capability in every system 20-channel capacity as a minimum. This requirement is now (1976) being re-evaluated.

Microwave

In the category of wireless data paths, microwave offers a means of transmitting data without the necessity of converting the data into audible signals. Private microwave lines have been in use for a number of years, particularly by the railroads. But until recently, the only microwave facilities available to the public have been under control of the telephone and telegraph companies. Some years ago, a company called Microwave Communications, Inc. (MCI) applied for a construction permit to establish microwave facilities for public use from Chicago to St. Louis. The application was violently opposed by the telephone companies and Western Union. Hearings were held in 1967 and in July of that year the Common Carrier Bureau issued proposed findings of fact and conclusions favoring the application. On appeal to the full Commission, the Common Carrier Bureau's position was adopted by a four to three vote on August 14, 1969. The main argument in opposition, which the Common Carrier Bureau and the Commission would not accept, was that the proposal to provide a public microwave network in the busy Chicago/St. Louis corridor at rates cheaper than that charged by the telephone companies would result in skimming the cream of the market and would adversely affect the price-averaging policy of the established companies. The Commission found that there was a need for this additional communications capability, that the service would be sufficiently reliable, and that it would not unduly use up radio frequencies.

The MCI decision led to a rash of applications to establish common-carrier microwave service and, as might be expected, the telephone companies did not give up the battle; Bell appealed the MCI decision to the courts. To handle the new problems that had been produced by the microwave applications, the FCC decided to reevaluate its policies on the authorization of new common-carrier facilities by microwave. On July 15, 1970, it commenced an inquiry in which it described in detail the two main applicants (Datran and MCI), discussed the problems involved, and requested comments.

On May 25, 1971 the Commission issued its First Order and Report.* It found that with respect to a policy on the entry of new common carriers into the market,

> there is a public need and demand for the proposed facilities and services and for new and diverse sources of supply, competition in the specialized communications field is reasonably feasible, there are grounds for a reasonable expectation that new entry will have some beneficial effects, and there is no reason to anticipate that new entry would have any adverse impact on service to the public by existing carriers such as to outweigh the considerations supporting new entry. We further find and conclude that a general policy in favor of the entry of new carriers in the specialized communications field would serve the public interest, convenience, and necessity. [par. 103.]

On the question of the need for hearings on economic exclusivity among the applicants, the Commission concluded,

> Since new entry by more than one private line applicant appears reasonably feasible in a potential market of this nature, we deem the marketplace to be a more reliable and effective instrument than the comparative hearing process for

---

*Specialized Common Carrier Services, 2 CLSR 788, 29 FCC 2d 870.

determining how many and which new entrants may succeed. Considering the desirability of avoiding delay in the institution of services needed by the public now, the benefit to the public in the availability of diverse options, and the lack of public detriment in the event some fail, we will decline to hold such hearings on the pending applications. Our policy determination [on the question of new entry] rests essentially on our judgment, based on circumstances shown by this record, that competition is reasonably feasible and offers benefits to the public such as to outweigh any risk that some new entrants may fail. We would be very reluctant at this time to foreclose future applicants from an opportunity to compete with the present applicants, perhaps with a different or better service or by developing a new submarket. [pars. 121-2.]

As regards frequency interference, the Commission will require that organizations seeking to enter the business "coordinate the technical aspects of their proposals with other certified carriers," with previous applicants (par. 128), and with the later filer required to remove conflicts (par. 135). Rules for frequency allocation are set forth in a 1972 order.

The Commission reached no conclusion on the question of ensuring quality service to the user, and will study the matter further; it will also give further study to the problem of local distribution of new specialized services, but reaffirmed its position that "where a carrier has monopoly control over essential facilities we will not condone any policy or practice whereby such carrier would discriminate in favor of an affiliated carrier or show favoritism among competitors" (par. 157).

There was considerable opposition to this policy by the established carriers; requests for reconsiderations were denied, and the National Association of Regulatory Utility Commissioners appealed the ruling to the Ninth Circuit Court of Appeals in San Francisco. The matter was argued on February 15, 1973 and almost two years later, the court affirmed the FCC. In the meantime, several construction permits had been granted under the general policy, and the FCC began a general inquiry into the economic effects of competition.

Although the specialized common carriers handle the long distance aspects of data communications, the path between the user and the microwave system is supplied by the telephone company. There has been a running battle between the Bell System and MCI, the first of the specialized common carriers, as to what "local loop" services must be provided by the telephone company. One of the major questions was whether the original Commission ruling in favor of MCI included two types of data paths, Foreign Exchange Services (FX) and Common Control Switching Arrangements (CCSA). The Commission ruled that Bell must provide this kind of service; in mid-September 1974 the Commission's position was upheld by the Third Circuit Court of Appeals in Philadelphia. The federal antitrust suit brought against the Bell system in November 1974 will also consider this competition.

Satellite

The international satellite as a data path has had increasing use, but the negotiations involved in arranging for the use of this medium can be exhausting. Robert V. Evans, general counsel of CBS, noted that in order to transmit programs internationally, his company had to deal, at one time or another, with the Communications Satellite Corporation (COMSAT), the FCC, AT&T, the international carriers (RCA, IT&T, Western Union International), the International Telecommunications Satellite Consortium (INTELSAT), the Postal, Telephone and Telegraph (PTT) Administration of each foreign nation, and the Conference of European Postal and Telegraph Administrations (CEPT)!* The role of COMSAT as manager of INTELSAT has been decreased; the comparative values of satellite and cable communications are under continuing study by the FCC.

On the domestic scene, satellite communications have been proposed for some time, and an application to establish domestic satellites was made as early as 1965. In March 1966, the FCC instituted an inquiry regulating the establishment of domestic communications satellite facilities by nongovernmental entities in which it asked for comment on the Commission's authority to set rules for

---

*Robert V. Evans, "Satellite Communications—The Legal Gap, 11 *Jurimetrics J.* 92 (1970).

the establishment of domestic satellites by noncommon carriers; what the effect of such rules might be on the Communications Satellite Act; whether as a matter of public policy noncommon carrier's domestic satellites should be allowed; and whether such satellites were technically feasible.

The first filings on this inquiry excluded questions involving the common carrier's authority to construct satellites, but the initial response to the March notice convinced the Commission to broaden the inquiry to cover this question, the interrelationships of carriers, and the comparative advantages of satellites and other communications media and systems.

In August 1967, President Johnson established a Task Force on Communications Policy. Chaired by Undersecretary of State Eugene V. Rostow, the Task Force submitted its final report on December 7, 1968; it recommended the establishment of a pilot domestic satellite program under the management of COMSAT. In January 1970, the White House sent a memorandum to the FCC stating that in its view no natural monopoly condition existed in satellite communications and recommending relatively open entry and rate competition for such services during the next three to five years.

In March 1970, the FCC handed down its report and order in the Domestic Satellite Inquiry [1 CLSR 472 (70-306), 22 FCC 2d 86]. It decided to "consider applications by all legally, technically, and financially qualified entities proposing the establishment and operation of domestic communications satellite systems designed to provide the capability for multiple or specialized communications services" (par 19). Concurrently, the Commission issued a notice of proposed rule-making "on the policies to be followed in the event of technical or economic conflicts between applications, the appropriate initial role of AT&T in the domestic communications satellite fields, access to earth stations, and what, if any, policies, should be adopted with respect to procurement" (par. 23). In March 1972, the Commission released its staff's proposals, and in June of that year issued its Second Report and Order, concluding that multiple-entry policy was desirable. The decision was 4-3; the dissenters did not agree with the majority's treatment of AT&T and COMSAT. The Commission settled these difficulties by the end of

1972, and in the Final Opinion and Order (3 CLSR 1070, 38 FCC 2d 665) modified the prohibitions against Bell and COMSAT to permit them to participate in domestic satellite communications under certain restrictions.

Confusion was added to the satellite situation in the summer of 1974 when IBM proposed to buy a major interest in a domestic satellite company. Both government and competitors filed objections to this proposal with the FCC, which in early 1975 allowed IBM to acquire an interest in the company, but not a majority interest. IBM has now joined with Comsat and Aetna Casualty & Surety to form Satellite Business Systems, Inc.

MANAGEMENT OF COMPUTER/ COMMUNICATIONS SYSTEMS

Let us now turn to the legal problems of the management of computer/communications systems. Although the communications industry is to a large degree regulated directly, government regulation of the computer industry is for the most part indirect, and the legal problems of computer people are frequently those of their own making. These are discussed in other chapters of this book; the addition of data communications is a complicating factor.

Tariffs

The data communications industry is a continuing battlefield between the regulated companies typified by the telephone companies and the unregulated companies like time-sharing providers who wish to maximize their own portion of the available communications facilities without the need to clear their use with federal and state authorities.

The regulated companies—both the regular telephone companies and the specialized carriers—are governed by the tariffs they file with the state and federal commissions.

Tariff is a term used by public utilities for their rules and rate schedules that are filed with federal and state regulatory authorities. The carrier sometimes gives the customer the impression that these tariffs are handed down by the regulatory authority. Actually they are filed by the utility and are very seldom subject to hearing after filing. Generally, only in major rate cases, or when some member of the public (or more recently, a competitor) complains to the regulatory authority is a hearing held on whether the tariff is reasonable. Most tariffs are not challenged.

A thorough study and understanding of the tariffs can be very helpful to you, the data communications manager. Not only will you be able to talk with the carrier in its own language, but you may well find that by making minor adjustments in your company's communication system you can qualify for a lower tariff.

When a customer concludes that a tariff, as filed, is unreasonable or perhaps unlawful under the rules applying to common carriers, he can usually arrange a hearing before the state or federal commission. He should be prepared for a long and expensive legal battle in which the carrier's lawyers are very familiar with the battlefield. However, the threat of such a battle will sometimes encourage the carrier to compromise and file new tariffs that will accomplish the user's objectives—perhaps not as fully as a customer might like, but certainly a better result than would have been achieved without any fight.

Multiple Suppliers

Competition in the communications industry has led to the emergence of multiple suppliers and of different ways of providing the same service. If you deal with only one supplier, you avoid the problem of placing the blame when the system goes down. However, it is not always the cheapest method and there may be great economies achieved by shopping around for the most cost-effective combination available. The manager who does this must be prepared, when the system breaks down (as it will sometime), to have each supplier disclaim responsibility for the breakdown. These problems are discussed in Chapter 10 in connection with acquisition of computer equipment from multiple suppliers. They are also touched upon in Appendix C, dealing with interconnection. The fact that at least one of the suppliers in a communications environment will be regulated by the government adds an additional complication, since these companies may be inclined to answer complaints about service with the argument, "We cannot do this under the law because our tariffs won't let us." As noted above, this statement is seldom true.

Network Legal Problems

In considering network legal problems, it is sometimes helpful to differentiate between the computational remote access system and the informational remote access system. Legal problems seem to arise most frequently in the information type of network; they include determinations of (1) whether the source is legitimate, (2) whether the information is accurate, and (3) who is authorized to extract the information.

Probably the most widely discussed legal problem today in the information-supply industry is the question of privacy. Privacy questions generate much emotion, because the data in the file relates to individuals. But the legal problems involved can generally be classified under one of the three areas noted in the preceding paragraph. The privacy aspects of information networks do, however, often illuminate some of the problems faced by the manager of a multiaccess network, and the material in Chapter 12 may be helpful if the reader substitutes business data for personal data as he thinks about these problems.

Network Regulation

While the Securities and Exchange Commission regulates the operations of automated stock-price-quotation systems, and has ruled that a computerized stockholder's service is a broker-dealer, the major aspect of federal regulation of computer networks has been the FCC inquiry into computer use of communications facilities. This considered a fourth question: Who is authorized to do data processing?

This inquiry began on November 9, 1966 and raised questions as to whether the FCC had the power to regulate computer utilities, whether common carrier practices should be revised, whether common carriers should be permitted to provide computer services, and what measures should be taken to protect privacy in computer utilities. Over 3000 pages of comments were filed; these were analyzed by the Stanford Research Institute, further public comments were received, and in April 1970, the FCC issued its tentative decision.

The Commission invited comments on its tentative decision, received these, and in March 1971 issued its final decision (1 CLSR 692, 28 FCC 2d 267). The Commission held in substance that it would not regulate computer services; that public computer services owned by communications common carriers must be entirely separate organizations from the parent; and, by a split decision, that the data processing affiliate of a common carrier could not use the carrier's name or logo or supply it with computer services. Upon appeal, the Second Circuit affirmed the Commission generally, but struck the requirements prohibiting the affiliate from using the parent's name or performing services for it. Final rules were thereafter adopted by the Commission (3 CLSR 867, 38 Fed. Reg. 8744). The problems are far from settled, however, and it seems likely that a new study of the interrelationship will begin in 1976.

Antitrust Problems

Even without the FCC rules, and whether or not Congress enacts legislation directly regulating computer networks, the provisions of the antitrust acts must be given consideration. (The IBM suits are not directly concerned here.) However, a computerized reservation system between Atar Computer Systems and eleven major airlines drew the attention of the Justice Department which called it a "collective boycott" and a violation of the Sherman Antitrust Act. Apparently partly because of antitrust noises by another time-sharing service, IBM transferred its Information Marketing Department from the Data Processing Division to the Service Bureau Corporation, before the latter was transferred to Control Data Corporation as part of the settlement of the CDC-IBM antitrust case.

Another antitrust problem could arise in the operation of multi-access computer networks when communications lines cross company boundaries. If these computerized systems can be programmed to divide markets, there might be an antitrust violation.

Consideration should also be given to the provision of the consent decree in the first telephone antitrust case, United States v. Western Electric Co., 1 CLSR 24 (1956). Under this decree AT&T is enjoined from engaging "in any business other than the furnishing of common carrier communications services." Many commentators have stated that this prohibits the Bell System from providing commercial time-sharing services unless those services are regulated.

However, the consent decree also provides that the injunction does not apply to "businesses or services incidental to the furnishing by AT&T or such subsidiaries of common carrier communications services." It is interesting to note that the National Bank Act permits banks "to exercise . . . all such incidental powers as shall be necessary to carry on the business of banking" (12 USC 24, 7th). It is under this banking law, as interpreted by the Comptroller of the Currency, that national banks have been able to perform data processing services for their customers. And whether their providing such data processing services is an *incidental, necessary* power was the question involved in the ADAPSO case (397 U.S. 150, 2 CLSR 594). Although this case was withdrawn because of the 1970 amendments to the Bank Holding Act and the Federal Reserve rulings thereunder, if a court should decide that providing commercial data processing services for customers is *incidental* to a regulated business, it is certainly arguable that AT&T's furnishing commercial time-sharing services to its customers is incidental to providing common-carrier communications services. The implications of a decision upholding such an argument should be given serious consideration. Not only would this permit the Bell System to compete, but it might also imply that a commercial time-sharing service is subject to regulation which might well be coextensive with that regulating the communications industries.

In November, 1974, the federal government began another antitrust suit against the Bell system, naming as defendants AT&T, Western Electric, and Bell Laboratories; named as "co-conspirators" but not defendants are 22 operating subsidiaries and an operating affiliate. While the government complaint relies heavily on AT&T's activities in the voice communications area, particularly interconnect, the government also claims that Bell competed illegally with the specialized common carriers and domestic satellite companies in the private line area. The government has initially asked that AT&T dispose of its Western Electric stock, that Western Electric dispose of sufficient manufacturing capability to provide competition in the making and sale of telecommunications equipment, and that the Long Lines (long distance) Department of AT&T be separated from the operating companies.

A further complication on the horizon may be the proposal of Senator Philip A. Hart (93rd Cong, S 1167) to establish a commission and a court to eliminate abuses by monopolies and oligopolies in seven areas, one of which is computers and communications. Initial hearings were held in the spring and summer of 1973.

chapter 5

*Taxation**

A knowledge of the rules of taxation of computer hardware, software, and services is important to people involved with the management of data processing operations. Federal and state tax authorities have discovered that computers can be excellent sources of revenue for hard-pressed governmental budgets, and they are eagerly exploring every possible avenue for levying taxes upon the unsuspecting computer manufacturer and user. Particularly in the field of software taxation the interests of the federal government and the state governments, because of the different nature of the taxes imposed, lead to conflicting characterizations of the item to be taxed.

---

*Portions of this chapter are excerpted from Robert Bigelow, "Federal Software Taxation," *Modern Data,* April 1972, p. 42. © Modern Data Services, Inc.

CASH FLOW

The Federal Internal Revenue Code provides two methods by which a business can recover its investment in business property. One of these is Section 162, which says that the business can deduct from its gross income "all the ordinary and necessary expenses paid or incurred during the taxable year in carrying on any trade or business." Section 167 of the Code provides that a business can deduct "a reasonable allowance for the exhaustion, wear and tear (obsolescence) . . . of property used in the trade or business, or of property held for the production of income." In general these two situations mean that if an item of property has a useful life of less than a year, it can be expensed (i.e., used in full as a tax deduction immediately) under Section 162; but if it has a useful life of more than a year, its cost must be amortized under Section 167 over the useful life of the item.

The determination of whether the money paid for an item can be expensed (deducted immediately) or whether it must be capitalized and amortized (cost recovered over several years) can have a profound effect upon the cash requirements of a company. Let us assume that a corporation develops its own software, that the corporation is profitable, and that it spends $300,000 in its first year for software development, increasing this expenditure $100,000 per year. (Obviously, the relationships between the figures we have selected are unrealistic. But by avoiding fractions, we make the examples more understandable.) The current corporate tax rate is very close to 50 percent, so that every dollar which the company spends and which can be deducted as an expense on the tax return really costs the company only fifty cents, while the government, in effect, pays the other half.

Table 1 indicates the cash the company must, as a practical matter, generate when it deducts its entire software cost in the year in which it was incurred. This shows that the new cash which the company must supply to pay its creditors is only half the amount the company spends on development (disregarding the slippage which occurs because the company has to pay salaries weekly or monthly and cannot get tax credit until the quarterly estimated tax returns are filed). So the company has to generate $150,000 in new money in the first year, $200,000 in the second year, and so forth.

TABLE 1

EXPENSING SOFTWARE EXPENDITURES

Year	Cost of Development (a)	Cash Recovered by Tax Deduction (b)	New Cash (c)
1	300	150	150
2	400	200	200
3	500	250	250
4	600	300	300
5	700	350	350
6	800	400	400
	3300	1650	1650

NOTES: All figures in thousands of dollars
(a) Development costs are used as tax deductions in year incurred.
(b) Because of 50% tax rate.
(c) Amount the developer must find from other sources, e.g., sales.

Table 2, on the other hand, assumes that programming costs are capitalized and amortized over a period of five years. This table is based on what is called the *straight-line method*. The depreciation allowable in the first year is only a portion of that year's development cost because we assume that one-twelfth of the year's software expenditures are made each month; therefore, while the company has received almost a full year's use out of what was spent in January, it has received only a month's use out of what was spent in December. This results in an average "real" expenditure of only $150,000 in the first year and the government will permit amortization only on that amount. Since we can deduct only 20 percent of $150,000 in the first year, we have to pick up the other $30,000 in the sixth year.

Table 2 shows that the cash recovered by tax deductions in the first year is only $15,000 and the company must find $285,000 in new cash. The next year, when the company spends $400,000, it can take a full year's amortization on what it spent the first year (one-fifth of $300,000 = $60,000) plus one-fifth of $400,000/2. Based on a 50 percent tax rate this generates a $50,000 tax credit and requires the company to come up with only $350,000. By the end of the sixth year, the company has made a cash outlay of $3,300,000 for which it had to generate $2,500,000 in new cash. Table 1 shows

TABLE 2

AMORTIZING SOFTWARE EXPENDITURES (STRAIGHT LINE METHOD)

Annual Amortization

Yr.	Cash Paid Out	Yr. 1	Yr. 2	Yr. 3	Yr. 4	Yr. 5	Yr. 6	Total Amortization (a)	Cash Recovered by Tax Deduction (b)	New Cash (c)
1	300	30(d)						30	15	285
2	400	60	40					100	50	350
3	500	60	80	50				190	95	405
4	600	60	80	100	60			300	150	450
5	700	60	80	100	120	70		430	215	485
6	800	30	80	100	120	140	80	550	275	525
7			40	100	120	140	160	560	(280)	(280)
8				50	120	140	160	470	(235)	(235)
9					60	140	160	360	(180)	(180)
10						70	160	230	(115)	(115)
							80	80	(40)	(40)
11	3300	300	400	500	600	700	800	3300	1650	1650

NOTES: All figures in thousands of dollars.
(a) Each year's expenditures amortized over 5 years, 20% per year.
(b) Because of 50% tax rate.
(c) Amount the developer must find from other sources, e.g., borrowing.
(d) 20% of average cost during first year.

that, when the software costs were expensed for the same period, the company had to generate only $1,650,000 in new cash. Of course, during years 7-11 in the Table 2 case, the company recaptures the $850,000 difference (if we can assume that software expenses level off or cease, neither of which is particularly likely).

So it is obvious why the Internal Revenue Service tries to capitalize expenditures whenever possible. It reduces the amount deductible and increases the government's "take-away pay."

FEDERAL HARDWARE TAXATION

There has been very little, if any, dispute that computer hardware is a capital item and must be amortized over a period of years. However, hardware is tangible or touchable and therefore alternative methods are available to the user. Table 2 shows a straight-line amortization approach for software—a simple 20 percent per year. However, under Section 167, there are some other methods available which give the taxpayer a better break. One of these is a declining balance approach in which the taxpayer deducts a fixed percentage of the undepreciated cost each year during the estimated life of the item. This is frequently done at a double rate, so that if the item had a five-year useful life, the first-year deduction would be 40 percent of its cost instead of 20 percent; this would increase the tax deduction, and decrease the amount of new cash the company must find.

Another common method is called the *sum of the year's digits,* which applies a changing fraction each year to the original cost. The numerator of the fraction represents the remaining life of the asset; the denominator (which is constant) is the sum of all the digits representing the years of useful life. For example, for a central processing unit with a five-year life, sum the digits 1 through 5 for a denominator of 15. There are five years left in the first year, so the numerator is five and the taxpayer is entitled to deduct 1/3 of its cost. The next year he is entitled to deduct 4/15ths and so on, until in the last year he can deduct 1/15th of the hardware cost.

When *new* equipment is acquired, an *investment credit* is sometimes available; this is an offset against the actual tax payable rather than a deduction from income. There has been considerable criticism of the investment credit as an unfair tax advantage, and its availability for any particular purchase should be discussed with a tax advisor during the negotiating stage to see what the current law is. If hardware is to be leased through a third party, the contract should specify who gets the investment credit. In a full pay out investment situation, the credit will often be available to the user. Leasing arrangements in which the lessors are individuals procured through a lease broker may, however, depend on the investment credit being available to the lessor.

STATE AND LOCAL HARDWARE TAXES

At the state level, seller and buyer, lessor and lessee, must all consider the effect of sales and use taxes, and of local property taxes. The standard computer lease or rental contract passes on all taxes to the user, and so the user must consider these costs in his procurement procedures. In one case Honeywell rented computer equipment to the federal government in California and was held subject to the California tax. Honeywell's contract with the government provided that it be reimbursed for such taxes. The government contracting officer denied reimbursement on the ground that the tax was imposed not on the use of the computer, but on the manufacturer's use of machine components, i.e., on the value of the components purchased by the manufacturer and used within the State of California. However, the General Services Administration's Board of Contract Appeals held that computer equipment was tangible personal property within the meaning of California law, the manufacturer as owner was liable for payment, and the federal government must reimburse the manufacturer (Honeywell, Inc., 1 CLSR 760).

Local property taxes are assessed on tangible personal property and the taxing officials attempt to include within this term everything they can think of. This has created a considerable amount of controversy in the software field as we shall see later. The laws under which these taxes are assessed vary from state to state; Ohio even assesses personal property taxes on computers built for export and awaiting shipment by the manufacturer (Kosydar v. NCR, 417 U.S. 62, 5 CLSR 419, 94 S. Ct. 2108). The user should always consider the additional local property tax that will be encountered, especially when there is a change from a manual to a machine system.

FEDERAL SOFTWARE TAXATION

At the federal level software taxation is controlled by Revenue Procedure 69-21 which became effective in October 1969. This procedure defines software as "all programs or routines used to cause a computer to perform a desired task or set of tasks, and the documentation required to describe and maintain those programs," a definition which includes everything from operating systems to application programs. Since Section 174 of the Internal Revenue Code permits the taxpayer to expense research and experimental outlays under Section 167 over a period of not less than five years, Washington decided that Section 174 might also serve as a guideline for the tax treatment of software: "The costs of developing software in many respects so closely resemble . . . research and experimental expenditures . . . as to warrant accounting treatment similar to that accorded such costs . . ." Thus, the IRS "will not disturb a taxpayer's treatment of costs incurred in developing software either for his own use or to be held by him for lease to others," where the taxpayer consistently either expenses all software costs or capitalizes them and recovers the costs through "rateable amortization . . . over a period of five years from the date of completion of such development or over a shorter period where such costs are attributable to the development of software that the taxpayer clearly establishes has a useful life of less than five years."

When the taxpayer buys rather than develops his software, however, he is up against another problem. If the software costs are "bundled" with the hardware costs, the taxpayer must treat the software as part of the hardware, capitalize it, and amortize it over the life of the hardware. On the other hand, if the cost of the software is separately stated, the taxpayer has to treat it as an "intangible asset, the cost of which is to be recovered by amortization deductions rateably over a period of five years" or such shorter life as the taxpayer can prove. (If the user acquires his software under lease, he takes the lease payments as deductions against income under Section 162 and doesn't have to worry about capitalization at all!)

Now, this looks fairly simple and solves a lot of problems. But, unfortunately, Procedure 69-21 creates problems of its own. One of these is caused by the phrase "rateable amortization." What it means is that the amortization deduction must be taken on a straight-line basis, because the IRS takes the position that software is an intangible.*

The Internal Revenue's position that software is intangible can place a cruel burden on the taxpayer if the courts should rule against the government's reliance on Section 174 as a procedure for determining useful life. Under Section 174, the *minimum* period of amortization is five years, but under the Revenue Procedure, this seems to be the *maximum*. If the Revenue Procedure should be held invalid, but the concept of intangibility approved, the taxpayer will have to prove that the software has any useful life at all. Why? Because the government presumes that an intangible asset is good forever unless there is clear evidence (such as the statutory time limit in the case of a patent or copyright) that the intangible wears out. And while some programs become obsolete fairly quckly, others—which are machine-independent—are likely to last more than five years. No amortization, no deduction—and the company has to find more cash to pay for its programming!

Software Definition

The IRS Procedure has created another problem by its limited definition of software ("programs or routines used to cause a computer to perform a desired task or set of tasks, and the documenta-

---

*One of the autnors has argued vehemently that software should be considered tangible, as it is at the state level; see Robert Bigelow, "Federal Software Taxation", 1 CLSA, Section 2-3.2, Article 1.

tion required to describe and maintain these programs") because it specifically excludes "procedures which are external to computer operations, such as instructions to transcription operators and external control procedures."

The Treasury Department has chosen to ignore the federally adopted definition for software: "A set of programs, procedures, and possibly associated documentation concerned with the operation of a data processing system, e.g. compilers, library routines, manuals, circuit diagrams" (FIPS PUB 11, December 1, 1970). The Internal Revenue Service applies one definition of software to itself, and another to its victims.

The Revenue Procedure even permits the computer manufacturer (but not the independent software developer) to determine whether a program is tangible or intangible. It has been held that if you buy a computer from a bundled manufacturer, the software provided by the manufacturer is part of the hardware and can be depreciated over the same period and by the same depreciation method. And if the investment credit is restored, the software, by being bundled with the hardware, is eligible for investment credit (Ruling 71-177).

But if the computer manufacturer is unbundled, the software is intangible, and only straight-line amortization is available. This means that if you buy a computer from the manufacturer and buy a sort package from Joe's Packaged Software Inc. (which does the same job as the sort package you would get bundled with the hardware), you must capitalize Joe's package and amortize it on the straight-line basis over five years.

Some Other Difficulties

Another point that both developers and users of packaged software should keep in mind is that the IRS has ruled (Revenue Ruling 60-122) that it can study the terms of the lease agreement and, if the amount which is paid under the lease equals or exceeds the purchase price of the item, it may decide that a sale has been made.

The effect of such a ruling in the software field is hard to predict, but it could include a determination (if the amount received during the first year exceeds thirty percent of the total to be paid under the "lease") that the entire transaction must be treated as a sale during the first year; this would shift the right to take depreciation from the seller to the buyer, and would affect the investment credit if such were available.

For the program developer who leases out his programs, but pays a commission to his salesmen at the time of installation, a 1969 IRS ruling may have an unexpected impact. The ruling involved a gas company which leased hot water heaters for a five-year period to users and paid commissions to its salesmen for installing the heaters. Apparently the gas company paid the salesmen their commission based on the value of the lease and sought to deduct these payments as current expenses. The Internal Revenue Service ruled that "the lease is for five years. Thus the taxpayer has acquired contracts from which income will be derived in the future. The commission and bonuses paid played a direct, significant part in the acquisition of the leases and should properly be recovered over the term of the lease" (Revenue Ruling 69-331). In other words, the gas company had to capitalize these sales costs and recover them through amortization, even though it had to pay commissions in cash "on the barrelhead."

Certain software packages are licensed with an installation fee. These one-time charges provide quite a bit of room for negotiation. How should they be treated for tax purposes? The practical answer probably depends on the ratio of the installation fee to the monthly charge. If it is about equal to one or two months' charge, the IRS will probably allow it to be expensed. But what if the installation fee is equal to two years' rent? From the point of view of the manufacturer or developer, such an arrangement can have a considerable cash flow advantage. From the point of view of the user, the ability to write off such an expenditure could have a considerable tax advantage. If the installation or initial charge is particularly high, the government will probably require the user to amortize the amount over the term of the license. If the installation fee is high enough, the IRS might consider it a sale right at that time rather than a lease. Where there is a single charge for the license period payable in advance, and the license period is more than a year, the Internal Revenue will probably require the user to treat the transaction as a purchase of software; the seller will probably be allowed to treat it as a sale of stock in trade.

STATE SOFTWARE TAXATION

California assessors have been particularly energetic in their efforts to tax software at the local level by treating it as tangible property. The California Legislature amended the tax law to remove software from the assessors' grasp, but the definition of "basic operational programs" by the State Property Tax Department succeeded in including a number of programs that many considered were far beyond the proper meaning of the phrase. Further legislation was enacted in 1973; this provided that the storage media for computer systems would be valued as if there were no programs on the media unless it was a "basic operational program" which is defined as a program "fundamental and necessary to the functioning of the computer . . . that part of an operating system including supervisors, monitors, executives and control of master programs which consist of the control program elements of that system".* This is the first time that a legislature has seen fit to distinguish between systems programs, utility programs, and applications programs.

Other states have shown much interest in software taxation; the tax authorities frequently make a ruling that is not good for computer users or vendors and then leave it up to the industry to take the question to court or get the law changed. Management should stay alert in this area; sometimes a bad rule can be softened before it is issued.

CUSTOMS DUTIES†

The movement of information in a machine readable form across international boundaries can create some interesting problems. For example, a program can be a deck of cards or a reel of tape that can

---

*California Revenue Taxation Code, Section 995.2, as amended by Chapter 998 of the Acts of 1973. The definition is actually considerably longer.

† Reprinted from the *Computer Law Service,* Section 9-2.3.

be moved in tangible form across the border, or it can be transmitted over communications lines.

If the program is carried across in punched cards, it might be treated for customs duties as used goods, or it might be taxed at its sale value in the country of import. (See Business Automation, November 1970, p. 96.)

It was reported in July of 1969 that when a computer program on magnetic tape form was valued by Canadian customs officers at the program value ($15,000), rather than its tape value ($30), the importer refused to accept the shipment. The importer then arranged to have the program transmitted over telecommunication lines to a terminal in Montreal, thus avoiding tax. (The Financial Post, as reported in Computers and Automation, September 1969, p. 16). The Canadian government has since decided to value programs for customs purposes at the value of the media on which the program is stored.

Of course, when information of this nature is transmitted over communications lines, it is not unlikely that a citizen of the importing country, working for the importing company, may report the act to the customs authorities, with obvious consequences.

TAXATION OF COMPUTER SERVICES

As a general rule, states do not levy excise or property taxes on receipts from personal services directly; these are usually picked up as part of the income tax. However, some state property tax decisions have resulted in the direct taxation of services. For example, in one Massachusetts case, a memory drum was used by the taxpayer to store information on securities prices, which were available to stockbroker subscribers over telephone lines. It was held that the information was the taxpayer's stock in trade, that the drum was machinery involved in producing this stock in trade, and was therefore subject to local taxation (Ultronic Systems Corp. v. Boston, 355 Mass. 284, 2 CLSR 97, 244 NE 2d 318). Ohio has been particularly active in computer taxation; in a case involving another stock quotation service, it was held that the dissemination of this information to customers in Ohio would be treated as a sale under the sales tax law because there was a license to use of terminals which were tangible personal property; the transfer of this information was not a personal service which was exempt from taxation (Bunker-Ramo Corp. v. Porterfield, 21 Ohio St. 2d 231, 2 CLSR 629, 257 NE 2d 365. See also General Data Corp. v. Porterfield, 21 Ohio St. 2d 223, 2 CLSR 621, 257 NE 2d 359 where a similar result was reached with respect to a hotel reservation system).

The personal-service exemption received considerable attention in a 1973 case in Ohio, Accountant's Computer Services v. Kosydar, 35 Ohio St. 2d 120, 4 CLSR 554, 298 NE 2d 519. In this case, standard service bureau operations were held subject to Ohio sales taxes since the personal services rendered were minor, but where the data was analyzed by the company's professional workers who used data-processing equipment for their own assistance, the personal-service exemption was applied. It is possible that under some state statutes a separate maintenance contract, with its costs separately stated from hardware costs, might avoid sales taxes on the maintenance, even when the maintenance is an integral part of the acquisition of the hardware or software.

In some states such as Hawaii and New Mexico, there are gross-receipts taxes which apply to personal services. Knowledgeable tax planning may permit some companies to have such personal services performed and paid for in states which do not have gross-receipts taxes.

part three

Proprietary Rights

chapter **6**

An Overview of Proprietary Legal Rights

PROPRIETARY LEGAL RIGHTS IN HARDWARE AND SOFTWARE*

The computer manager examines the proprietary rights of the owner of hardware and software from two points of view. Sometimes you are the buyer, and sometimes you are the supplier. When hardware is acquired, the supplier should guarantee to defend the buyer and pay any damages if someone else claims that the buyer is using their property. Often the right to use software is acquired by lease rather than sale, so that the supplier retains ownership, primarily in order to protect his rights as an inventor; a

---

*Introductory material based on a portion of Chapter 11 of *the Information Systems Manager's Handbook*, published in Homewood, Ill. © 1975 Dow Jones Irwin.

similar guarantee is needed here. If the user's company develops software—or a data base that has marketable value—consideration must be given as to how to protect the company's legal rights in that information.

There are basically three ways of protecting legal proprietary rights in hardware and software: by patent, by copyright, and by trade secret. Sometimes the law of trademark or the law of unfair competition can apply.

The legal basis for patents and most copyrights is found in statutes enacted by Congress. The copyright law currently provides that an author or copyright owner has the exclusive control for 28 years of the right to reproduce the form of expression (it is not a violation of copyright to express the same idea in other words). Under patent law, Congress gives an inventor the exclusive right to control the use of his invention and the methods embodied therein during the 17-year period that the patent is in force.

Since the patent law gives the inventor a monopoly, it is generally strictly construed. The Government Patent Examiner determines, insofar as he can, whether the invention is original, useful, and not obvious to a person "skilled in the field"; if so, a patent may be granted. The Patent Office, which is very overloaded with work and considers programs to be mental rather than physical manifestations, has consistently opposed the patentability of programs. Despite this, a number of program patents have been issued, frequently by order of a court.

There are nonstatutory methods of protecting proprietary rights. If an author severely limits the circulation of an article and does not "publish" it, a common-law copyright applies which in some ways is broader than a statutory one. A process, be it a program or a procedure, that is kept extremely confidential may qualify as a *trade secret* under the law of your state. This term has often been defined to include "a confidential formula, pattern, device, or compilation of information which is used in one's business and which gives the owner an opportunity to obtain advantage over competitors who do not have it." (Milton Wessell, "Legal Protection of Computer Programs", *43 Harvard Business Review,* p. 97 March/April 1965.) Preserving a trade secret can be a very difficult job; the developer should make sure to discuss protective methods with a lawyer before starting the development of any program procedure or data base that is likely to have commercial value.

The development of software or a data base with commercial value calls for working closely with the company lawyer to prepare a contract form that will protect the developer's rights to control the use of this information. It is possible to license it as a trade secret, provided that sufficient sanctions are imposed upon the customer; such a method may be more effective than copyright and much cheaper than a patent.

It has been suggested that trademark is a means of protecting computer languages and program names. IBM has proposed a registration system combining aspects of both patent and copyright law.

PROGRAMS DEVELOPED BY TWO PARTIES

A software package may be leased by a developer with the source code included so that a user can debug it if problems occur. Frequently, modifications made by a user result in an improved product. What are the relative rights of developer and user in this improved program? Similarly, an employee of a company may, perhaps on his or her own time, improve one of the company's programs. Does this employee have any proprietary rights?

The 1972 IBM program product license provides:

> The Customer may modify any licensed program and/or optional material, in machine readable form, for his own use and merge it into other program material to form an updated work, provided that, upon the discontinuance of the license for such licensed program, the licensed program and optional material supplied by IBM will be completely removed from the updated work and dealt with under this Agreement as if permission to modify had never been granted. Any portion of the licensed program or optional material included in an updated work shall be used only in the designated CPU . . . and shall remain subject to all other terms of this Agreement.

The Customer agrees to reproduce and include IBM's copyright notice on any copies, in whole or in part on any form, including partial copies in modifications of licensed program or optional materials made hereunder in accordance with the copyright instructions to be provided by IBM.

Since IBM ties the use of each program product to a specific CPU and requires that the user return the program in unmodified form at the end of the license, the company says, in effect, that the user may do what he wants with his improvements. But since the user must return the original unchanged, the improvements, without the basic program, probably have little value. IBM will, however, as a practical matter, negotiate with the user to acquire such modifications and distribute them for the financial benefit of both parties. It is better not to leave the question for later negotiation; if the user wishes to be able to realize commercially any improvements it makes, this should be specified in the agreement under which it acquires the use of the software.

With respect to employee-developed programs, the employee involved is probably working for the company and is subject to the law of trade secrets. If the employee has made a valuable breakthrough and the employer has taken appropriate steps to preserve trade secrets, and if there has been a confidential relationship between employer and employee, the employee should not be able to take the improvement with him when he leaves, even in his head. If, on the other hand, the program improvement is not a trade secret, the employee can take it when he leaves; an employer cannot stop a former employee from using his general knowledge even when it is gained from the employment. In either event, however, an employee is not entitled to take from a former employer the tangible items on which the program resides, such as discs, punch cards, or tape. The status of the employee and his rights should be negotiated at the beginning of the employment and written out in full to avoid future misunderstandings.

chapter 7

Common Law Methods
of Software Protection

Most of the problems that have arisen so far concern the legal protection of proprietary rights in software. Hardware is generally protected by patent and presents little in the way of unique problems. The following discussion, therefore, emphasizes software, but the laws of copyright, patent, and trade secret also apply to hardware.

While most of the public discussion in the United States with respect to the legal protection of computer software has been about statutory methods, the protective techniques derived from the common law are in wide use today. In none of these does the developer achieve a legal monopoly; his competitors have the right to develop the same software, by independent and honest means.

COMMON LAW COPYRIGHT

In the United States, an author can obtain copyright protection in two ways: by common law, or by statute. Under traditional Anglo-American common law, as continued in force by the individual states of this nation, an author has a right to control the distribution of his unpublished writings. The key question in common-law copyright problems is whether there has been publication. Wide distribution, uncontrolled by the author, is publication and, unless the requirements for statutory copyright have been met, results in the dedication of the writing to the public, and loss of any right by the author to control its use in any way. This type of publication has been defined by one court as "a communication, disclosure, or circulation of a work to members of the public without restrictions as to the person or use of such publication" (Shanahan v. Maco, 224 Cal. App. 2d 327, 36 Cal. Rptr. 584).

Distribution of the writing to a select group for comment or to a limited group under contract may not destroy the common-law copyright. The courts have been quite favorable to authors in finding that there has been only "limited" publication, and the authors' common-law rights are preserved. Under common-law copyright the author has not only the rights that apply to a statutorily copyrighted work, as discussed below, but also the right to control distribution, and this common-law copyright lasts until general publication. With respect to a computer program, this could be interpreted to grant the author a right to control the use of the program.

TRADE SECRETS

The law of trade secrets has developed over many years, and varies from state to state. The most widely quoted definition of trade secret in American law is that promulgated by the American Law Institute in Section 757, comment b, of the Restatement of Torts (1930):

b. *Definition of trade secret.* A trade secret may consist of
any formula, pattern, device or compilation of information
which is used in one's business, and which gives him an opportunity to obtain an advantage over competitors who do not
know or use it. It may be a formula for a chemical compound,
a process of manufacturing, treating or preserving materials, a
pattern for a machine or other device, or a list of customers. It
differs from other secret information in a business (See Section
759) in that it is not simply information as to single or
ephemeral events in the conduct of the business, as, for
example, the amount or other terms of a secret bid for a contract or the salary of certain employees, or the security invest-
ments made or contemplated, or the date fixed for the
announcement of a new policy or for bringing out a new model
or the like. A trade secret is a process or device for continuous
use in the operation of the business. Generally it relates to the
production of goods, as, for example, a machine or formula
for the production of an article. It may, however, relate to the
sale of goods or to other operations in the business, such as a
code for determining discounts, rebates or other concessions in
a price list or catalogue, or a list of specialized customers, or a
method of bookkeeping or other office management.

The American law on liability for misuse of trade secrets varies
from state to state. In some instances, intentional unauthorized
use is a criminal offense. In at least one instance, attempted sale of
a program by an employee was held to be grand larceny, the value
of the program being determined from testimony by the owner that
it far exceeded the value of the media on which it was recorded
(Hancock v. Texas, 1 CLSR 562, 402 S.W. 2d 906; Hancock v.
Decker, 1 CLSR 379 858 F. 2d 552).

The protection accorded the trade secret holder is against the
disclosure or unauthorized use of the trade secret by those to
whom the secret has been confided under the express or
implied restriction of nondisclosure or nonuse. The law also
protects the holder of a trade secret against disclosure or use
when the knowledge is gained, not by the owner's volition, but
by some "improper means," which may include theft, wire-
tapping, or even aerial reconnaissance. A trade secret, however, does not offer protection against discovery by fair and
honest means, such as by independent invention, accidental

disclosure, or by so-called reverse engineering, that is by starting with the known product and working backward to define the process which aided in its development or manufacture. [Kewanee Oil Co. v. Bicron, 416 U.S. 470, 94 S. Ct. 1879, 4 CLSR 1203.]

In another case, Data General Corporation provided uncopyrighted engineering drawings of its unpatented Nova 1200 to its customers, subject to a nondisclosure agreement in the contract of sale; the drawings bear a legend that they contain proprietary information of Data General not to be used by the purchaser for manufacturing purposes. At trial, the Delaware court held that these facts could be purposes. At trial the Delaware court held that these facts could be the basis of a finding that trade secret protection had been preserved (Data General Corp. v. Digital Computer Controls, 5 CLSR 1073 (Del. Ch. 1975).

A person who independently develops a product that is the trade secret of another may use it, sell it or do whatever he wishes with it. And to the extent that the new developer publicizes his development, the trade secret of the first discoverer will be destroyed.

UNFAIR COMPETITION

Unfair competition is a common-law doctrine that has been called the "Book of Rules of the Business Game." It is a doctrine developed primarily by the state (rather than federal) courts for protection against a competitor appropriating to the competitor's use the fruits of the businessman's hard work. The law of unfair competition developed in favor of the businessman over the years. But in 1964, the United States Supreme Court held "that when an article is unprotected by a patent or copyright, state law may not forbid others to copy that article. To forbid copying would interfere with the federal policy . . . of the Constitution and in the implementing of federal statutes, of allowing free access to copy whatever the federal patent and copyright laws leave in the public domain" (Compco Corp. v. Day-Brite Lighting, Inc., 376 U.S. 234, 237).

Broadly interpreted, these statements could mean that if a product were not patented or copyrighted, anybody could copy it, unless by contract they have given up that right. This problem is discussed in more detail later; there has also been a continuing effort to get Congress to enact a federal law prohibiting unfair competition.

LEASE AND CONTRACT CONSIDERATIONS

An outright sale of property ends the seller's dominion; under basic common-law rules, the seller cannot control the buyer's use of that property. Like most general statements, this one is beset with exceptions, but on detailed examination these exceptions often demonstrate that the seller has not made an outright sale.

Because of this loss of control, software is very seldom sold, but rather is leased or licensed. The distinction can sometimes be important. The law governing leasing stems from the feudal land law of England; the law governing licenses comes from the law of contracts as developed by English businessmen in a later time. The emphasis in feudal law was on the superior right in the land holder—subject only to very defined limits—and the courts approached the problems with deference for the person rightfully occupying the land. In contract law, the parties were generally considered equal, and so appeared to a court that decided a dispute between them.

A lease of real property, under the old land law, usually conveyed a "complete estate" for a period of years, giving the tenant the right to exclude the landlord from the premises. This concept carried over into personal property lease, and gave the lessee under a written document a high standing. There has, however, been a trend recently in the courts to examine leases of personal property to see if they are actually disguised sales. If the amount paid during the term of the lease approximates the market value of the product, especially if much of this amount is paid at the beginning, the courts have tended to find that there was a sale in fact, no matter what the parties called it. From taking this step it has not been too difficult for the courts to apply the warranty provisions of the Uniform Commercial Code to actual long term leases.

These difficulties of leasing have often caused lawyers to use a license or contract method for protecting the developer's proprietary rights. Frequently such contracts include provisions that the user recognizes that the program is the developer's trade secret and will enforce specified measures. Violation of these agreements gives the developer the right to sue on the contract. The damages are limited to those that the developer can prove, but the contract may include an agreement for stipulated damages and an agreement for the entry of an injunction. Additionally, some states may allow punitive damages for particularly unfair treatment of the vendor.

If the decision in the Data General case—that trade secret protection survived the outright sale of the computer—is sustained on appeal and is followed in other states, the need to lease or license may be diminished. Of course the warranty problem will then be clearly presented, at least as to those parts of software that can be found to be *goods** within the definition of the Uniform Commercial Code.

SOME SUGGESTIONS ON PROTECTING PROPRIETARY RIGHTS

To protect proprietary rights under common-law concepts of copyright and trade secrets, considerable care must be given—from the very beginning—to make sure that the item to be protected is not widely disclosed. If a common-law copyright is being considered each copy should include the words "not for publication" at least on the title page and even scattered through the manuscript. Each copy might also be numbered so that if copies are made it may be possible to determine who was the original source. Alternatively, each copy could have a different minor bug that did not affect its validity.

Goods means all things (including specifically manufactured goods) which are movable at the time of identification to the contract for sale other than the money in which the price is to be paid, investment securities and things in action, U.C.C. Section 2-105 (1).

Similar considerations apply to trade-secret protection, except that greater care must be taken. Access to the office or other space where the product is kept and developed must be severely limited. There should be sign-in and sign-out sheets and identification should be required. If the trade secret is disclosed to a third party, a record should be kept of this disclosure; the third party should be required to sign an agreement that he realizes that the item is a trade secret and will not disclose it further. Particularization of each copy disclosed might also be considered, for example, the use of a superfluous branch instruction if the program is disclosed in source code.

Computerized data bases are a frequent subject of trade secret or common-law copyright protection. Mailing lists are a very common example. To protect against the unauthorized use of the list, dummy names are inserted at random intervals, so that the owner will receive a copy each time the list is used.

It is very important to move promptly to protect one's rights when unauthorized use is made of a trade secret. Courts will, after notice to the alleged unauthorized user, grant an injunction against the use if the owner can make a good showing that he protected his rights to the fullest. (For a good discussion on this, and some of the difficulties the lawyer faces, see J. Thomas Franklin, "Proprietary Protection of Computer Data Bases," 3 *Computer Law Service,* Section 4-4, Article 3.)

chapter *8*

Statutory Methods of Software Protection

The statutory methods discussed here, primarily copyright law and patent law, are those by which a developer may obtain a monopoly and thereby exclude competitors from the use of the product. The statutory basis for copyright and patent protection comes from Article I, Section 8, Clause 8 of the United States Constitution, which provides that,

> The Congress shall have Power . . . to promote the Progress of Science and useful Arts, by securing for limited Times to Authors and Inventors the exclusive Right to their respective Writings and Discoveries.

Under this power, Congress enacted the Copyright Law, which, in its current version, gives an author or other copyright owner exclusive control for 28 years of the right to reproduce the form of expression. But it is not a violation of copyright to express the same idea in other words. The major effort in Congress to change this law will be discussed later.

Under the Patent Law, Congress gives an inventor the exclusive right to control the use of his invention and the methods embodied therein during the 17-year period the patent is in force. Because of these essential differences, copyrights are registered and questions as to the validity of the copyright (including originality) are litigated only after the registration. In patents, the patent is applied for, the Patent Office searches through the records to determine if the application has not already been invented and is not obvious, and then issues the patent. Patents, which confer a full monopoly, can be attached before issuance and after.

Generally an invention that can be patented cannot be copyrighted, though in some cases it is possible to obtain a copyright of an ornamental design that has been patented.

STATUTORY COPYRIGHT

Under the constitutional clause quoted above, the Congress has legislated protection to authors for their writings if certain actions are taken at the time of first *public* distribution, known as publication. The major requirement is "publication thereof with the Notice of Copyright required by this title; and such notice shall be affixed to each copy thereof published." The type of notice and location are specified in the statute, and this notice (essentially: ©, author's name, date) *must* appear on every copy. Failure to include it can end the author's copyright. It is the publication with notice that secures the copyright, and not the required deposit of copies in the Copyright Office; however, the copies must be deposited before the copyright holder can bring suit for infringement. Copyright protection now lasts for 28 years, renewable for an additional 28 years.

Program Copyright Registration

For some years there was question in the legal profession whether computer programs could be registered for copyright under the federal law. There has been no court determination of this question yet, but in May 1964, the Copyright Office decided that computer programs could be registered if certain requirements were met. Currently these include requirements that:

(1) the elements of assembling, selecting, arranging and editing—in other words, the literary expression—going into the compilation of the program must be sufficient to constitute original authorship;

(2) the program must be published with the regular copyright notice;

(3) the copies deposited for registration must, at the least, include reproductions in a language intelligible to human beings; in any case, where the program or its publication is in machine-readable form, something more, such as a printout of the entire program, must be deposited;

(4) in most cases, a brief explanation of how initial publication occurred should be filed.

The complete requirements are set forth in Copyright Office Circular 61, reprinted in Appendix D.

The Copyright Office keeps an informal record of programs registered for copyright. During the years 1964-1971* inclusive, only 201 programs were so registered. But during 1972, 247 programs were registered, 280 registrations were recorded in 1973, and 266 in 1974. The upsurge may indicate that organizations that had distributed programs with copyright notices, notably IBM, during the period following "unbundling" have now decided to enforce these copyrights. As noted earlier, registration is a prerequisite to an action for infringement, but it is not required to obtain a copyright.

---

*Fiscal years ending June 30.

The Copyright Holder's Statutory Rights

The rights of a copyright holder are spelled out in 17 U.S.C. Section 1; computer programs are considered as a "literary work" and therefore the copyright holder has:

> the exclusive right: (a) to print, reprint, publish, copy, and vend the copyrighted work; [and] (b) to translate the copyrighted work into other languages or dialects, or make any other version thereof, if it be a literary work . . .

But the copyright holder would seem to have no right to prevent a person from using the ideas expressed in the copyrighted work. This was pointed out in testimony on the scope of program copyright protection by George Cary, Deputy Registrar of Copyright, in 1967:

> . . . the Supreme Court decision in the case of *Baker v. Selden,* . . . handed down in 1879 . . . involved a book on accounting systems and the question was whether or not the copyright of the book included protection against anyone using the particular system.
>
> The Supreme Court made it very clear that this did not cover the system that was set forth in the book, that anyone could take the system and use it. [Hearings on Data Processing Management in the Federal Government, July, 1967, p. 170.]

The effectiveness of a program copyright has also been thrown in doubt by the recent decision of the United States Supreme Court in Gottschalk v. Benson, discussed later in this chapter in the section on patents. Even though the Court did not cite Baker v. Selden, the reasoning was quite similar.

Mr. Cary, in his testimony, also pointed out two other problems facing the copyright holder attempting to enforce his right:

I would think that in many cases there is a problem of difficulty of proof. Because a copyright proprietor who brings suit has to prove to the satisfaction of the court that the defendant had access to his particular work. And then, if he can prove access, and the court is satisfied that access was available, then he has to prove whether or not there was an unjustified appropriation, as it were, of the copyright material that is involved, or whether it was merely a fair use. So these are not always simple matters and they do require considerable amount of proof. [Ibid. p. 168.]

Mr. Cary's comment about access points up a major difference between patent protection and copyright. A patent gives an exclusive monopoly, even against an independent inventor who stumbles on the idea without knowledge of the patentee's action. But in copyright, the holder is protected only against those who copy or use his form of expression with knowledge of the author's writing. The independent author has an equal right to obtain and to enforce copyright protection. In the area of algorithms, particularly moderately simple ones, proof of access may be difficult. Several commentators have felt that the copyright holder's right to translate prohibits others from transforming a computer program in one language to the same program in another, such as COBOL to FORTRAN or even COBOL to assembly language. Others have felt that such transformation can be considered fair use, as mentioned by Mr. Cary above.

Fair Use

Fair use is a doctrine developed by the courts to get around the strict letter of the copyright law. One of the better summaries was written in February 1972, when a Commissioner of the United States Court of Claims recommended a decision in a copyright infringement action brought by a magazine publisher against the United States Government. At issue was the government's right to photocopy and distribute to scientists and others upon request, articles that had been published in the plaintiff's magazine. The defendant argued that making a single photocopy was fair use. In refusing to accept this argument, the Commissioner said:

> "Fair Use", a judicially-created doctrine, is a sort of "rule of reason" applied by the courts as a defense to copyright infringement when the accused infringement acts are deemed to be outside the legitimate scope of protection afforded copyright owners. . . . What constitutes "fair use" cannot be defined with precision. . . . Principal factors considered by the courts in deciding whether a particular use of a copyright work is a "fair use" are (a) the purpose of the use, (b) the nature of the copyrighted work, (c) the amount and substantiality of the material used in relation to the copyrighted work as a whole, and (d) the effect of the use on a copyright owner's potential market for his work. While these criteria are interrelated and may vary in relative significance, the last one, i.e., the competitive character of the use, is often the most important. [Williams & Wilkins Company v. U.S., 172 U.S.P.Q. 670, citations omitted.]

Unfortunately, the recommended decision of the Commissioner was not adopted by the Court of Claims itself which ruled, in a 4-3 decision, that the particular use which gave rise to the case was fair use. The Williams & Wilkins Company appealed to the Supreme Court, which heard the case in the Fall of 1974, and split 4-4 (one judge not sitting), thus affirming, but without opinion or discussion.

Copyright Infringement

Since a copyright includes the right to control translation of the copyrighted work, some interesting legal questions have arisen, and have not yet been resolved, about copyright infringement by means of a computer. Some have taken the position that the conversion of copyrighted material into machine-readable form is translation and therefore an infringement of copyright; others have said that the infringement does not occur until a print-out is made.

Many reference books, particularly in the engineering and chemical fields, are compilations of formulas, relationships, and other data that are used on a selective basis by the consumer. If a treatise on engineering were, for example, converted into machine-readable form accessible by a time-sharing system and the user made only selected abstracts, would his use be an infringement of the copyright or only fair use? It is certainly arguable that in such a situation the copyright infringement was in the "translation" to machine-readable form. And what happens if the output is on a CRT rather than on hard copy? When the user browses through the various documents looking for the one he wants, has he actually "used" the ones that he did not want, the false drops?

These are questions that have not been answered, but are typical of those that must be considered by the computer manager who is using copyrighted material in a data base. And in one major data base program in Canada, the implementers decided to provide reasonable compensation to those who held copyrights on the documents they planned to put into the system. But study disclosed that it was sometimes difficult to determine who had the copyright. (Lawford, "Copyright in Large Information Systems: A User's View," CLS Section 5-3, Article 3.)

The scope of fair use, as noted above, was considered by the United States Supreme Court in the Williams & Wilkins case. While the decision of the Court provided no guidance on copyright-infringement questions, they may be clarified by specific legislation.

New Copyright Legislation

The Copyright Law was enacted in 1909, and for many years there have been efforts to revise it to handle properly such inventions as photocopiers, cable television, and computers. In the winter of 1975, Senator McClellan introduced a compromise bill (S. 22) that appears to have a good chance of passage in 1976. Some of its provisions handle the problems discussed above. Copies are defined as "material objects . . . in which a work is fixed by any method now known or later developed, and from which the work can be perceived, reproduced, or otherwise communicated, either directly or with the aid of a machine or device." There can be no copyright protection for any idea, plan, procedure, process, system, method of operation, concept, principle or discovery. Fair use is defined and permitted by the bill; the Williams & Wilkins situation is handled explicitly.

Section 117 of S.22 says that the copyright owner does not get "any greater or lesser rights with respect to use the use of the work in conjunction with automatic systems capable of storing, processing, retrieving or transferring information, or in conjunction with any similar device, machine or process, than those afforded the works under the law, whether [federal statute] or the common law or statutes of a State, in effect on December 31, 1976, as held applicable and construed by a court in an action brought under this [statute]." Whether these rights should be changed is being investigated by the Commission on New Technological Uses of Copyright (CONTU), which is scheduled to report at the end of 1977.

Another section of the bill appears to abolish all state copyright laws if the subject matter *can be* copyrighted under the new law. Thereafter, unpublished works would have the same legal protection as works published with proper copyright notice. The length of copyright protection for works published after January 1, 1977 will generally be fifty years after the death of the author.

The new bill also provides that if copyright notice is omitted on only a few copies, or if registration is made within five years after publication without notice but the notice is added to all copies thereafter distributed, or if the notice was omitted in violation of an express requirement in writing that the copyright owner's notice be displayed, the copyright will still be valid. This will prevent accidental loss of copyright by many authors who, under the present law, have unwittingly lost their rights.

PATENTS

The issuance of patents to inventors to enable them to exploit their inventions for their own profit has been considered policy of the United States since it was founded. Over 3,500,000 patents have been issued in the two hundred years this nation has existed. The purpose of the patent monopoly is to encourage invention and the prompt implementation of that invention for the benefit of society, since, after 17 years, any person may use the invention without compensation to the inventor. This policy of a 17-year monopoly conflicts with another public policy of the United States—that monopolies and cartels are bad and should be struck down in favor of competition. United States antitrust policies, discussed in Chapter 16, may weaken an invention patent monopoly.

The Statutory Background

The history of patent protection of computer programs is complex. Before we review the position of the United States Patent Office and some of the cases that have been decided, it is helpful to quote selected portions of the Patent Act (Title 35 United States Code) that set forth the requirements for patentability:

> Section 100. Definitions . . . unless the context otherwise indicates—
>
> (a) The term "invention" means invention or discovery.
>
> (b) The term "process" means process, art or method, and includes a new use of a known process, machine, manufacture, composition of matter or material . . .
>
> Section 101. Inventions patentable. Whoever invents or discovers any new and useful process, machine, manufacture, or composition of matter, or any new and useful improvement thereof, may obtain a patent therefor. . . .
>
> Section 102. Conditions for patentability; novelty and loss of right to patent. A person shall be entitled to a patent unless—
>
> (a) the invention was known or used by others in this country, or patented or described in a printed publication in this or a foreign country, before the invention thereof by the applicant for patent, or
>
> (b) the invention was patented or described in a printed publication in this or a foreign country or in public use or on sale in this country more than one year prior to the date of the application for patent in the United States, or
>
> (c) he has abandoned the invention, or

(d) the invention was first patented or caused to be patented by the applicant or his legal representatives or assigns in a foreign country prior to the date of the application for patent in this country on an application filed more than twelve months before the filing of the application in the United States, or

(e) the invention was described in a patent granted on an application for patent by another filed in the United States before the invention thereof by the applicant for patent, or

(f) he did not himself invent the subject matter sought to be patented, or

(g) before the applicant's invention thereof the invention was made in this country by another who had not abandoned, suppressed, or concealed it. In determining priority of invention there shall be considered not only the respective dates of conception and reduction to practice of the invention, but also the reasonable diligence of one who was first to conceive and last to reduce to practice, from a time prior to conception by the other.

Section 103. Conditions for patentability; non-obvious subject matter. A patent may not be obtained though the invention is not identically disclosed or described as set forth in section 102 of this title, *if the differences* between the subject matter sought to be patented and the prior art are such that the subject matter as a whole *would have been obvious* at the time the invention was made *to a person having ordinary skill in the art* to which said subject matter pertains. . . . Patentability shall not be negatived by the manner in which the invention was made. [Emphasis supplied.]

The Patent Office Position

Since the beginning of the computer age, applications have been filed, and patents issued, for computer hardware and systems. The idea of obtaining patent protection on computer programs was advanced in the late 1950s to the dismay of the United States Patent Office, which was already overworked and doubted it had either the manpower or the expertise to investigate the patentability of software. In August 1966 the Commissioner of Patents issued proposed Guidelines to Examination of Programs; the proposal was never implemented. The Patent Office, in October 1968, issued revised Guidelines that in essence denied the patentability of computer programs.

The Court Cases

The Patent Office position set forth in the Guidelines had actually been in effect for some years, and patent applications dealing directly or indirectly with computer programs had been rejected by examiners in the Patent Office. Their rejection had been sustained by appeal boards within the Patent Office. From these boards, a disappointed applicant could appeal to United States Court of Customs and Patent Appeals, and a number of cases were so appealed.

The first case to reach this court was the application of Messrs. Prater and Wei for an apparatus and program that would analyze data for mass spectrographs. The decision of the court was announced August 14, 1969 (2 CLSR 32, 415 F. 2d 1393, 162 U.S.P.Q. 541), and was unanimous. The patent was granted as an apparatus (machine) but rejected as a process. From the standpoint of software protection, the most significant statement was footnote 29, which read:

> No reason is now apparent to us why, based on the Constitution, statute, or case law, apparatus *and* process claims broad enough to encompass the operation of a programmed general-purpose digital computer are necessarily unpatentable. In one sense, a general-purpose digital computer may be regarded as but a storeroom of parts and/or electrical components. But once a program has been introduced, the general-purpose becomes a special-purpose digital computer (i.e., a specific electrical circuit with or without electromechanical components) which, along with the process by which it operates, may be patented subject, of course, to the requirements of novelty, utility, and non-obviousness. Based on the present law, we see no other reasonable conclusion. [Emphasis by the Court.]

The court's decision led to a withdrawal by the Patent Office of the Guidelines it had adopted in 1968. The Prater and Wei decision was followed by a number of opinions in the Court of Customs and Patent Appeals, each reversing a rejection by the Patent Office and granting a patent.

In the midst of these cases, on May 6, 1971, the Court of Customs and Patent Appeals decided Benson & Tabbot (441 F. 2d 682, 2 CLSR 1030, 169 U.S.P.Q. 548). The claimed invention was a program for converting binary coded decimal (BCD) numbers to binary numbers. The program was very simple, and the application was rejected by the Patent Office Examiner primarily on the ground that a program was mental and nonstatutory. This rejection was affirmed by the Board of Appeals on the grounds that the claims "set forth mental processes and mathematical steps." The Court of Customs and Patent Appeals reversed the Patent Office, and the case was appealed to the United States Supreme Court.

On November 20, 1972, Mr. Justice Douglas, writing for a unanimous court (only 6 of the 9 justices heard and decided the case) reversed the Court of Customs and Patent Appeals, and struck down the application (Gottschalk v. Benson, U.S., 409 U.S. 63, 3 CLSR 256).* The Supreme Court limited its discussion to whether the method claimed was a "process" within Section 100(b) above. After reviewing some earlier patent cases that discussed the patentability of scientific truths and natural phenomena, the Court pointed out that the claim of Benson and Tabbot was "abstract and sweeping" and not limited to specific applications or machinery. The Court then said:

> We do not hold that no process patent could ever qualify if it did not meet the requirements of our prior precedents. It is said that the decision precludes a patent for any program servicing a computer. We do not so hold. It is said that we have before us a program for a digital computer but extend our holding to programs for analog computers. We have, however, made clear from the start that we deal with a program only for digital computers. It is said we freeze process patents to old technologies, leaving no room for the revelations of the new, onrushing technology. Such is not our purpose. What we come down to in a nutshell is the following.

---

*The complete opinion is reprinted in Appendix E.

It is conceded that one may not patent an idea. But in practical effect that would be the result if the formula for converting binary code to pure binary were patented in this case. The mathematical formula involved here has no substantial practical application except in connection with a digital computer, which means that if the judgment below is affirmed, the patent would wholly pre-empt the mathematical formula and *in practical effect would be a patent on the algorithm itself.* [Emphasis by the Court.]

It should be noted that the Court dealt only with process claims, and that Section 101 of the Patent Act also provides for patents of machines. A number of software patents, cast in terms of a machine or apparatus have been issued. In this connection the case of Bernhart and Fetter (2 CLSR 359, 417 F. 2d 1395), which was decided before the Supreme Court decided Gottschalk v. Benson, is interesting. Here the Court of Customs and Patent Appeals ordered a patent issued for an apparatus in which a computer, connected with a plotter and using a specified set of equations, plots selected views of a three-dimensional object. The court rejected the process or method claims, but allowed an apparatus or machine claim. The following language from the opinion shows the court's philosophy:

We think it is clear that in enacting section 101 Congress meant to exclude principles of laws of nature and mathematics, of which equations are an example, from even temporary monopolization by patent. Accordingly, no rule of law should be announced which would impress a monopoly upon all uses of equations disclosed by appellants here in their patent applications. To allow the claims in issue here would not prohibit all uses of those equations. As we have pointed out above, a member of the public would have to do much more than use the equations to infringe any of these claims. He would have to use them in the physical equipment recited in the claim. Moreover, all machines function according to laws of physics which can be mathematically set forth if known. We cannot deny patents on machines merely because their novelty may be explained in terms of such laws if we are to obey the mandate of Congress that a machine is subject matter for a patent. We should not penalize the inventor who makes his invention by discovering new and unobvious mathematical relationships which he then utilizes in a machine, as against the inventor who makes the *same machine* by trial and error and does not disclose the law by which it operates. The mandate of Congress in [Section] 103 is that "patentability shall not be negatived by the manner in which the invention was made." For the foregoing reasons we conclude that under the statute the apparatus herein claimed constitutes statutory subject matter. [Emphasis by the Court.]

In the same opinion the court also amplified its footnote in Prater and Wei, saying:

There is one further rationale used by both the board and the examiner, namely, that the provision of new signals to be stored by the computer does not make it a new machine, i.e., it is *structurally* the same, no matter how new, useful and unobvious the result. This rationale really goes more to novelty than to statutory subject matter, but it appears to be at the heart of the present controversy. To this question we say that if a machine is programmed in a certain new and unobvious way, it is physically different from the machine without the program; its memory elements are differently arranged. The fact that these physical changes are invisible to the eye should not tempt us to conclude that the machine has not been changed. If a new machine has not been invented, certainly a "new and useful improvement" of the unprogrammed machine has been, and Congress has said in [Section] 101 that such improvements are statutory subject matter for a patent. It may well be that the vast majority of newly programmed machines are obvious to those skilled in the art and hence unpatentable under [Section] 103. We are concluding here that such machines are statutory under [Section] 101, and that claims defining them must be judged for patentability in light of the prior art. [Emphasis by the Court.]

The first programming case to be considered by the Court of Customs and Patent Appeals after Benson & Tabbot was Knowlton (4 CLSR 799, 481 F. 2d 1357), in which the patent application disclosed a system for the computerized processing of list information such as business inventories, personnel files, business accounts, etc. The invention consisted of a number of computer program listings for use with a general-purpose digital computer; the application itself referred to the IBM 7049 System as one type of apparatus which could process the programs. The court held that a patent should be issued saying, ". . . when appellant's program is fully loaded into the computer the stored pattern of signals transforms the unprogrammed machine into a new structure, with all the necessary hardware elements being physically interrelated so as to enable them to perform their specified function." In support of this decision the court cited the Bernhart & Fetter case.

A week later in Comstock & Gilmer (4 CLSR 818, 481 F. 2d 905), the same court, in a similar case, said, "The specific computer itself, physically altered by the disclosed specific modifications and especially as altered by the operation of the disclosed program, is the structure to which appellants properly direct attention as the actual, practical embodiment of the invention." In this case, the Board of Patent Appeals (the inferior tribunal that denied the patent) "alluded to the proprietary nature of the structure of the IBM 1620 and the lack of access to information concerning that structure." The applicants offered to supply such information, and also contended that the technical manuals that would be supplied would encumber the application unnecessarily. The court agreed, saying, "We think it is somewhat unrealistic to suggest that the specification would become nonenabling in the future by change of manufacturer's requirements . . . In any event, if there were no way to convert programs designed for one model of computer to other models which replace it, the art of data processing would be thrust into a state of havoc far more detrimental to the public than the disadvantage which would flow from the particular invention here involved becoming nonenabling."*

Patent Validity

The issuance of a patent by the United States Patent Office means only that so far as that Office's examination has disclosed, the invention is novel, useful and unobvious. Currently, some 1500

---

*A late note. The CCPA followed this rule in Johnston, (4 CLSR 1491, 502 F2d 765); the U.S. Supreme Court, on appeal, invalidated the patent for obviousness, 5 CLSR 1133, 44 LW 4463 (March 23, 1976).

patents are being issued each week. It has been estimated that only 2 percent of these become the subject of litigation, but since 1966, more than 72 percent of those patents whose validity has been litigated in the courts of appeals have been found invalid, (Bruce B. Wilson, "Patents and Antitrust: How Clear is the Water," Nov. 30, 1972 speech before the Philadelphia Patent Law Association). In a speech in June 1974, to a conference sponsored by the Federal Bar Association and the Bureau of National Affairs, the Commissioner of Patents argued that only 50 percent were held invalid, counting *all* court cases, and this was a proper figure "since parties will not go to court unless they think they have a chance to win, and plaintiffs and defendants on the average will each be right half the time."

Action to enforce a patent is brought by the patentee in a United States district court, against the alleged infringer. The defendant will frequently defend on the ground that the patent is invalid because the invention is not new (Section 102), or is obvious (Section 103), or that the application did not disclose sufficient information.

Patent enforcement litigation is extraordinarily expensive and protracted. Two cases, commenced in May 1967 to test the validity of the Eckert-Mauchley patent were finally concluded in October 1973 when the federal court in Minnesota held the patent invalid. (Honeywell, Inc. v. Sperry Rand Corporation, 5 CLSR 79, 180 U.S.P.Q. 673.) The trial ran for 135 days; there were 160 witnesses and more than 30,000 exhibits! The defendant is frequently in a position to research the question of prior invention more thoroughly than the Patent Office, and to discover "prior art" which defeats the novelty of the invention. At the end of the trial, the judge found the patent invalid; one reason was that the patentees, Eckert and Mauchley, were not the original inventors.

In the computer field, the problem of previous invention is complicated by the fact that many procedures can be done with either software or hardware. One commentator has noted:

> . . . much prior art is already available in existing patent search facilities. In the same manner that software may anticipate hardware, so may hardware and the use thereof anticipate software. Many issued patents include extensive program description, even though the subject matter thereof is not

claimed in the patent. [Spencer, "Retrieval of Programming Technology for Patent Purposes," 52 *JPOS* 125, 127, (February 1970).]

Some Suggestions on Applying for a Patent

The critical point in getting a patent often occurs before the inventor sees a lawyer. Therefore, the best time to start thinking of patent protection is when the inventor starts thinking of the invention. As soon as an idea can be reduced to pictures and writing the inventor should write it out and sign it. The inventor should also, at as early a stage as possible, explain the invention and this written explanation to an outsider who can understand the invention. This outsider should also sign and date the written explanation. This provides an independent witness in case there is an argument over the date the invention was developed. The outside witness is important because the Patent Office gives very little weight to the uncorroborated testimony of the inventor when the issuance of the patent is contested.

It can be very helpful, particularly for a complex invention, if the inventor keeps a daily notebook or diary. This is best done in a hardbound notebook with numbered pages. Additional authenticity is provided to the diary by having each page dated and signed by another person.

There is often a tremendous desire on the part of the financial and marketing arms of the company to get the invention into public use as soon as possible. What is public use and what is private demonstration is a very difficult distinction and it frequently cannot be decided without a court battle. Two courts reached opposite results on this question in the ENIAC case.

The public use of the invention or offering it for sale in the United States, more than one year before the patent application is filed, prevents the issuance of a valid patent. The validity of a major software monitor patent has been contested on this ground. It is very important that the patent application be filed as soon as possible after the invention is made, preferably before any public disclosure. Under the present law, patent applications are kept secret by the Patent Office, so there is little danger of public disclosure through that agency.

Preparing a patent application and shepherding it through the intricacies of Patent Office procedure require the assistance of a specialist. Most lawyers are not trained to do this work and will hire patent counsel to work with them on these problems. Many large companies have their own patent counsel and the regular lawyer for every company should have little difficulty in finding competent patent counsel for a particular invention.

TRADEMARKS

Trademarks in the United States are the subject of both federal and state statute. By complying with these statutes, the trademark owner may obtain exclusive right to use the trademark for his product. Most trademark registrations are under a federal statute known as the Lanham Act, 15 U.S.C. Sections 1050-1127, which gives international protection. The use of a trademark by another company for commercial purposes can subject the infringer to heavy liability. The application of trademark protection to computer programs seems somewhat limited. The name of at least one language has been registered (TRAC), and the manuals describing it copyrighted (see Calvin N. Mooers, "Accommodating Standards and Identification of Programming Languages," 3 CLSA, Section 4-5, Article 1). Dr. Mooers brought suit against DEC and Western Electric to enforce his trademark and copyright. The names of a number of programs, such as Autoflow, have also been registered.

SOME PROBLEMS OF INTERRELATIONSHIP

There are two areas in which conflicts in legal authority or doctrine have particular pertinence to the question of legal protection of software. The first is the interaction between federal and state governments, the second is the conflicting monopoly philosophies of the United States government.

Federal Preemption

The Compco case quoted in Chapter 7 raised a question as to whether the law of unfair competition would be applicable when an article that could be patented or copyrighted, but had not been, was copied. This problem was compounded in 1969, when several judges of the United States Supreme Court indicated that the same reasoning might apply to trade secrets protected by contract (Lear, Inc. v. Adkins, 395 U.S. 653, 2 CLSR 235 (1969)).

In 1970, a federal judge in New York applied Lear and Adkins extraordinarily broadly to strike down a trade secret contract (Painton & Co. v. Bourns, Inc., 2 CLSR 550, 309 F. Supp. 271, 164 U.S.P.Q. 595). On appeal the Court of Appeals for the Second Circuit reversed, holding that Lear and Adkins did not upset the law of trade secrets (Painton & Co., Ltd. v. Bourns, Inc., 2 CLSR 558, 442 F. 2d 216). In 1973 the Court of Appeals for the Sixth Circuit in Kewanee Oil Co. v. Bicron Corp. (4 CLSR 37, 478 F. 2d 1074), held, however, that the trade secret law of Ohio was preempted by the operation of the federal patent law.

With this clear conflict between different federal circuits, the United States Supreme Court accepted the Kewanee case for review and on May 13, 1974 left no doubt that the law of trade secrets at the state level is in full operation (Kewanee Oil Co. v. Bicron Corp. 416 U.S. 470, 4 CLSR 1203, 94 S. Ct. 1879). It adopted the definition of the Restatement of Torts given in Chapter 7 and distinguished the objectives of the patent infringement and trade secret doctrines:

> The stated objectives of the Constitution in granting the power to Congress to legislate in the area of intellectual property is to "promote the Progress of Science and useful arts." The patent laws promote this progress by offering a right of exclusion for a limited period as an incentive for inventors to risk the often enormous costs in terms of time, research and development. The productive effort thereby fostered will have a positive effect on society through the introduction of new products and

processes of manufacture into the economy, and the emanations by way of increased employment and better lives for our citizens. In return for the right of exclusion—this "reward for inventions" . . . the patent laws impose upon the inventor a requirement of disclosure. To insure adequate and full disclosure so that upon the expiration of the 17-year period "the knowledge of the invention enures to the people, who are thus enabled without restriction to practice it and profit by its use" . . . the patent laws require that the patent application shall include a full and clear description of the invention and "of the manner and process of making and using it" so that any person skilled in the art may make and use the invention. When a patent is granted and the information contained in it circulated to the general public and those especially skilled in the trade, such additions to the general store of knowledge are of such importance to the public weal that the Federal Government is willing to pay the high price of 17 years of exclusive use for its disclosure, which disclosure, it is assumed, will stimulate ideas and the eventual development of further significant advances on the art . . .

The maintenance of standards of commercial ethics and the encouragement of invention are the broadly stated policies behind trade secret law. "The necessity of good faith and honest, fair dealing, is the very life and spirit of the commercial world."

. . . Trade secret law and patent law have coexisted in this country for over one hundred years. Each has its particular role to play, and the operation of one does not take away from the need for the other. Trade secret law encourages the development and exploitation of those items of lesser or different invention than might be accorded protection under the patent laws, but which items still have an important part to play in the technological and scientific advancement of the Nation. Trade secret law promotes the sharing of knowledge, and the efficient operation of industry; it permits the individual inventor to reap the rewards of his labor by contracting with a company large enough to develop and exploit it. Congress, by its silence over these many years, has seen the wisdom of allowing the States to enforce trade secret protection. Until Congress takes affirmative action to the contrary, States should be free to grant protection to trade secrets.

The decision was written by Chief Justice Burger and concurred in by Justices Blackmun, Marshall, Rehnquist and White. Justices Douglas and Brennan dissented, saying that the decision was "at war with the philosophy of" the Compco case.

Antitrust Considerations

As noted at the beginning of the discussion of patents, public policy in the United States favors competition and looks with disfavor on monopolies. Antitrust law is discussed in detail in Chapter 16.

The basic American antitrust policy was established by the Sherman Antitrust Act enacted in 1890 in response to a general public fear over the great business trusts and combines of the period, which threatened to dominate and control the economy. Other antitrust acts—Clayton, Robinson-Patman, Federal Trade Commission—followed; they are really supplements to the Sherman Act.

There has been discussion for some years about whether bundled software is a tie-in sale in violation of the Sherman and Clayton Acts.

In March 1969, Donald I. Baker, then a high-ranking official of the Antitrust Division of the Department of Justice (and perhaps the antitrust lawyer in the federal government who knew the most about the computer industry) discussed the tie-in question extensively.* He defined the term *tie-in* as follows:

> . . . any arrangement which forces a customer to take an undesired product in order to obtain the one he wants. The old IBM case was a classic: if you wanted to use an IBM tabulating machine, you had to use IBM's tabulating cards. (IBM v. U.S., 298 U.S. 131 (1933)). But the rules are not confined to dominant companies. A tie-in is illegal under the Sherman and Clayton Acts where: (1) two products are involved; (2) the

---

*Mr. Baker's full paper appears in 4 CLSA, Section 7-1, Article 1.

seller has some measure of economic power of the so-called 'tying product'; and (3) the other product (the so-called 'tied product') can only be obtained in conjunction with the tying product. In addition, there must be some reasonable amount of commerce involved. The economic evil of the tying arrangement is that it forecloses competition in the tied product, which no longer has to survive in the marketplace solely on its merits.

Mr. Baker summarized his discussion of tie-in sales as follows:

The implications of this broad tie-in rule for the computer software field are pretty obvious. The common existing practice of providing computer programs on a package basis has not seemed a source of major concern so long as computer programs have only been protected as trade secrets; since successful programs can be largely duplicated by others, a particular program is less apt to be a source of the type of economic power necessary to make it a tying product. (Indeed, most of the complaints to date have been based on the theory that computer programs were the *tied* product in a hardware-software tie-in).

However, all this will change if software becomes subject to some type of patent or copyright protection. A particular patented program may become indispensable to users in a particular field; it will thereby become a real source of economic power—and antitrust will have to be vigorously applied to prevent its use as a tying device. The fact that it is patented will at least assist in such enforcement, since the patent will enable a court to presume that the software supplier has the necessary economic power to be guilty of illegal tying.

Even though the purpose of a patent is to promote invention, there is no requirement in the United States Patent Law that a patentee must use his patent, or that he must manufacture or vend the patented apparatus or process, or that he pay to the United States any fees after that paid upon the initial issuance of the patent. A number of patents have been obtained, not for protection of an invention to be sold to the public, but merely as a defense against other inventors. This defensive use of patents has resulted in much litigation between the federal authorities and patentees, often resulting in mandatory licensing of the patent. And since alleged patent infringers often raise antitrust as a defense, the patentee who violates these laws cannot recover for the infringement, since he has misused his patent. The Sperry Rand-Honeywell case in which the Eckert-Mauchley patent was held invalid because it was not novel, also included an antitrust defense by Honeywell based on a questionable market-sharing agreement between Sperry Rand and IBM.

An unpatented or uncopyrighted product or program, protected only by contract, would not appear to differ, insofar as the antitrust laws are concerned, from statutorily protected programs. If a contract should require that an organization acquiring hardware use only software supplied by the vendor, it would seem subject to attack under both the Sherman and Clayton Acts. From several recent cases, it may be deduced that any provision in the contract prohibiting the user from attacking the validity of such a tie-in clause would be invalid. If hardware or software is sold, the seller releases his rights:

> If a manufacturer seeks to exercise control over the subsequent use or disposition of his product after he has sold it, it is per se an unreasonable restraint of trade. In general, he cannot condition his sale to a customer on any agreement or understanding limiting that customer's freedom as to how he will use or to whom he will resell that product. [Robert L. Werner, "Antitrust, Social Responsibility and Changing Times," RCA, New York (March 1974).]

For this reason alone, the lease or license of software with continued manufacturer support is almost mandatory if nonstatutory proprietary rights are to be protected.

part four

Contracting
for EDP

chapter 9

The Law of Contracts

As a computer manager, it is very important that you understand the law of contracts as it applies to the sale or lease of computer products. Properly drafted contracts assure that the intent and expectations of each party as to the subjects covered, the terms, and the product's or service's performance will be plainly stated in the agreement. Moreover, a clear understanding of the rights and duties arising from the contract enables each party to obtain maximum benefit from the relationship.

The actual drafting of the agreement is usually undertaken by the legal department or legal counsel for one or both parties. These specialists are the best qualified to assess the legal sufficiency of all terms incorporated in the agreement. But it is seldom that counsel are sufficiently familiar with the products or services bargained for to include, from their own experience, all requirements critical to satisfaction at the technical level. The first draft of a contract for software, for example, might not include specific reference to updates, such as subsequent releases or versions. The lessee might think this reference was present by implication, while the lessor had deliberately excluded it. Similarly the expectation of an imminent product announcement might be important in contracting for hardware. By telling counsel the terms and conditions most critical from a technical or operations standpoint, you can avoid potential disappointment and costly renegotiation or conversion.

When you participate in the contract process, it is particularly helpful if you know the legal meaning of terms widely used in contracting, the types of contracts which are available, and the rights and duties of parties thereunder.

CONTRACT FORMATION

The classic definition of a contract is "an agreement, upon sufficient consideration to do or not to do a particular thing." (2 *Bl. Comm.* 442.)

Formation of a contract requires (1) mutual assent and (2) consideration (usually money) or its substitute. Performance of a contract is the fulfilling of the duties created by it. When the duties are not fulfilled, remedies can be invoked to compensate the injured party for his losses.

MUTUAL ASSENT

Mutual assent or a meeting of the minds is accomplished by one party making an offer to another; acceptance of this offer forms an agreement. The concept is simple, but determining what is an offer that is capable of acceptance and what constitutes a valid acceptance can be tricky.

An offer must include a manifestation of a present intent to contract. It does not exist when the words or acts represent only preliminary negotiations or an invitation to accept offers such as "Are you interested?" Sales order forms which say, "This contract subject to approval at seller's home office," are not contracts at all; they are only offers which the seller may accept or reject. Likewise offers made as a joke or in anger such as "These disk drives have been nothing but trouble. I'm so fed up you can have them all for a dollar apiece!" are not valid offers. This is because a reasonable man would know that the speaker did not really mean to sell the drives for a dollar each, and there could be no meeting of the minds at that price.

An offer must be communicated to the offeree, because an offer is a promise, and the very nature of a promise necessitates communication. If a buyer finds out in a roundabout way that a seller has prepared an offer for him, he cannot go ahead and tell the seller he accepts. That effort is, at best, an offer to the seller which the seller may then accept or not as he chooses. When an offer is communicated to an offeree, but there has been an error introduced in the transmission and the offeree is unaware of that error, the offeror will usually be bound to the terms communicated. However, as noted in Chapter 11, data transmitters may be liable for negligence as well as for breach of their own contract with the offeror to transmit his message correctly.

The Acceptance

Mutuality of assent requires in addition to the offer, a valid acceptance of that offer.

An assent to be effective must be unequivocal and unqualified. Otherwise it is no assent at all, just a counteroffer which, by implication, rejects the original offer. Mere grumblings about the terms or inquiries for a better deal, however, are not rejections as long as they stop short of a real "no." For example, "I agree, but I'd rather have had better terms," a grumble, stops short of the counteroffer, "I agree to work for you, but I want $10 more a week."

The Uniform Commercial Code (UCC) which governs the sale of goods (but not the sale of land or contracts for personal services) is less restricting. The UCC construes the contract as made on the terms upon which the offeror and offeree do agree and treats the additional terms as proposals for additions to that contract. Further, as between "merchants" (persons specially skilled or experienced in dealing with the kind of goods involved in the transaction, UCC 2-104) the new terms do become part of the contract unless they would materially alter the contract or unless they are promptly rejected by the offeror. This provision illustrates the general purpose and effect of the UCC to expedite business dealings such as the sale or lease of computer hardware and software.

As with the offer, the acceptance must be communicated to the offering party. Contrary to the beliefs of many laymen, silence is not generally equivalent to assent. The exceptional situations where silence can operate as acceptance include: where the silence shows the intent to accept in accordance with the offer—"I'll take your silence as acceptance"; where having had an opportunity to reject, the offeree takes the benefit of goods or services; where the offeree has solicited the offer; or where in previous dealings between the parties they have in each case dispensed with the formality of an acceptance.

Other Factors in Deciding Whether an Agreement Has Been Reached

Sometimes an agreement that on the surface appears to be clear and precise may actually be full of misunderstandings. The effect of these misunderstandings on the existence or terms of the contract will vary with individual circumstances. Such misunderstandings can arise from the use of ambiguous terms, mistakes by either one or both parties, and errors in transmission.

The classic example of ambiguity was decided in the 1864 British case of Raffles v. Wichelhaus. There two parties contracted for a load of cotton to be shipped on the *Peerless* from Bombay. Neither party knew there were two ships named *Peerless,* and each party was thinking of a different ship. Since neither was aware of the ambiguity, and each had a different ship in mind, there was no meeting of the minds and no contract. Today such a possibility could result from a supposed contract for COBOL when each party has in mind a different COBOL.

The legal effect of a mistake will depend on whether it is a mutual mistake or the mistake of only one party, and whether the other knew or should have known of it. Unilateral mistakes by the offeror, if unknown to the other party, will generally result in a binding contract on the terms proposed. This makes accuracy of computation on which bids are based the responsibility of the bidder who should carefully check all proposals for mathematical and typographical errors.

Effect of Writings on the Existence or Enforceability of an Agreement— the Statute of Frauds and the Parol Evidence Rule

The Statute of Frauds is a law that requires certain kinds of contracts to be in writing. These include contracts for the sale of land, guaranty contracts, contracts for the sale of goods of $500 or more, and contracts which by their terms are incapable of being performed within one year. In most states oral contracts for these purposes are voidable. A few states consider them absolutely void.

The Parol Evidence Rule prohibits the use of oral statements to vary or add to the terms of a written contract entered into at the same time or after the oral statements were made, when the parties intend the written contract to be the complete agreement. This rule is important to remember when you negotiate for the sale of computer products and services. Parties should be careful to include in the written agreement all the terms and conditions important to the sale.

CONSIDERATION

This is the second major component of a contract; the bargained-for exchange of something of value. From the legal viewpoint, there are two important aspects to consideration. First, it must have been bargained for; second, it must be legally sufficient, i.e., have legal value.

Because it must be bargained for, consideration is not present when the agreement is based on something already done before the new promise is made. For example, a promise to deliver additional parts or help with installation after a computer is delivered, when the contract for the computer did not include those promises, is unenforceable; it lacks consideration. Similarly, an agreement to do something as a moral obligation is not enforceable in some states.

However, there is an important qualification. If the person to whom the promise is made changes his position in reliance on that promise, then the promise may be enforced by operation of law to the extent that justice requires. The courts substitute what is called promissory estoppel for the missing consideration in order to achieve a fair result.

Consideration is legally sufficient when each party gives up something of value which was his legal right to keep, or does something it was his legal right to refrain from doing. This is most often money, but could be an agreement to share confidential information, extend credit, extend the time for payment of a debt, or serve as a test site for a new product.

Generally the law will not look into the adequacy of the consideration when the parties have made a contract. This is because it would be too difficult for a court to assess the relative value the parties had placed on the exchanged acts or promises. Furthermore, it is fundamental to the law of contracts that parties of like sophistication deal with each other at arm's length. Therefore, in the absence of fraud, duress, and other inequalities in the negotiating process, the courts will not interfere to relieve a party of his own bad bargain.

THIRD-PARTY RIGHTS

There are three types of third-party agreements, and the distinction can be important. There are third-party beneficiary contracts, assignments, and novations.

In a third-party beneficiary contract, at the time of entering into the contract one of the parties tells the other to render performance to someone else—the third-party beneficiary. The most common example of this is the beneficiary under a life insurance policy. In an assignment, however, the introduction of the third party takes place after the original agreement has been formed. One of the original parties subsequently assigns his rights or delegates his duties to another. Thereafter the other original party must perform to or accept performance from the assignee, but the assignor is liable to the other original party for the assignee's failure. Novation is a three-way agreement whereby one of the original parties is replaced by a third new party, and the other original party agrees to accept the substituted performance without recourse to the re-placed party.

Most computer contracts have a clause which prohibits assignment without the written consent of the other party.

This is reasonable, because in the absence of such a provision parties are free to assign without notice to the other. By inserting this provision in their contract, the parties agree to incur liability for breaching the promise not to assign. However, it should be noted that in many cases the assignment itself will be valid; the other party to the contract is left with a claim against the assignor if the assignee does not perform. This result is predicted on the theory that prohibitions against assignments impede the flow of business.

WARRANTIES

A warranty is a stipulation that a certain fact related to the subject of a contract is, or will be, as it is stated or promised to be. Warranties can be express or implied. Express warranties are created by explicit statements; implied warranties come from the nature of the transaction or the relative situation and circumstances of the parties.

Under the UCC which governs the sale of goods, there are two types of express warranties: (1) those made by a statement of fact or promise, and (2) those made by description or sample. Two implied warranties are also included in contracts governed by the code: (1) a warranty of merchantability, which is a warranty created by law that the goods are of fair or average quality and suitable for the ordinary purpose the buyer would use them for, and (2) a warranty of fitness for a particular purpose known to the seller. The code, however, provides for the exclusion or disclaimer of warranties by words and actions which warn the buyer that goods are sold without warranties (as is) or with only those warranties specifically stated. Computer vendors make extensive use of this provision and commonly include a clause in bold-face type that excludes the implied warranties of merchantability and fitness as well as any other express warranties not referred to in the written agreement.

PERFORMANCE

The goal of a contract is the performance agreed upon. Hopefully the contract will be performed as agreed and no further problems will arise. But many contracts made in good faith are not performed for a variety of reasons. In response to these situations the law has developed a host of rules directed to the various reasons for nonperformance or incomplete performance and the degree to which performance has failed. First, it is important to decide when a party is under an absolute and present duty to perform. Many terms that look like absolute promises are, in fact, conditioned upon the happening of some event. For example, a vendor may agree to replace parts or perform unscheduled maintenance *when* notified that the equipment is inoperative.

Given an absolute duty to perform, the law recognizes nine ways by which the contract can be discharged other than by the party's performance. These are impossibility, frustration of purpose, modification, substituted contract, rescission, written release, accord and satisfaction, operation of law and account stated. The determination of the existence of a cause for discharge and the responsibilities of the parties in these various situations are too complex and diverse for a fair discussion in this volume. As a general rule, if either party cannot go forward for any reason with the performance bargained for, the parties should consult their lawyers immediately.

REMEDIES

Under the appropriate circumstances a party may recover money— either what he expended on the contract, or what the other party unjustly gained, or the value of his commercial expectation. When money damages are inadequate, a party may be able to compel performance.

The most frequently sought remedy is for damages for the benefit of the bargain, the value of commercial expectation. This is called compensatory damages and is made up of two elements: standard damages and consequential damages. The first of these are derived from formulas applied by the law to all contracts of a certain type, e.g., goods, personal services. For example, the standard measure of damages for breach of contract for the sale of goods is the difference between the contract price and the market price for the goods at the time and place where the goods were to be delivered.

Consequential damages are all losses resulting from the breach, which both parties as reasonable persons should have foreseen (when the contract was made) as likely to result from the breach. In computer contracts there is traditionally a clause inserted by the supplier expressly excluding liability for consequential damages. The effect is that each user then bears the risk of these losses personally even though the other party knew the damage might occur as a result of his breach. If the user is an intermediary, he then inserts a similar clause in his contracts with his users. For example, the hardware vendor protects it from claims for loss of programs and data resulting from machine malfunction, and the customer service bureau similarly protects itself against the end user.

chapter *10*

Some Special Aspects of Computer Contracting

Many contract considerations are specific to the particular computer product or service bargained for; however, some generalizations can be made. And two important factors common to all negotiations are not legal technicalities, but rather the use of good judgment and the application of system analysis techniques to the contracting process.

Of basic importance is specific knowledge of what is desired or expected from the other party and what you can reasonably provide in turn. Every vagueness or uncertainty must be identified and accounted for in some way in the agreement. For example, in a first-time software application, it may be more useful to require completion of a pilot or experimental project rather than to proceed directly to a full commitment. This will provide more complete data on which to determine reasonable parameters of elapsed time, man and machine hours, resulting costs, and necessary warranties. When uncertainties are unavoidable, it is better to select a procedure which takes these uncertainties clearly into account, such as a fixed price contract if you are a user, or a cost-plus agreement when you serve as a supplier.

After deciding what you want and what can be performed, you must make sure that these decisions are effectively incorporated into the agreement. An important legal principle here is the rule that one deals at arm's length when contracting with another. Only in special circumstances where injustice would otherwise result, e.g., fraud, duress, and certain mistakes, will the courts intervene to relieve you of your bad bargain. If a salesman's representations are what clinched the deal, those representations should be included in the final agreement. Otherwise, it will be difficult (if not impossible because of the Parol Evidence Rule) to show that they were relied upon as the basis of the contract. This is particularly true in a written agreement which specifically excludes external representations from its terms and warranties. If a new machine, for example, is supposed to give twice the throughput for the same job stream as the former machine, and that is why the new one was chosen, that understanding should be stated in precise and quantitatively measurable terms.

A supplier concerned about the aggressive enthusiasm of its sales force and knowing the limits of its product's performance, should state clearly in the agreement the performance for which it agrees to accept responsibility. This is very helpful in counteracting the legal liability that might result from undue "seller's puffing."

Finally, you must be diligent to hold off the execution of the agreement until you are satisfied with all its terms; this should be a nondelegable duty for every person or organization responsible for performing some action under the contract. In addition to the obvious occasions for persistence (such as when the parties disagree on a particular term and one eventually gives way) there are more subtle cases where firm insistence is called for. A written contract that omits an important representation may, as the other party says, have resulted from a typist error. But it might not have! In any event, the error should be corrected and not genially waived away on the understanding that the parties will perform their oral commitments.

STANDARD OR "BOILER-PLATE" CONTRACTS

Hardware vendors typically have formal and widely-used written contracts which define with particularity the basic relationship between the vendor and the customer, see for example, the IBM contract, Appendix F. When confronted with a printed form contract and what has been called the one-two punch of a take-it-or-leave-it attitude on the part of the vendor's contract negotiators and the smiling intimation on the part of the sales force that the agreement will be interpreted loosely at the local level, the buyer is apt to be confused. He may be unsure of the outcome if he does sign the form contract, or if he insists on negotiating a special contract. What if he tries to cross out or insert one or two terms on the form agreement, or if he chooses to sign nothing and attempts to do business by individual purchase orders?

At the outset of unbundling, June 1969, a number of lawyers, unsure of the impact on their clients, advised them to sign the new form contracts and wait and see how it worked in practice. Their advice was predicated on an equity consideration which enables courts to relieve a party from the onerous burdens of an unconscionable, one-sided contract. The feeling at that time was that the vendors had thought through the terms and conditions from their vantage point and then essentially presented these to the relatively unsophisticated user who was dependent on the vendor and thus in a weak, if not helpless bargaining position. That advice is now outdated. Many users now have years of experience with unbundling and in some instances now carry greater corporate weight than the suppliers. The better course now is to negotiate a contract fully, using the vendor form as a starting point at most, and turning a politely deaf ear to the importunings of the sales side of the vendor organization.

As part of the user education process, there have been published a number of helpful clause-by-clause analyses of vendor contracts. A selected list of these sources is included as Appendix G.

The authors' view, however, is that your organization's combined departmental checklist will indicate the terms and conditions you will wish to incorporate into your contract, along with a ranking of their importance. From this, your organization's lawyer can draft the "ideal" contract, and the negotiating personnel will know on which terms to insist and on which to compromise.

NEGOTIATING THE CONTRACT

Effective negotiation requires a blend of skills. These include a thorough understanding of the needs of the organization and of the technical and financial aspects of the product or service involved. At the same time, the negotiator must have strong interpersonal skills to arrive at an agreement most beneficial to his company. One such attribute is sensitivity to the timing of insistence or concession.

Often the blend of necessary skills is achieved by using a team made up of EDP personnel, a lawyer, and a finance officer. A critical factor in this structure is team solidarity. A team leader must be appointed and should brief his group on the overall strategy and the goal of each meeting, if there is more than one. It should be understood that the leader controls the participation of his group members in the meeting and can recess or terminate the discussions on behalf of his organization. For further reference, a most practical if somewhat cynical view of contract negotiating, is "Project Management Games" by Werner W. Leutert, which first appeared in the September 15, 1970 issue of *Datamation,* and is reprinted in *Computer Law Service,* Section 3-2, Article 2.

CONTRACTS FOR THE SALE OF HARDWARE

Hardware items, except for the hand calculator miniature computers, are priced over $500 and are thus within the purview of the Uniform Commercial Code (Sec. 2-201) which requires contracts for the sale of goods priced over $500 to be in writing. Because of the Parol Evidence Rule described in Chapter 9, the parties should take care that the written contract includes all items important to the contract.

As described earlier, express warranties included by the parties will be supplemented by the warranties implied by law, of merchantability and fitness for the particular disclosed purpose. However, the UCC permits—and most hardware vendors include—a clear, prominent statement of exclusion or disclaimer of all warranties except those specifically stated. This disclaimer may exclude warranties of merchantability and fitness in those vendor contracts. And, if the seller tenders a sample of the goods and the buyer does not inspect them, the seller is released from all warranties of quality that he had made and which an examination would have revealed, provided the goods equal the sample in quality.

Most buyers will initiate the procurement process through either a formal RFP (Request For Proposals) or an informal announcement to selected vendors that they are or might be in the market for a certain product, e.g., a front end processor, CRT terminals, or an entire system. This activity on the part of the buyer is the invitation for offers discussed in Chapter 9.

For a variety of reasons, such as price, appearance of impartiality, delivery schedules, weighing of technical features, and differing vendor warranties, the invitation will usually be circulated as widely as possible. However, the terms of specifications may be quite restrictive and favor one vendor over others. Where this is patently unreasonable, a thus foreclosed seller may have some recourse—for example, if the buyer is a governmental agency. From a marketing viewpoint, the seller may think it worthwhile to somehow let the buyer's top management know that the EDP department is not doing its best for the company.

The product and terms of sale of each vendor should be evaluated concurrently by the finance, legal, systems, operations, and management sectors of the user organization. A formal checklist should be used by each department as it evaluates each product and the supplier's terms with respect to the department's requirements. A sample checklist is included as Appendix H.

While there may be a tendency for one department of an organization to dominate in the selection process (frequently the pull is between the financial and technical sectors), the most functional approach is to write up a complete profile of each product being acquired and then to decide, after seeing all the information, which are the priority factors in the decision. Of course, in the interest of time, each product considered should have passed an initial threshhold of availability, price, and technical attributes.

Depending on the size and complexity of the procurement, there may need to be extensive bench marks and other tests run by the user or vendor on the proposed equipment, and site visits by the buyer to other customer installations using the product. Vendors frequently extend invitations to visit the manufacturing or test location as well. Requirements and vendor representations made during this preliminary process should be noted and retained for inclusion in the later contract.

Lease vs. Purchase

Someone in the user organization will do a lease/purchase analysis on equipment included in a procurement when this alternative is available under company policy. Trade-offs considered should include the legal position under each plan as well as financial and management considerations. Here again the organization's lawyer should provide specific information.

Generally, a lease differs from a sale in that title to the items leased remains in the lessor, while title in a sale passes to the purchaser. The importance of title concerns the rights and liabilities that the law attaches to ownership. These include risk of loss, creditor's rights to take over the property, power to transfer to a third party, and liability for taxes.

Because the risk of loss remains with the lessor-owner, as a practical matter lessees may find insurance provisions in their lease agreements which obligate them to protect against certain contingencies that the owner would find expensive to insure, e.g., riot, nuclear radiation.

Maintenance is customarily included in the rental and some operations managers have found that it tends to be superior to that performed under a supplementary agreement to maintain a purchased piece of hardware.

One important aspect of a well-drawn lease agreement is the clear differentiation between it and an installment purchase, which it closely resembles. Early participation by the company lawyer will guard against an intended lease being interpreted as a sale, with perhaps disastrous tax consequences.

The procurement checklist will have spelled out the type of acceptance tests required for the equipment and the minimal time period necessary to run the tests. It will also have listed the acceptable performance criteria including mean time between failure and mean time to repair. Thereafter the user will notify the lessor of his acceptance and commence payment under the lease.

A similar process takes place under a sale, but the sale contract also should resolve the time for passage of title and the transfer of risk of loss. Risk of loss most appropriately shifts upon installation and certification in writing by the vendor to the user. Title usually passes upon receipt of the full purchase price by the vendor and acceptance by the purchaser.

Vendor vs. Third-Party Leases

Third-party leasing has had its ups and downs since it first became a procurement alternative in the 1960s. The advantages of leasing from one who bought the equipment from the vendor rather than leasing directly from the vendor are mainly financial. Attractive savings are possible over the manufacturer's rental because these third-party leases are not full payout leases; that is, the lessor does not recover the full cost of the equipment during the lease, but relies on his ability to lease the remaining useful life of the equipment, which is longer than that of the first lease. In a rental situation, the owner usually has to take back the machine on short notice; this can be a major risk in as rapidly developing a field as computer technology.

Recently new forms of leasing (sometimes called leveraged leasing), in which the lessor is a group of individual investors and the lease is procured and managed by a fourth party, have appeared. The investors are particularly interested in tax savings, and the user-lessee should be sure to protect himself against the disinterest of the lessors in the performance of the system.

Insurance coverage can vary. Some contracts contain all risk coverage carried by the lessor (passed on to the lessee in his monthly payments). Others are less expensive but leave more remote risks to the lessee. Costs for identical insurance coverage by different lessors vary and a cost analysis should include this aspect of the procurement decision.

Tax considerations are also different in a third-party rather than a manufacturer's lease. Sales taxes in each case are usually passed to the lessee, but property taxes are frequently absorbed by the manufacturer-lessor and not by the third-party lessor.

Restrictions as to site relocation or return of equipment should be specifically negotiated. Normally the user cannot relocate equipment on lease and must return it as directed by the lessor at the end of a third-party lease. Manufacturers usually limit return to the place of original manufacture.

A danger of the third-party lease is something called a *hell or high water* clause. An example of such clause is "lessee agrees that its obligations are absolute, and shall continue in full force and effect, regardless of any disability of the lessee to use the equipment because of War, Act of God, government regulation, strike, loss or damage, obsolescence, breach of contract or warranty, failure of or delay in delivery, missed delivery or any other cause, and that its obligations shall not abate due to any claim or set-off against Lessor". In essence the lessee pays come *hell or high water;* hence the nickname.

Unpleasant as they are, these clauses have been held to be legal, see, e.g., Leasco Data Processing Equipment Corporation v. the Starline Overseas Corporation, 346 NYS 2d 288. When the lease is just a financing vehicle analogous to a bank loan such provisions are reasonable, because the lender need not let the user off the hook just because he made a bad deal and got a defective product. The wise user who finances his computer by lease will make certain that the manufacturer's responsibilities extend directly to him and that seller's warranties are not excluded by the lease agreement.

SOFTWARE CONTRACTS

Software contracts include agreements to obtain existing software or to develop software specifically for the individual user. Although software perhaps can be considered "goods" for the purpose of UCC coverage, personal service contracts for software development cannot.

Following unbundling the industry became familiar with differences among program products. These range from fully debugged programs accompanied by full documentation including user manuals, vendor support for updates and error correction on the one hand, and bare undebugged tapes at the opposite extreme. Similarly, contracts to develop software (sometimes known as contract programming) can also vary. These contracts can be for a total application, for specific work on a given application, or for programmers to work on one or more projects as assigned and supervised under user direction.

Program Products—Licenses

Because of the need to control dissemination and use of programs, software developers normally license software rather the contract for an outright sale. While the price may be a one-time cost, other terms such as the right to updates and "fixes" and statements of proprietary rights should differentiate this from a sale. But if the vendor gives little continued service, a court might still treat it as a sale. The reader will recall that a sale transfers all rights including title from the vendor to the vendee. Under a contract for sale of software the vendee could copy his purchased program and compete in the marketplace with his seller. Licensees, however, are usually restricted in the number of copies they can make for internal use and are prohibited entirely from knowingly distributing copies to others. Present limitations with respect to computer security have been ackowledged by licensors who now increasingly accept a *best-efforts clause* in a contract which obligates the licensee to protect the licensed software to the same degree and extent as its own proprietary products. The critical question concerning ownership of additions and changes to the software by the licensee are discussed in the chapter on intellectual property.

Software Development

Contracts for software development usually can be analyzed as (1) contracts for personal services or "warm-body" contracts, (2) cost-plus-a-margin-of-profit contracts—for specific but speculative projects, and (3) fixed-price contracts—for specific jobs which are more easily costed out by the bidder or on which he is willing to risk a loss. Each of these contract choices carries advantages and drawbacks for customer and supplier.

The "warm-body" contract is advantageous from a unit cost standpoint since the employer can select personnel and utilize a pay scale he determines appropriate to the level of the task. However, the degree of supervision required and the variation in talents available may operate to negate expected cost savings in the long term. A cost-plus agreement protects the supplier from the risk of under-bidding a job but lacks certainty for the customer's budgeting process. The fixed-price contract benefits the customer because he knows exactly what the job will cost. It is the least certain for the contractor who must insure himself against mistakes in assessing the parameters of time, material, and other cost factors on which he bases his bid. As the degree of price certainty rises for the customer, so does the cost for the same project to offset the accompanying risk to the supplier.

Contract Considerations

Contracts for both program products and development should include detailed specifications, written progress reports when applicable, a requirement for full documentation for both internal and user needs, acceptance tests, and signoffs. Along with these items, warranties, rights in data, indemnification for consequential damages, defense of infringement claims, and security precautions should be negotiated.

The customer may need only a nonexclusive license or may insist on full ownership rights in a program developed exclusively for him. A program which malfunctions can result in loss to third parties. The contractor will want to disclaim any liability for this occurrence; the user will wish to be held harmless by the supplier. Presently the standard measurement of liability offered by suppliers is the amount paid by the customer under the contract.

Programs may infringe the proprietary rights of other program owners. Current vendor policy is to defend these claims at vendor expense. This seems fair to both parties.

Program security is a current unsolved problem. A recent and interesting solution is proposed by a company which offers to serve as escrow agent when the supplier chooses not to provide source code with his program and the buyer wants the security of having source code available should the need arise. The source code is kept in a designated bank vault by the escrow agent.

In software development contracts the agreement should specify which party has control over selection and management of personnel. The closer the programmers will work with the user's own people, the more the user should be able to control the additional work force. Since the supplier will want to allocate its manpower as it chooses, some conflict can arise. One compromise solution is to provide the user with the right of refusal of any one or more particular people supplied. And, if the user wants certain individuals, their participation can be spelled out in the contract. Another concern of the user is the space and support allocated to the outside people. A clause which states the outside cost to be allocated to their "room and board" will safeguard against unanticipated collateral expenses.

SERVICE BUREAUS

Service bureaus are computer installations which offer a range of services to external organizations. Such services range from companies which sell only computer time and access to their application programs, to those which take raw data, place it in machine-readable form, process it and return an edited, finished output in the form of payrolls, invoices, or management reports.

Service bureaus are true middlemen between the end user and the hardware and software suppliers. Their products can be either a service or goods or a mixture of both. To the extent that they deal in goods, their contracts may be subject to the Uniform Commercial Code.

Depending on the type of service offered, the service bureau may have custody or possession of the user's data and programs. (The distinction can be important for a possessor may owe a higher duty of care to the owner than would a mere custodian; see "Torts," Chapter 11.) It may also be serving competing user companies.

The warranties that service bureau customers will want to have expressly stated will be fitness of the service for their particular purpose and merchantability. Other user-oriented provisions are expressions of responsibility for security to prevent loss, alteration, or improper access to customer's data; minimal guarantees of correctness of information furnished; and assumption of liability for other consequential damages.

The service bureau, however, will wish to limit its liability by omitting these provisions from the contract, and where appropriate, specifically disclaiming liability therefore. The bureau may wish to include covenants which permit it to terminate the service to the customer at will; it may require a money payment for user-caused systems crashes or other interruptive activity; and it may want to get an agreement from the user to keep confidential data and proprietary programs owned by the bureau or leased by it from a third party.

TIME-SHARING NETWORKS

Time-sharing networks range from full-service centers analogous to service bureaus to message-switching services more like the telephone companies.

Since the phrase *time-sharing network* is essentially ambiguous and lacks an established meaning, the service actually bargained for is what controls in determining the legal aspects of the agreement.

Assuming that the service offered is truly time-sharing, i.e., the simultaneous use of a computer system from multiple terminals, some generalizations can be made. The parties will have to decide whether the user is to supply his own terminal and data communications equipment and what choices of line speeds and communications codes, etc. are available under this approach, or whether the customer must agree to lease or purchase a network-supplied terminal. In the latter case, there must be provision for housing and maintenance of the equipment at the user's site and provision for billing for use of the equipment as well as for use of the system from installation through termination and removal. Communication costs will normally include current telephone charges passed on to the user. Some agreements will specify the times of day the user may access the system. If proprietary programs or data are on the system, there should be a promise by the network to keep these confidential and by the user to abide by network security provisions, such as proper use of user identification numbers. These items supplement the considerations covered in the section on service bureaus, above. Readers are also referred to Chapter 4, "Data Communications," for further treatment of this area.

FACILITIES MANAGEMENT

As originally offered, facilities management was a service by which a team of computer professionals assumed responsibility for operation of a customer's home-site computing facility on a long-term basis. Variants of this concept now include providing for a customer's computing needs off site using the supplier's in-house nonsaturated system, like a service bureau, or delivering a turnkey system that the supplier also agrees to maintain.

Some computer organizations have achieved significant success in offering the original form of the service, notably Electronic Data

Systems of Dallas, Texas; and in 1973 Tymshare, Inc. contracted with the Stanford Research Institute to manage its node on the ARPA network. However, in its original form facilities management has not generally proved as attractive an undertaking for suppliers or users as was initially hoped. Problems have included financial instability of the managing organization, lack of control by the facility owner, the facility manager's need for familiarity with the customer's particular business, and inflexibility of the arrangement to meet changing business or technical requirements.

Contracts for pure facilities management, as opposed to remote batch or time-sharing use of a supplier's home computer, deserve particularly close scrutiny by negotiating teams from each party. An important instance of the facilities management-user company relationship is the degree to which the fortunes of one affect the other. For example, if the supplier has provided for a too narrow profit margin, in a squeeze it will cut back on the cost areas under its control—personnel and software development. This has a direct impact on the user organization that expects the best quality performance for its dollar commitment. Similarly, the user organization that fails to specify its needs is likely to blame the facilities management company when these needs aren't met. It is in the clear and immediate interest of both parties to develop a contract which is sensitive to the expectations of the other side. The user's standard checklist for contracting should be expanded to include information as to the supplier's long-term financial status, provision for reports on mid- and long-term plans for software development, and progress reports related thereto. It should certainly contain provision for operating reports and cover the unique problems in the personnel area.

Termination provisions are particularly important. The dissolution of a facilities management relationship is extremely difficult, since the management company is almost embedded in the customer. Such a company should be willing to agree to simple and clear terms on this issue, because its primary selling point is the argument that it can do the job more effectively than the customer. If at any time the customer can do the job a better way, the facilities manager is not living up to its prime purpose.

The supplier should supplement its checklist by insisting on periodic review of the user requirements by an appropriate level of user management.

MAINTENANCE AGREEMENTS

Owners of hardware have the option of performing their own maintenance, or of procuring service from the equipment manufacturer or from a third-party maintenance organization.

The decision analysis should include the standard service acquisition checklist and should also take into account

(1) an objective determination of the user's real ability to serve himself;

(2) the projected impact on resale if equipment is maintained by someone other than the manufacturer;

(3) provisions for obtaining vendor coverage at a later time;

(4) the ability to control or influence assignment of personnel (so as to avoid serving as a training center for a succession of customer engineers);

(5) response time for service (on call and emergency);

(6) flexibility of preventive-maintenance scheduling; and

(7) responsibility in a mixed-vendor installation.

This analysis is essentially a business evaluation. From a legal standpoint the contract should reflect the decisions made during the analysis in a form that is sufficiently definite and certain that enforcement will be relatively easy.

On the critical issue of acceptance by a computer manufacturer of maintenance responsibility for equipment previously maintained by a third-party service organization, the CDC Field Engineering Contract for third-party maintenance could serve as a model. This contract is included as Appendix I.

PROBLEMS WITH MULTIPLE VENDORS

The multivendor computer room is a phenomenon of the 1970s. The availability of plug-to-plug compatibles and add-on or extended memories, coupled with significant cost savings, have prompted growing numbers of mixed-equipment configurations. Most of the experience has been good, and the one-vendor shop is becoming increasingly rare.

However, only the prudent have reaped the real rewards promised by lower prices. The careless planner is still a sorry statistic that the mainframe vendor can use to warn its customers from straying from the single manufacturer's fold.

One of the authors has operated a multivendor shop and it can work. We suggest adding as part of the contract checklist, the experiences that others have had with the combination proposed, such as an add-on memory by X to a specific model of computer Y; or a front-end processor from A with a mainframe by B and I/0 devices by C. Peculiar and trivial quirks can result in a good merger with some products—and can cause chaos with others.

The technical checkout should be followed by a supplier responsibility check. Will mainframe manufacturer X still respond to the user's statement that down time is X's problem when the organization uses a foreign communication controller? Or will each supplier point the finger at the other while the system is down and unproductive. What about a third-party maintenance contract? Will the customer engineers be as agile with the new equipment as with those on which they were originally trained?

Will the "foreign attachment" cause any contractual problem with a mainframe supplier, either as to present warranties or the user's ability to return or sell a machine with assurance that the manufacturer will agree to maintain it? The mainframe companies are reluctant to cooperate in some situations, and there has been litigation on the question of allowing the connection of foreign add-on memories. Whether it is worthwhile to the user to become embroiled in such a battle depends to a good degree on comparing the probable savings from this equipment with the time that will be lost from productive work if the mainframe is not serviced by the manufacturer, or if the user becomes involved in litigation between manufacturers—as a witness or even as a party.

part five

Computer Errors

chapter *11*

Tort Law

Tort law covers the civil injuries caused by individuals and organizations to the person or property of others. Tort law differs from contract law in that the injury usually arises from a breach of a duty created by law rather than from the agreement of the parties. It differs from criminal law in that the injured party has a right to sue the *tort-feasor* (one who does the wrongful act) for compensation for the injury, while in a criminal situation the state prosecutes the perpetrator and invokes penal sanctions (such as fines or imprisonment) against him but usually makes no award to the victim.

The categories are not exclusive. The same act may be both a breach of contract and a tort. For example, the incorrect transmission of a message may be a breach of a contract provision to deliver it properly and at the same time a breach of duty to exercise due care in the performance of an obligation—a possible tort. Similarly, wrongfully taking a program of another can be both a criminal theft and a tort of unfair competition or conversion.

TORTS

Torts are usually classified as (a) intentional, (b) negligent, and (c) strict liability or liability without fault. *Intentional torts* are those in which the actor actually intends to do harm or is substantially certain that his act will cause injury. *Negligence* is a careless act that injures the person or property of another, such as failing to see a red light and hitting another car in an intersection. *Strict liability* or *liability without fault* is imposed on activities which are inherently dangerous, such as blasting, and in recent years, for some injuries from defective products.

Intentional Torts

Intentional torts require the doing or failure to do an act intending thereby to harm another, and findings that the harm is inflicted, that the injured person has not consented to the act and that the actor is not privileged in any way to have committed the act (e.g., handcuffing a person pursuant to a valid arrest). Because an intentional tort is a purposeful injury, the plaintiff does not have to prove actual damages in order to recover something from a legal action. Moreover when willfulness can be proved, courts' will often allow punitive damages both to punish the defendant and to compensate the plaintiff, such as in the Ford Motor Credit Company case discussed later.

Negligence

Negligently caused injuries are inflicted without malice. Therefore, the law doesn't seek to punish the wrongdoer, but only to compensate the injured from the assets of the careless person (or his insurer). In striving for fairness the law has evolved several tests which must be passed before the plaintiff can recover. The defendant must have done or failed to do something that a reasonable man in the circumstances should have done; this duty must have been owed to the plaintiff. The breach of the duty must have actually caused the injury. The injury itself and the way it happened must have been foreseeable to the defendant. The plaintiff must have suffered damages and must (in most states) have been free of contributing to his own harm.

Failure to act in an appropriate instance is as wrongful as is doing an affirmative act. The classic case involves a tugboat that lost its barges in a storm because it could not hear the weather forecast. The court held the tug owner had a duty to have aboard, and use, a radio to hear weather reports. The T. J. Hooper, 60 F 2d 737 (1932). One can conceive of occasions when modern courts will require that one have and use computers for certain functions in order to avoid liability.

The reasonable man described above is as artificial as the average American family of 2.4 children. But it serves a similar function as a measuring device, in this case the reasonableness of the actions of persons. There are two key extensions of this rule. One is that people of superior knowledge or skill will be held to a standard reasonable for one of their capabilities. Thus a computer professional might be negligent in a computer environment when a layman would not. Secondly, the test is reasonableness under the circumstances. Emergencies require different responses than normal daily activities, and knowledge of an existing condition increases responsibility.

Breach of the duty, the act unreasonably done or omitted, is often obvious. Sometimes, however, it has to be based on a surmise of what happened. The doctrine of *Res Ipsa Loquitur* (the thing speaks for itself) holds that when an injury occurs which, in the normal course of events would only happen through the negligence of someone, *and* the instrument causing the injury was within the exclusive control of the defendant, *and* the plaintiff was free from fault, then a court will treat the occurrence of the incident as permitting the jury to infer negligence. Computer components or systems used in a closed shop environment may fall within this rule.

The duty of care must be owed to the plaintiff. This is one way of limiting responsibility for unintentional injuries. A simple example of lack of duty to the plaintiff is that of a defendant shipwrecked on a desert island. After searching the island for people and finding none, the defendant threw a coconut over his shoulder and hit a person who had just been washed ashore from a second wrecked ship. There being no one on the island originally, there was no duty to anyone; the second person being washed ashore was totally unforeseeable and his injury a true accident. However, the presence of other drivers is foreseeable to automobile drivers. Lessees and end users are foreseeable to computer owners and thus owed a duty of due care. They are, as Justice Cardozo said in the famous Palsgraf* case, "within the orbit of the risk."

Once the duty of care and its breach have been established the court looks to see if the defendant's act actually caused the injury. If so, the second policy limitation of liability for unintentional injuries is applied. Was the defendant's act the proximate cause of the injury? Unless both the result and the means of harm are foreseeable, courts are reluctant to find the actor liable. Likewise, when a third person has had the opportunity and duty to defuse the harm and doesn't, this supervening act will discharge the defendant. For example, if defendant negligently leaves dynamite caps where a young child could find them and one does, but the father sees them and fails to take them from the child, a subsequent injury will be attributed to the father's failure to act rather than to the defendant's original negligence.

In many states the injured party must not be contributorily negligent: he must have been totally free from fault in order to recover. This is a harsh rule as applied in many instances, so some courts have softened this requirement by providing that if the defendant has the last clear chance to avoid the injury and fails to, he will be liable even when the plaintiff also has been negligent. Some states (and many foreign countries) have adopted a comparative negligence view, under which the plaintiff, if his negligence was less

---

*The facts of Palsgraf v. Long Island R.R. Co., 248 NY 339, 162 N.E. 99 (1928), were that a passenger was running to catch one of the defendant's trains. Defendant's employees, trying to assist her to board it, dislodged a package from her arms, and it fell upon the rails. The package contained fireworks, which exploded with some violence. The concussion overturned some scales, many feet away on the platform, and they fell on the plaintiff injuring her. The Court found no negligence to Mrs. Palsgraf who was unforeseeable, beyond the orbit of danger created by defendant's employees' acts.

serious than defendant's, can recover to the extent that he was innocent.

Third-Party Responsibility

Owners, employers, and parents of minors are the persons most likely to have responsibility for the negligence of others. This is called vicarious liability and subjects one to full liability for the damages due to an injury caused by another whom the law determines is under the supervision and control of the defendant. An employer, owner, or parent may also be personally liable for his negligence in hiring or assigning certain duties to an employee or in entrusting a car to a known bad driver or in failing to control a vicious child.

Strict Liability

The difference between strict liability and ordinary negligence is that in strict liability the duty of care is an absolute duty to make safe, and contributory negligence is no defense. The keeping of vicious dogs and dynamiting are examples of ultrahazardous activities for which one can be held strictly liable. The activities have just enough usefulness to society not to be outlawed, but they are so intrinsically dangerous that any harm proximately resulting will be deemed to have come from the breach of defendant's duty of care. While the defendant usually cannot claim that the plaintiff was contributorily negligent, he may show that plaintiff assumed the risk. Assumption of the risk means that plaintiff recognized and understood the danger involved and voluntarily chose to encounter it. The assumption may be express—as in the exchange, "Don't ride that horse it's wild." "I don't care, I'm not afraid"—or implied, such as from passing a gasoline truck on a blind curve.

Products Liability

Products liability is essentially consumer oriented. Its application emanates from another famous Cardozo decision, MacPherson v. Buick Motor Co. 217 N.Y. 382, 111 N.E. 1050 (1916). In that case the court held the Buick automobile manufacturer liable for injuries caused when a defective wheel that was part of the original equipment collapsed resulting in injuries to the purchaser even though the buyer's contract was with a dealer, not with the manufacturer. Since that time the duty owed to third parties has been extended to persons other than ultimate purchasers—even to bystanders under some tort theories—and to property as well as to persons. Similarly, liability has been extended to persons who supply components of an article, e.g., circuit boards in a computer, to those who sell under their brand name goods manufactured by others, and to second-hand dealers who recondition goods. The defendant is usually not liable if the product causes injury only when used in an unforeseeable way or when an intermediate seller (retailer) knows of the defect and fails to correct it or warn the purchaser.

Depending on the state in which the lawsuit occurs, the kind of product and the relation of the injured person to the supplier, different theories will be relied on by plaintiffs to recover. These can include strict liability, negligence, intentional harm, or a breach of warranty, express or implied. (See "The Law of Contracts," Chapter 9, for a discussion of warranty.) Every vendor of a computer product that could cause harm through a design or manufacturing defect is potentially affected by products liability law. When the injury is to human beings rather than to property or an economic interest, many courts will somehow find liability notwithstanding warranty disclaimers.

Unfair Competition

This category of torts concerns injury to business interests and relationships. The defendant may have caused people not to deal with the plaintiff; interfered with existing business relationships; passed off his goods as plaintiff's; or taken plaintiff's ideas, designs, etc. and improperly passed them off as his own. In so doing, defendant may have defamed plaintiff or disparaged his business; caused a third party to breach a contract with plaintiff; infringed plaintiff's patent, copyright or trade name rights; or misappropriated a trade secret. The remedies in these cases may be money damages, injunction (an order from the court to stop the unfair competition), or both.

One case that received considerable publicity involved the theft of a program by an employee of the defendant through wrongful remote access to plaintiff's files at a service bureau. The employee was convicted of theft;* in a civil suit the jury found his employer liable for over $200,000 for its unfair competition.

Defamation

Defamation is the intentional or negligent publication to third parties of statements which injure the reputation of plaintiff or his goods. The words must be capable of a defamatory meaning; they must have been understood to defame plaintiff, and in most instances must have resulted in specific injury. The statement must be untrue and the plaintiff must not have consented to its publication. These statements may be oral (slander) or written (libel).

Some defamations are privileged. For example, absolute privilege extends to any remarks made on the floor of Congress, to statements pertinent to judicial proceedings and high executive officers of the government, and to communications between spouses. Conditional or qualified privilege extends to inferior legislative bodies and inferior executive and administrative officers. Newspapers have a qualified privilege to report accurately legislative, judicial, executive, and other newsworthy proceedings, e.g., National Computer Conference. Conditional privileges may be lost if the defamer acts with malice, or with lack of belief in the statement.

Two other privileges are important. There is constitutionally based privilege to comment on public officials, public figures, and people in the public eye. This privilege has been applied to the media, but arguably can extend to face-to-face comments by private individuals. This privilege is lost if the statement is false and either deliberately misstated or made recklessly without regard to its truth or falsity. The second privilege is protection of private interests and is applicable to one's personal interest, family, employment, or a common interest in business affairs. The privilege requires that the

---

*See Ward v. Superior Court, 3 CLSR 206 (1972).

alleged defamer have a reasonable belief that an important interest of his own, of the reader or listener, or of a third person is being threatened, that the defamation is relevant to the interest involved, and that the publication was made believing that the recipient could protect or assist in protecting that interest. This privilege covers advice not to extend credit, and comments on employee performance which are made internally or to prospective employers.

Because of constitutional requirements of freedom of speech, injunctions will not normally be given to restrain threatened defamation of individuals. However, damages are available after the defamation.

Disparagement

Disparagement differs from defamation in that it applies to non-defamatory falsehoods such as "Plaintiff does not sell tape drives" (when he does) or that X is no longer in business (when he is active in business). Disparaging a product can take place when a competitor tells a customer that X Co.'s equipment is poorly made. Again there are privileges such as protection of others and a privilege to claim honestly that one's product is better than someone else's.

Interference

Interference with contract requires an intention to induce a third person to breach a contract with the plaintiff or an act to make a contract more onerous to fulfill, e.g., crashing a service bureau system so that it can't process its customer's work.

Interference with prospective business involves an abuse of competition such as violence, lies, and bribery.

Misrepresentation

Misrepresentation is a tort in which the defendant intentionally or negligently represents to the plaintiff material statements of a past or present fact which are false and on which the plaintiff justifiably relies to his detriment. Normally there is no duty to disclose information, but in positions of trust or unequal dealing, the duty to speak may be present, for example, if a manufacturer announces a substantial product change three days after signing a contract with a customer, and the supplier knows that the customer would have waited for the new product if it had known of its existence and imminent availability. In such a case, the manufacturer would have to rewrite the contract, or face a lawsuit for damages.

A leading case concerning misrepresentations in the computer service industry is Clements Auto Co. v. Service Bureau Corp., 2 CLSR 102, 298 F. Supp. 115 (1969) aff'd. 2 CLSR 143, 444 F.2d 169 (1971). There the customer, Clements Auto Co., successfully sued Service Bureau Corp. for fraudulent misrepresentations made to induce Clements to purchase data processing services. These misrepresentations included statements by salesmen that it was necessary for them to automate their accounting. The court found that the statement were false for there were in fact other alternatives. The statements were of a past or present fact, not a mere opinion or prediction, and were made with the intention that plaintiff rely on it in deciding to purchase the services, which plaintiff did to its detriment as the system failed to work properly.

TORT LAW AND THE COMPUTER

So far there have been few cases of intentional torts involving computers. Those that did occur were largely of sabotage to computer systems, of conversion (the civil corollary of theft), or of forms of unfair competition.

The potential for unintentional tort liability increases as the computer becomes more widely used. Computer-operated machines are capable of causing physical injury in a plant and conceivably to nearby persons and property. Malfunctioning systems can endanger medical patients in a variety of ways from diagnosis through treatment; the chance for error affects (among others) those connected to computer-controlled lifesaving devices and those taking prescription drugs prepared in reliance on computer-generated drug interaction reports. Computer systems in control centers or aboard vehicles can endanger airline or train travelers; reservation systems can oversell space. Third parties injured in such situations might well recover on a theory of *Res Ipsa*. Computer error can cause faulty input to credit bureaus to adversely affect credit ratings, and careless proprietors of information data banks may breach a duty to secure the privacy of individual data subjects.

Persons may become liable for failing to use a computer, as the tugboat owner was liable for failing to use a radio, and conversely persons may be liable for using a computer when they should have performed a function personally, i.e., where human judgment is required. A classic case is Ford Motor Credit Co. v. Swarens (2 CLSR 347, 447 SW 2d. 533), in which a computer error caused the company to believe that Mr. Swarens had not been making payments for his new car. Twice the company employees visited the plaintiff and told him he was delinquent, twice he showed cancelled checks establishing currency. The third time he showed a shotgun and invited them to leave. Thereafter his car was repossessed. The Kentucky courts held for Mr. Swarens and awarded him punitive damages as well as compensatory damages. The Court of Appeals emphasized the importance of establishing liability in the case, saying:

> Ford explains that this whole incident occurred because of a mistake by a computer. Men feed data to a computer and men interpret the answer the computer spews forth. In this computerized age, the law must require that men in the use of computerized data regard those with whom they are dealing as more important than a perforation in a card. Trust in the infallibility of a computer is hardly a defense, when the opportunity to avoid the error is as apparent and repeated as was here presented.

Liability for undue reliance on computer output could also extend to internal or independent auditors who certify a company's financial status without knowing the truth or falsity of records generated by machine.

A products-liability theory of recovery is quite likely when hardware or systems errors proximately cause an injury to a user. Strict liability is likely with experimental equipment, certain types of process control computers, and for those under certain statutory duties, such as the duty to provide secure personal information systems.

As a prudent computer manager, you should be alert to the potential of intentional harm to your organization by social malcontents, disgruntled employees, or business competitors (see Chapter 14, "Security," for further discussion of computer abuse). You should also be alert to the activities of zealous employees who may take programs from competitors (see, e.g., Ward v. Superior Court 3 CLSR 206) or compromise another's system to give your organization a business advantage.

Because liability for negligence results from carelessness, you, the computer manager, must emphasize proper performance of tasks; regular inspection of equipment and testing of systems; warning of suspected or known defects; and limitation of warranties to others when appropriate. In so doing, you not only help protect your organization from liability for negligent acts, but minimize your company's risk in liability without fault situations.

chapter *12*

Privacy

The computer trade press has, through the years, along with the newspapers and magazines of general circulation, published a number of articles, often of a scare nature, on how "Big Brother Computer" invades the citizen's privacy. There is no doubt that the computer's ability to store vast quantities of information and retrieve selected items almost instantaneously does, by its efficiency, affect the collection and distribution of personal information. However, the problem of privacy is more a question of public policy and social conscience than a technical question involving the computer, though there are many technical problems still unsolved. There are now a few laws within the United States regulating the storage of personal information in computerized form*; others will

---

*See the discussion below of the Privacy Act of 1974 and the state statutes and local ordinances in Appendix 5-2b and c of the *Computer Law Service.*

undoubtedly be enacted. Computer people should be familiar with the questions involved and should be prepared to discuss the effect of the computer on personal privacy with both management and the general public.

A corporation should, in any of its automation projects that might adversely affect personal privacy, give serious consideration to these aspects so that its response to possible criticism not only will cool the criticism, but improve the corporate image. Similarly, with the general public, computer people must be able to respond to fears of the average citizen and to point out the advantages of the computer in our modern economy.

The personal information which is in data files, be they ones maintained by the Internal Revenue Service, law enforcement agencies, credit bureaus, or insurance companies is already there to a large degree, but the expense of searching through the documents for pertinent information has, so far, acted as a brake upon the development of extensive individual dossiers. The advent of the computer and its ability to sort data relatively cheaply has changed the economic equation and has made feasible the construction of the large personal data bank for governmental or private purposes.

Personal data, tax returns, and questionnaires in government files have historically been considered confidential and their disclosure has been limited to authorized sources. In theory this type of data should be very difficult for other government agencies or for private individuals to obtain. But the current thinking is that its unauthorized acquisition or copying may be easier when the data is in machine-readable form than when it is printed.

The accuracy of data within the data base is important from several aspects. The accuracy of the source of the data may be suspect. For example, a statement that a man is an habitual drunkard could have as its source either the man's physician or a jealous co-employee. The report from the former would probably be accurate, the report by the latter might well be suspect.

The completeness of the data is another area of difficulty. The simple report that a girl aged 20 is arrested for disturbing the peace does not say whether she was drunk and disorderly, was protesting the Vietnam War, or was a right winger protesting the protesters of the Vietnam War. If the entry does not state the disposition of the young lady's case, a person reviewing the record cannot properly evaluate it; a full acquittal after a jury trial certainly means something different from a conviction and a sentencing to six months in jail.

A third aspect of accuracy is the currency of the data. What was useful credit information once—perhaps the fact that a programmer is employed by Company A at $18,000 per year—may be meaningless after five years, when he has left that company, formed his own firm, and sunk his life savings therein.

Systems designers are considering these points more and more but their procedures may work well on paper, and not work out in practice. It should be emphasized that not only must privacy procedures be designed, but they must be followed. Particular attention must be given to insuring that corrections and deletions of data called for by the update procedures are actually executed. Security can be compromised internally as well as externally, and the enforcement of prohibitions against unauthorized use must be audited on a regular basis. The system must include quality-control checks built into the input, and search phases to insure the accuracy of data. Breakdown of these procedures is caused by laziness, time pressures, a search for shortcuts, and the like; the EDP manager, as well as management, must resist these temptations and insist on audits on a regular basis to insure that the system has not been harmed.

One of the more widely read reports on the question of computer privacy is that issued by a special committee established by Elliot Richardson when he was Secretary of Health, Education and Welfare, and chaired by Willis Ware of the Rand Corporation. The report* was released July 30, 1973 and recommends: (1) federal legislation guaranteeing an individual's right to find out what information is being maintained about him in computerized systems, and to obtain a copy on demand; (2) that the legislation also allow a person to contest the accuracy, pertinence, and timeliness of any information in a computer-accessible record about him; (3) that record-keeping organizations be required to inform individuals, on request, of all uses made of information that is being kept about

---

Records, Computers and the Rights of Citizens, Report of the Secretary's Advisory Committee on Automated Personal Data Systems, U.S. Dept. of Health, Education and Welfare, July 1973.

them in computerized files; and (4) that with respect to Social Security numbers, (a) Congressional action should give each individual a right not to disclose his or her number to any person or organization not authorized by federal statute to collect and use the number and (b) organizations with authority to use the number be prohibited from disclosing it to organizations lacking such authority.

Numerous bills were introduced in Congress to enact these recommendations into law.

On January 1, 1975, President Ford signed the Privacy Act of 1974 (Appendix J, P.L. 93-579). The new law applies only to federal agencies and excepts law enforcement activities generally, and certain related activities specifically.

> The law requires federal agencies:
> - To notify an individual on request if there is personal information about the individual contained in the agency's records,
> - To permit the individual to examine and copy most of those records and,
> - Under designated procedures, to dispute the contents of the record and to place a statement of the dispute in the file.

Agencies are required to publish notice of the existence of the files, to keep records of accesses and disclosure, and to refrain from disclosing information without the data subject's permission unless the disclosure is to one of the eleven excepted "disclosees." Agencies are required to take reasonable precautions to protect the security of the records. Private companies that operate a records system for an agency are considered part of the agency, and their employees are subject to the same rules as federal employees.

Willful failure to conform to the requirements of the Act results in civil liability of the agency to the individual harmed for actual damages of not less than $1,000. There is a criminal penalty of a $5,000 fine for an agency employee's willful failure to comply with the requirements of the Act. Unauthorized requests for and accesses to records under false pretense are likewise punishable by a $5,000 fine.

The Act set up a Privacy Commission charged with a two year study of information systems and data banks in all sectors. The study concludes with recommendations to the President and Congress as to which requirements and principles of the Act should be extended to regional and private organizations.

The Act prohibits the use of the Social Security number by federal, state, or local government agencies except as required by federal law or as was required by law prior to January 1, 1975. The Act became effective January 1, 1975, except for sections 3 and 4 (agency requirements set forth in 5 USC §552a) which became effective September 27, 1975. Six states have privacy laws, which, like the Federal law, affect only the public sector.

Similar bills have also been introduced in a number of states. Unfortunately such bills are often written without proper consideration of the particular needs of the various interests affected or without sufficient thought as to how, if at all, the requirements of the new law can be economically implemented.

As one example, California Assembly Bill 2656 of 1974 had significant drawbacks from a technical point of view. First, the bill imposed a duty of care on those maintaining automated personal data systems to "ensure" that certain things occurred or did not occur. One of these was a requirement that no use of individual identifiable data be made that was not within the stated purposes of the system as reasonably understood by the data subject. The system proprietor could escape liability by showing that when the alleged violation took place, reasonable procedures were in use to ensure compliance. Such a reasonable procedure would doubtless require a log of access and attempted access to the data. Yet the log itself might be sensitive. The people interested in one's personal data are often as revealing of one's privacy as the factual information in the data file. Thus the problem is recursive, requiring logs kept of logs kept of logs . . ., each of which might be sensitive. And the bill provided that liability for *un*intentional violation of the act include consequential damages to the individual injured; willful violation subjected the violator to punitive damages and criminal penalties.

Second, Bill 2656 provided that when an item of information is disputed (potentially the entire file) the dispute must be noted and included in every subsequent disclosure or dissemination of the disputed data. It also required provision for a 100-word statement by the data subject as to each unresolved dispute to be included either in full text or by an accurate summary in every subsequent disclosure of the data. Compliance with such a provision requires extensive reprogramming for any system which does not currently maintain this capability in context. Would a separate file of disputes and statements, without direct pointers from disputed items, satisfy the requirements of the act? Perhaps not, because the legislation intended that the law be literally construed.

Third, the systems owner was required to make certain that any system to which data is transferred meets the security requirements that are specified for the first system. The bill gave no guidelines as to adequate security standards, but failure to comply was a misdemeanor.

Fourth, the bill required the data bank proprietor to eliminate data when no longer timely. Again, no guidelines as to timeliness were specified, nor any duty imposed on other state officials to define timeliness in any context; but failure to comply was a misdemeanor.

These points make it clear that resources and time are required for system proprietors to comply with such legislation. Yet the bill provided no grandfather clause exempting existing systems and no grace period in which they could comply. As of the data of enactment, every nonconforming system would function at its peril. AB 2656 was not passed by the California legislature but three new bills are now pending in California.

EDP management should be alert to pending legislation and keep informed of what bills are being introduced and what they require. EDP management must participate during the legislative process and hearings on the bills.

In testimony before the United States Senate, one of the authors stated* that the computer has been a very positive force in favor of privacy. The computer's effect has been two-fold: first, it has been

---

*Modified and abridged from the statement of Robert P. Bigelow, before the Subcommittee on Constitutional Rights, Senate Committee on the Judiciary, 92d Congress, 1st Session, *Hearings on Federal Data Banks, Computer and the Bill of Rights,* March 9, 1971, pp. 680-707.

a catalyst in making citizens and legislators conscious of the dangers of governmental and private data banks; second, its electronic capabilities make economically possible the updating, correction, and deletion of individual data. Data banks have been with us for years—court records, birth and death records, real property records—all have been publicly maintained by the government and have been available to whoever was interested. The life insurance industry for many years has maintained its Medical Impairment Bureau as a guard against those who would seek to cheat it. Credit bureaus have been in existence for decades, sponsored by the merchants in each community. But generally these files have been separated and the computer promises an economical way of bringing them together and making them more useful. One of the finer examples of the computer as a beneficial device is the National Crime Information Center, which gives a patrolman in his cruiser the opportunity to check stolen car records before he approaches a suspected vehicle.

In commenting on the problems of the computer and privacy, Thomas J. Watson, Jr., former Chairman of the Board of International Business Machines Corporation stated,

> Today the Internal Revenue Service has our tax returns.
>
> The Social Security Administration keeps a running record on our jobs and our families.
>
> The Veterans Administration has medical records on many of us, and the Pentagon our records of military service.
>
> So in this scatteration lies our protection.
>
> But put everything in one place, computerize it, and add to it without limit, and a thieving electronic blackmailer would have just one electronic safe to crack to get a victim's complete dossier, tough as that job would be.
>
> And a malevolent Big Brother would not even have to do that: he could sit in his office, punch a few keys, and arm himself with all he needed to know to crush any citizen who threatened his power.
>
> Therefore, along with the bugged olive in the martini, the psychological test, and the spike microphone, the critics have seen "data surveillance" as an ultimate destroyer of the individual American citizen's right to privacy—his right to call his soul his own. (Speech to the Commonwealth Club of California, April 5, 1968).

Mr. Watson called upon his audience to face up to the threat to privacy and work for "understanding—massive and incisive public understanding."

Computer people and lawyers have long been concerned about computer privacy, and the two professions cooperated in defense of personal privacy in the position taken by TRW Credit Data Corp. in its dealings with the Internal Revenue Service. The Internal Revenue Service attempted to subpoena personal information in the credit files and Credit Data resisted. Unfortunately, the courts upheld the government's position (United States v. Davey, 2 CLSR 352, modified 2 CLSR 355, 426 F. 2d 842). Nevertheless, this action of Credit Data contrasts with the generally poor record of credit bureaus and inspection services with respect to maintaining the accuracy of data and the privacy of the individual. Public concern about privacy and accuracy in credit bureau records has been generated with the advent of the computer; companies like Credit Data that use computers as a basic tool have been an asset in restoring public confidence.

What should be done to protect the citizen against data-bank invasion of his personal privacy, of "the right to decide for himself how much he will share with others his thoughts, his feelings, and facts of his personal life," of "the right to call his soul his own"? Obviously, data banks are necessary for the advancement of society. Government needs information to administer its programs, to plan its future direction, and to improve the administration of justice. Business needs data banks to operate profitably, to prevent fraud, to improve the quality of society. The individual needs privacy to develop himself spiritually, to improve the quality of his life, and to enjoy his existence, or as the Continental Congress put it, his "Life, Liberty, and the pursuit of Happiness." Data banks provide an opportunity for better service, but they need some regulation.

A noted authority in the field has suggested a three-fold approach: (1) regulation of the information which may be collected about individuals and disclosed; (2) a writ of "habeus data" under which the individual can find out what is in his file, challenge its accuracy, and contest those items which he feels are in error; (3) a public agency charged with reviewing the operation of data banks and providing a source of appeal for the individual (Westin, "Computers and the Protection of Privacy," *The Technology Review,* Vol. 7, No. 6 (April 1969) pp. 32, 36, 37). More recently, Westin has suggested that a "privacy impact statement" should be regained from each personal data bank.

The regulation of data which A can collect about B is a difficult project for any government, whether it is controlling other branches of government or the private sector. While this should be a matter for continuing study, and perhaps legislation, the practicality of politics suggests that legislative efforts might be more productive, sooner, in the second and third areas suggested by Professor Westin.

The right of an individual to examine a data bank can be approached in two ways: (1) by giving everyone the right to examine the data bank, thereby practically ensuring that there will be public surveillance of the bank; or (2) by giving an individual the right to examine any entry about himself. Although the first method may not be practical (obviously it cannot be used in certain sensitive fields, such as some law-enforcement records), giving an individual the right to examine every entry which concerns him personally does commend itself as a method of individual enforcement; the necessary corollary is to give an individual the right to require that the entity maintaining the file correct erroneous data.

The burden should be upon the person maintaining the data bank to show that an individual should not have the right to examine his file, or, if he does have that right and alleges erroneous entries, that the information is not wrong. There is no question that this will add to the cost of maintaining the data bank, but for a person to enforce his right, either of inspection or correction, will cost him time and money, too. It is inequitable to require him to bear the burden of proof when the entity maintaining the data bank is the one receiving the prime benefit therefrom.

As noted above, the computer has been a positive force in favor of privacy because, with computerized records, the expense of editing and correcting data becomes economically feasible. Dr. Harry C. Jordan, president of Credit Data, once testified, ". . . the computer not only can forget, but must forget, if storage costs to a private corporation are not to become prohibitive. Consequently, Credit Data builds a case of amnesia into its computer programs" (*Hear-*

ings on Commercial Credit Bureaus before Subcommittee on Invasion of Privacy of Committee on Government Operations, House of Representatives, March 12-14, 1968, p. 90). Section 605 of the Consumer Credit Protection Act, Title 15 United States Code which became effective in 1971, requires the deletion of obsolete information from the ordinary consumer credit record. The use of computerized record-keeping techniques may well be the only way credit bureaus can comply with this law at a reasonable expense.

An individual should also be given information about the use to which a data bank is put. It has been suggested that he should be informed each time the file is interrogated and who the interrogator is. This certainly is a difficult requirement to impose on the operator of a data bank and, in many cases, the information may be such that the individual neither needs it nor wants it. For example, when a retail organization queries a credit bureau about the credit standing of an individual who has applied to the retailer for a charge account and who has authorized the inquiry, there is no particular reason for the data-bank operator to notify the individual of the inquiry. However, if the credit bureau is interrogated by some agency which does not have advance authorization, such as the Internal Revenue Service, the individual should be notified and given an opportunity to contest before the information is disclosed.

There might also be the requirement that a data bank proprietor maintain a record of each *person* who inquires about an individual, and that this record be available to the individual. Computerized data banks which now provide "on-line" service through telephone lines to a terminal often keep a record only of which terminal inquired about the data, not of the name of the individual who made the inquiry. The person initiating the inquiry should be willing to identify himself, and the investigated person's information should not be limited to the name of the inquiring organization or to its terminal operator.

A legislature or a regulatory authority must balance the cost of requiring a data bank operator to comply with regulations of the types suggested here against the likelihood of an unjustified invasion of privacy. Since the advent of the computer, updating and correcting records, adding explanatory matter, expunging obsolete material, keeping track of who uses the data banks, and notification of the individual, can all be accomplished more economically than before. The rules on data-bank operation can, therefore, be more stringent and still permit an economically feasible operation.

The administrative approach, by the establishment of a separate regulatory agency, may be easier and less expensive for the citizen and for the operator of a data bank, than an appeal to the courts. A government agency, required to provide standards for the establishment and maintenance of personal data banks, maintained by the Executive branch of the government, and authorized to enforce compliance with these standards, would be a starting point. This agency could be given equivalent powers with respect to personal data banks maintained by the private sector and by other governments.* Such an agency might also act as an arbiter between a citizen and the data-bank proprietor when there is disagreement as to the accuracy of the record; it could also be given authority to authorize access to a data bank by organizations such as the Internal Revenue Service and the Department of Justice. Hopefully, the cost to the citizen and to the government of such administrative proceedings would be less than if the matter were taken to the courts; the time saved might be considerable.

Where should this governmental entity be located? Some years ago Stanley Rothman asked, "Is there any single department constituted to tell IRS, Treasury, the Attorney General or Congress that they cannot under any circumstances (war or peace) have certain information?" (*Centralized Government Information Systems and Privacy,* prepared for the President's Crime Commission, September 22, 1966). The answer to Mr. Rothman's question is clearly, "No." Obviously another agency within the Executive branch will not fill the bill. An independent agency, such as the FCC or the SEC, would be more likely to have a detached viewpoint; or perhaps this new organization should be an agency of the Congress itself. The General Accounting Office, responsible to the legislature, provides a model. And every citizen has an elected legislator to whom he can appeal directly for assistance. If the legislature itself, or one of its committees, should request information from a data bank, which under the standards of the proposed

---

*A federal agency with authority over state-run data banks might have constitutional limitations, and vice versa.

agency would not be available to the Executive Department or one of the independent agencies, the legislation under which this new agency is established could provide for review by the courts.

Privacy and security are much discussed in the trade press, and top management is very concerned that the company be able to demonstrate to the public its concern for personal rights and to the stockholders its concern for efficiency. The data-processing manager must keep up to date on developments in both the privacy and security fields so that he or she may advise top management in time to take appropriate action.

part six

The EDP Manager

chapter *13*

Personnel

The EDP personnel of a corporation are subject to the same legal considerations as are other employees of the company, and the legal problems that the EDP manager will encounter are generally those that confront his counterparts in manufacturing and sales. Personnel management is not something that this book covers except as the subject is affected by the fact that we are talking about computer people. The primary areas in which the data-processing manager may run into such problems are in dealing with programmers and in countering possible unionization efforts in the department.

EXEMPT EMPLOYEES

In the early 1970s there was discussion in the industry on whether programmers were "exempt employees", as that term was used in the federal government's Fair Labor Standards Act. Exempt employees are defined in the Act as "any employee employed in a bona fide executive, administrative, or professional capacity." This is a dollars-and-cents question because exempt employees do not have to be paid overtime. In 1970 and 1971 the United States Department of Labor held hearings on the question, and, in the fall of 1972, issued its determination (29 CFR, Part 541.) As background the Department summarized the arguments of the proponents and opponents of exempt status as follows:

> The employer representatives contended that computer programmers and systems analysts should be considered professional employees. Some supporters of this position would include the position of junior programmer in this category. The testimony brought out, however, that a college degree is not a requirement for entry into the data processing field, that only a few colleges offer any course in a field designated as computer science, and that there are presently no licensing, certification, or registration provided as a condition for employment in these occupations. . . .
>
> On the other hand, employee representatives were opposed to expansion of the regulations to allow the professional exemption for data processing employees. They were in agreement that a prolonged academic background is not essential in this field. They also brought out that this relatively new occupation area is in a state of flux and that job titles and duties are not regularized and overlap and intermix in a confusing manner. They also felt that to expand the exemption was an invitation for employers to work such employees longer hours with no additional compensation.
>
> . . . at the present time the computer sciences are not generally recognized by colleges and universities as a bona fide academic discipline with standardized licensing, certification, or registration procedures. There is too much variation in standards

and academic achievement to conclude logically that data processing employees are a part of a true profession of the type contemplated by the regulations. (29 CFR, Part 541.)

Management

In its decision the Labor Department recognized that some programmers and analysts who might not be professionals, might nevertheless be managers and amended their regulations to cover this point:

> In the data processing field some firms employ persons described as systems analysts and computer programmers. If such employees are concerned with the planning, scheduling, and coordination of activities which are required to develop systems for processing data to obtain solutions to complex business, scientific, or engineering problems of his employer or his employer's customers, he is clearly doing work directly related to management policies or general business operations. [29 CFR 541, 205 (c) (7).]

Discretion and Independent Judgment

In certain cases when the work requires the exercise of much discretion and independent judgment, the individual may also be considered exempt. The Labor Department covered this as follows:

> In the data processing field a systems analyst is exercising discretion and independent judgment when he develops methods to process, for example, accounting, inventory, sales and other business information by using electronic computers. He also exercises discretion and independent judgment when he determines the exact nature of the data processing problem, and analyzes and structures the problem in a logical manner so that a system to solve the problem and obtain the desired results can be developed. Whether a computer programmer is exercising discretion and independent judgment depends on

the facts in each particular case. Every problem processed in a computer first must be carefully analyzed so that exact and logical steps for its solution can be worked out. When this preliminary work is done by a computer programmer he is exercising discretion and independent judgment. A computer programmer would also be using discretion and independent judgment when he determines exactly what information must be used to prepare the necessary documents and by ascertaining the exact form in which the information is to be presented. Examples of work not requiring the level of discretion and judgment contemplated by the regulations are highly technical and mechanical operations such as the preparation of a flow chart or diagram showing the order in which the computer must perform each operation, the preparation of instructions to the console operator who runs the computer or the actual running of the computer by the programmer, and the debugging of a program. It is clear that the duties of data processing employees such as tape librarians, key punch operators, computer operators, junior programmers and programmer trainees are so closely supervised as to preclude the use of the required discretion and independent judgment. [29 CFR 541, 207 (c) (7).]

The Department recognized that data processing is a changing field and indicated that its position on professionalization may change at a future time. However, at present the data-processing manager is best advised to follow the standards set out in the preceding paragraphs.

EQUAL EMPLOYMENT OPPORTUNITY

Under the Civil Rights Act of 1964, it is unlawful for an employer to hire or fire or otherwise discriminate against an individual with respect to compensation, terms, conditions, or privileges in employment because of the individual's race, color, religion, sex, or national origin. The same rules apply to employment agencies, labor organizations, and training programs.

Employers include any company engaged in an industry that affects commerce and has 15 or more employees. By Executive Order of the President, the federal government and all contractors who deal with the federal government are covered by the Act.

The laws are enforced by the Equal Employment Opportunities Commission which requires that an employer keep records relating to its hiring, discharge, and promotion of blacks, women, Mexican Americans, and persons of Asiatic extraction. It is sometimes necessary to separate this kind of information from an individual's personnel record as much as possible in order to insure that the person will be considered for a promotion for a new job without regard to these factors. Computerized personnel systems can be helpful in this type of situation by preventing access to color, religious, and sex information in preliminary displays of work histories.

The computer manager must also be sure that the system is not used as a tool to violate the law. There is at least one case on record of a personnel system that was programmed to eliminate black candidates in the selection process for new employees.

UNIONS

Unionization of the Data Processing Department

Employees who are not members of management have the right to organize themselves into unions and to bargain collectively. There have been a number of administrative agency and arbitration decisions, starting as early as 1962, involving the unionization of data-processing employees. These have included programmers, systems analysts, operators, and service or maintenance personnel.

If there are indications that unionization efforts are underway in the data-processing department, the managers concerned should talk immediately with the company's counsel because the managers' options in such a situation are severely limited by law. What might seem a logical answer or action to the manager could be the worst possible thing to do. Perhaps in this situation, more than in any other, a manager should move only on the explicit advice of counsel.

A strike by unionized data-processing personnel can have serious ramifications for a company. In the spring of 1974 the computer staff of the British Post Office went on strike. In the United Kingdom, as in many countries, the Post Office not only handles the mail but also provides telecommunications services. The strike lasted about seven weeks and became a major problem from a management point of view. About half the British telephone bills were not sent out; it has been estimated that the billing backlog for those seven weeks was £100 million or about $240 million. An additional complication arose because the Post Office maintained a computerized inventory-control system for its telephone equipment; the strike prevented the running of these programs and the supply of equipment for installations gradually ran down, but in an erratic manner.

In another case, the personnel of a data-processing manufacturer responsible for maintaining a user's system had a labor dispute with the manufacturer. To put pressure on their employer, the employees used their knowledge of the customer's codes to dump data stored at remote locations before it had been transmitted to the main CPU. This not only made it appear that the system was malfunctioning but caused considerable accounting difficulties to the customer. Eventually the individuals who caused the problem were caught and prosecuted.

The possibility that such difficulties could occur indicates the need for contingency planning against strikes by the data processor's own personnel or by the EDP suppliers. These plans should be worked out with management of the EDP department's "customers" and should be cleared with company counsel to ensure that they do not violate the laws that apply to labor-management disputes.

Automation and Process Control

The automation of functions has been a major cause of labor-management difficulties. Even though in the long run the computer may create more jobs, in the short run it may put people out of work or it may have a substantial effect on the nature of their work. For example, the interactive composition of newspaper copy using a CRT has led to major disagreements between the Associated Press and the telegraphers who work for it (Associated Press, 3 CLSR 321). Another problem occurs when work previously done in a unionized unit is assigned to non-union employees; this can occur particularly when process-control equipment is introduced. Employees can also be upset when jobs that have been done by union personnel are subcontracted out to a third party that uses a computer, for example a service bureau. Sometimes professional employees who are unionized, such as engineers, may find themselves put in the same union and bargaining unit as nonprofessional employees, or as happened in one case, computer and noncomputer professional employees were ordered into one bargaining unit (Boeing Co. v. Seattle Professional Engineering Employees Assn., 3 CLSR 542). This can cause morale problems and may lead to labor troubles.

Management's right to assign work, either by subcontract or by the use of new equipment, can be challenged before the National Labor Relations Board and before the courts. If there is any possibility that a new procedure might adversely affect union employees, it is well to talk with the company's lawyer at the very beginning. One of the authors recently heard of a major shipbuilding design program that had been challenged by the union involved and could not be implemented until the end of extensive litigation.

The unions have not been unaware of the situation. As long ago as September 1968, the International Association of Machinists recommended to their local branches procedures for negotiating contract provisions that would cushion the impact of technological change. The international union recommended provisions to include:

> (1) advance notice and consultation whenever employers plan major changes; (2) the right to transfer not only to other jobs within the plant, but to jobs in other plants, with adequate moving allowances provided; (3) training for new jobs or for old jobs which have not been eliminated at full pay and no expense to the worker; (4) preservation of the previous rate of pay for workers who have been downgraded supplemented by

such income protection devices as SUB or severance pay; (5) provision for early retirement with adequate pensions; (6) continuation of insurance and other fringe benefits during lay-offs; (7) negotiation of new job classifications and rates of pay when automation increases skill requirements, job responsibilities or work demands; (8) fair distribution of automation's productivity through increased wages, more leisure time, and greater security.

PROTECTING PROPRIETARY RIGHTS

Inventions

Frequently, particularly with respect to programmers, the employer wishes to make sure that any work the programmer does belongs to the employer. A great deal of litigation has arisen from these desires of the employer, and it is frequently advisable to have an agreement before employment commences, primarily to make sure that each party understands his rights and obligations. Such a contract should consider the employer's rights to inventions, on the job and off the job. It is probably best to limit a contract to inventions that pertain to the employer's business, perhaps even within specifically identified fields, and the contract should clearly specify any inventions the employee made prior to joining the company that are not to be included. To determine specifically when an invention is "made", it is often helpful to specify when the invention was "conceived" or when it was "first reduced to practice." Such a clause should cover the period of the agreement and perhaps a month or two thereafter to avoid disagreements when employment ends as to which inventions are covered. A statement requiring disclosure of all inventions, whether they become the employer's property or not, can also be helpful; this will encourage settlement of any disputes before they get out of hand. Material that could be copyrighted, such as programs, operating manuals, sales material, or the like, should be treated like inventions.

Confidential Information

The employment contract is an excellent time to specify, as much as possible, the confidential information that will be learned by the employee. Not only does this include trade secrets, discussed in Chapter 7, but other information that the business considers confidential, such as pricing practices, marketing plans, and perhaps even the company organization chart. The agreement should clearly state that this information is confidential, that it will not be disclosed except with permission of the employer, and that the employee will not use it for his own benefit.

Competition

In certain cases, an employer may want to obtain an agreement from an employee that the employee will not compete with the employer after employment ends. In most states these agreements are enforceable if they are reasonable as to the particular type of competition, the length of time, and the geographic area to be covered. For example, an agreement between a service bureau chain and the general manager of one of its branches prohibiting the individual from doing any work in the data-processing area for a period of five years anywhere in the country would be struck down by every court. However, an agreement providing that the individual could not, within one year after termination, run a service bureau less than 25 miles from the branch office that he had been running, might well be held reasonable. An agreement prohibiting a crackerjack APL programmer from doing APL programming for a competitor anywhere in the country for a period of six months might also be held reasonable.

A word of warning, however, on such contracts. While the courts will enforce an agreement to keep information confidential, usually without a time limit, an agreement that will prevent a man or woman from earning a living will not be enforced by the courts which look upon noncompete provisions with distaste. In fact, in California they are illegal.

CONSULTING CONTRACTS

In a contract with an outside consultant you should attempt to set standards for the work. The contracts should also be very specific about the expenses that are eligible for reimbursement. Consultants are well known for their desire to live well; if you are reimbursing them for hotel and travel expenses, you may find the cost considerably more than you had planned.

When you deal with an outside contractor, the caliber of personnel to be used is a matter for negotiation. If the contractor has a great deal of latitude in selecting personnel to get the job done, he will probably be able to quote a lower price. On the other hand, the job may not be done as well or as quickly as it would be if the contract set forth minimum experience or training standards for the personnel to be used. Sometimes the customer can obtain veto power over individuals used by the contractor; the customer will have to pay for this privilege, but it could be a worthwhile expenditure when prompt performance is a major consideration.

chapter *14*

Security

Computer security, a minor concern in the 1960s, is today one of the important responsibilities of a data-processing manager. Millions of dollars are being spent on security by vendors and users and a whole field of expertise and many businesses are dedicated to it. Because of the need to comply with statutory privacy requirements, security will have even more importance in the future.

A number of excellent publications are available which detail the security precautions you should consider for your computer installation (see Appendix K for a selected bibliography). Managers charged with instituting security measures or evaluating existing precautions might consider the following general approach.

First, analyze the value of the assets of the installation. For this analysis include people in the installation; hardware; software; data; the value of uninterrupted service including time-critical functions such as medical, payroll, and manufacturing applications; supplies; and the physical plant.

Then analyze the risks to those assets, such as physical destruction from sabotage, carelessness, or accident—including break-ins, fire, and power surges. The risks also include systems damage from simple usage overloads, wiping out of "vtocs", alteration of programs, and user-caused crashes. Other risks are intentional damage to computerized information such as by theft or by misappropriation of programs or data (e.g., trade secrets and personal information data); misuse of programs to steal money (in bank applications); and misuse of report-generating systems to mislead or defraud management, customers, or investors.

The value analysis may show some surprising results. IBM's Security Manager Robert Courtney has stated that customer lists are more valuable to his company than access methods to computer files. Algorithms to compile aggregate data from personal information may be more sensitive than the aggregated data. Some data centers have found that loss of one user's work was more costly than loss of the current version of the operating system, because routine backup procedures protected the installation's programs but not those of the user.

The first analysis is largely a policy determination that the EDP management should share with senior company officials and, for user data, with each user. The organization's legal representative should participate for the purpose of detailing the legal duties respecting assets; for example, privacy legislation may require a data-processing organization to guarantee the security of personal information with civil and criminal sanctions imposed for any breach, with or without fault by the data handler.

The installation's technical and financial staff should participate in assessing replacement costs in terms of time and money—including lost revenues for service disruptions—and loss of programs and data. Company insurance may cover some losses, but not others, and it may not cover every risk, e.g. riot, earthquake, or radiation.

Risk assessment should be undertaken by the people who know the installation's vulnerabilities and, where costs permit, by an outside security consultant who is familiar with common forms of security threats. This team should include both the staff and other organization employees who may have a keener eye for some soft spots than the operations group itself. There is a tendency in brainstorming sessions to get too elaborate (the James Bond syndrome) in imagining possible forms of attack. One of the authors recalls a meeting in which a senior participant seriously proposed that marauders might chop down nearby eucalyptus trees (5 feet in diameter), causing them to fall across the computer building, and enter via the trees. In fact, when an attack came, saboteurs simply placed extension ladders against a security fence and attempted entry over the fence.

Another difficult consideration to face is the possible presence on one's staff of a person willing to compromise the installation from within. The Stanford Research Institute (SRI) study of over 200 incidents of computer abuse* discusses a number of internally generated abuses. To be sure, many are perpetrated by operators and key-punchers, but the recent Westinghouse theft (Case # 73-37) was allegedly committed by a senior member of the data processing staff who had major responsibility for designing the security procedures. The SRI report further indicates that top management people are occasionally involved, including EDP vice-presidents. Some of these have worked independently, some in collusion with other data-processing personnel. The security risks include insiders at all levels, and security precautions must take this unhappy knowledge into account.

It is suggested that a draft plan for *physical* security be drawn by a small group of installation personnel, possibly led by the operations supervisor who can gather information and test products (fireproofing, alarm systems etc.). Their report will be presented to a larger task force for cost information and determination of priorities. Similarly, systems group representatives can study protective mechanisms for the *system* and report through the technical group to the larger task force. The installation manager, or senior company management in a small organization, should address the *people* problem—separation of functions, monitoring of activities, etc.

---

*Parker, Nycum and Oura, *Computer Abuse,* Stanford Research Institute Report to the National Science Foundation, Menlo Park, California, 1973.

We emphasize that at present there is no final technical solution to security problems. Realistic, attainable goals should be set and the best procedures, within financial capability, should be implemented to meet those goals. These decisions (but not of course the implementing procedures) should be communicated to users and other concerned parties so that no unrealistic expectations ensue.

Finally, it must be remembered that security is a constant concern; testing and updating of procedures should be a continuing effort, and major yearly reviews of assets and risks should be planned.

The legal aspects of security include sanctions against perpetrators and remedies for victims. Research indicates that in 1974 only 42% of the states had effective sanctions against theft of software, and 24% for theft of computer time. Sanctions against malicious mischief are common; however, these laws are directed toward tangible property and may not be particularly useful as sanctions against abuses to software and on-line data. The states are not uniformly good or poor at protecting these assets; thus the same state may have effective sanctions against theft of computer time, but may provide no specific legal deterrent to theft of software or data.

While new privacy legislation details the responsibilities of data custodians, and provides sanctions for perpetrators obtaining information under false pretenses, it is silent as to other damage perpetrated by these abuses, such as, alteration of data or destruction of systems. Therefore the presence or absence of state and federal laws addressing these activities may make a critical difference in privacy enforcement.

The question of legal protection of or remedies for victims of computer security breaches turns largely on privacy legislation, intellectual property laws (see Part III for a full discussion of patent, copyright, and trade-secret laws), and unfair competition (see Chapter 11 for a discussion of this common law tort).

In brief, if software has been stolen, and the owner of that software has a legally protected interest in it, there may be an action under the intellectual property laws or for unfair competition. If assets have been damaged, that loss may also be recovered under unfair competition laws. If personal information has been compromised, the privacy legislation in force at that time may provide money damages or an injunction on behalf of the individual whose data was disclosed or wrongfully altered.

In cases where an individual has perpetrated a wrongful act while in the employ of an organization, and the act benefits the organization, both the individual and the organization could be found liable.

Compensation to the victim is generally not available under criminal sanctions.

chapter 15

Insurance

There has been very little written about the special field of EDP insurance that gives helpful advice to the computer manager. One of the best general discussions is by Harry Chadwick, an underwriter with Chubb & Sons, who prepared a lengthy article for the *Computer Law Service**; Appendix L is an abridged version of that article, and much of the material in this chapter is abstracted from it. Most insurance brokers are not familiar with computers and their specialized requirements. Often you will find that you have to carry the ball in getting the EDP insurance you need.

Data processing equipment has its own particular risks and, for insurance purposes, should not be lumped with other office equipment such as copiers. For example, computers face higher risk of

---

*Harry Chadwick, "The Insurance of Electronic Data Processing Operations," *Computer Law Service,* Section 2-5, Article 1.

damage from electrical power surges and intentional or accidental employee acts, and many companies carry coverage for this damage.

Leased equipment may or may not be covered by the lessor's insurance. The lease should be carefully reviewed with the insurance underwriter to make sure that as many risks as possible have been covered, either by the lessor or by insurance. As noted in Chapter 10, the *hell or high water clause* in a lease may require continuation of the rental payments, no matter what happens to the machinery. Some of these risks, such as war, cannot be insured against.

The National Fire Protection Association has prepared a Standard for the Protection of Electronic Computer/Data Processing Equipment.* This small booklet has recommendations on:

> Building Construction
> Locating the Computer Area
> Computer Room Construction
> Fire Cutoffs
> Raised Floors
> Cable Openings
> Materials and Equipment Allowed in the Computer
>   Room
> Storage
> Fire Protection for Computer Room
> Fire Detection Devices
> Protecting Records in Machine Readable Form
> Evaluation of Records
> Duplication of Records
> Protection Against Building Collapse
> Air Conditioning and Cooling Systems
> Electrical Service
> Emergency Power Control
> Emergency Procedures

Guidelines such as the NFPA Standard can be particularly helpful in reviewing coverage required in such areas as building modification, and in valuing of hardware and software.

---

*NFPA Number 75, (1972), available from the Association at 470 Atlantic Avenue, Boston, Mass. 02110.

How much insurance is needed under any particular coverage is frequently a difficult decision. In the equipment area, one might use purchase cost, replacement cost, or market value (which is affected by obsolescence). The computer manager must be familiar with the rules of coinsurance which can be summarized as, "If you don't have enough insurance, you must pay a portion of every loss, even if the amount of that particular loss is less than the amount of your insurance." Valuing a data base is particularly difficult. In some cases it may be necessary to go back to the original records and input all the data over again. If a company has concluded an agreement with the Internal Revenue Service under Revenue Rule 71-20 (as discussed in Chapter 3 and reprinted in Appendix B), these original records may have been destroyed; and it may be necessary to go even further afield to find the data. Insurance on the replacement value of tapes and cards is often woefully insufficient; the cost of replacing the data must be included.

Interruption of a data processing operation should also be covered by insurance, and sometimes the cause of these interruptions may be beyond the control of the company. For example, in one case a fire for which the insured was not responsible caused damage to air-conditioning equipment in a building owned by and under the control of the data processor's landlord. The data-processing company shut down its equipment to avoid injury and had to sue its insurer to get reimbursement for interrupted earnings.

Protection against internal dishonesty is a particularly important consideration for the computer manager. Not only can one's own employees cause great financial injury to the company by dishonest conduct involving the computer, but for a company that processes the data of others, dishonesty can create a major liability.

The company that performs data processing services for others also must get coverage for the errors and omission that result from its work. For example, a service bureau in Illinois has been sued by a school district, whose building burned down and was allegedly underinsured because the service bureau failed to make proper calculations (Independent School District v. Marshall & Stevens Co., 3 CLSR 146, 337 F. Supp. 1278).

Failure of a company to insure its data-processing equipment and records against potential liability could result in a claim by stockholders against the directors and the responsible officers for wasting corporate assets. Such a claim might also be asserted by a trustee in bankruptcy.

Data processing insurance can be very expensive, sometimes more expensive than the risk justifies, but the computer manager must explore the risk, determine the cost of protecting against it, and make a judgment. It is better to make an erroneous but honest judgment, than for a court to find dereliction in duty by the corporate officers.

chapter *16*

Antitrust Considerations

Since the late nineteenth century, competition has been a principle of American economic policy. This competition is enforced both by the government and by private citizens (including corporations), who have been, or claim they have been, the subject of monopolization,* boycott,† unfair price cutting, and similar acts prohibited by law. Within the computer industry there have been, since 1968, one major governmental suit against IBM and numerous private actions, often against IBM though sometimes against other companies. The fact that IBM has won some and lost some is common knowledge, and it is not the purpose of this chapter to comment on the extensive—and expensive—antitrust litigation within the industry, nor upon the recently filed cases against the American Telephone & Telegraph Co.

---

*The state of being exclusively owned through legal privilege, command of supply, or concerted action.

†A concerted refusal to deal with a competitor.

Rather our purpose is to outline some aspects of antitrust law that computer people should be familiar with, and to make some suggestions so that you can avoid embarrassing, and perhaps penalizing, involvement at a later time. In practically no area of your efforts should you be more aware of the legal dangers involved and be ready to get yourself a lawyer. Doing your own thing can be very expensive for both you and your employer.

THE ANTITRUST STATUTES*

The antitrust laws in the United States are basically four and are remarkable in their simplicity. The earliest—the Sherman Act— became law in 1890. Section 1 of the Sherman Act (15 U.S.C. Para. 1) prohibits "every contract, combination . . . or conspiracy, in restraint of trade or commerce among the several States, or with foreign nations."

Section 2 of that Act (15 U.S.C. Para. 2) provides that "every person who shall monopolize, or attempt to monopolize, or combine or conspire . . . to monopolize any part of the trade or commerce among the several States, or with foreign nations" is guilty of a misdemeanor.

Section 7 of the Clayton Act (15 U.S.C. Para. 18) originally enacted in 1914 and amended in 1950, prohibits any merger or acquisition whose effect "in any line of commerce in any section of the country . . . may be substantially to lessen competition, or to tend to create a monopoly."

These three statutes are enforced by the United States Department of Justice, though with respect to the third—the antimerger statute—there is coordinate jurisdiction with the Federal Trade Commission.

The fourth basic antitrust statute of the United States is enforced solely by the Trade Commission. That statute, Section 5 of the

---

*Abridged in part from a speech by Bruce B. Wilson, Deputy Assistant Attorney General, Antitrust Division, before the Gottlieb Duttweiler Institute for Economic and Social Studies, Zurich, Switzerland, October 26, 1973.

Federal Trade Commission Act (15 U.S.C. Para. 45), declares unlawful "unfair methods of competition in commerce, and unfair or deceptive acts or practices in commerce."

These four statutes provide the legislative foundation for most of American antitrust law. They reflect a fundamental commitment to the proposition that the economy of the United States shall be governed primarily by the principles of competition.

To this listing should be added Section 2 of the Clayton Act, as amended by the Robinson Patman Act, (15 U.S.C. Para. 113), which prohibits unfair price discrimination in the sale of goods. It is also enforced by the F.T.C.

All these statutes also provide relief to persons who have been injured by their violation, although the scope of relief varies with each statute. Under the Sherman Act, certain violations are misdemeanors, punishable by very large fines and imprisonment; the Federal Trade Commission and Clayton Acts also include penalties. The government also can obtain major civil relief including injunctions, divestiture of portions of the company, dissolution and money damages. Private corporations and individuals can also enforce the antitrust laws if they have been personally injured; they can obtain injunctive relief and, in certain cases, not only the actual damages they have suffered, but three times that amount, the extra two hundred per cent being a punishment. Antitrust cases are extraordinarily expensive; if a private plaintiff wins his case, he is also entitled to reasonable attorneys fees.

SUMMARY OF PRINCIPAL TENETS OF ANTITRUST POLICY*

In the United States, the principal tenets of antitrust policy are:

1. Action against concerted restrictions.
   The law forbids concerted activity by which persons
   on one side of a transaction jointly seek to establish

---

*Condensed from a special report to the Council of Science and Technology, as printed in a special issue of *Honeywell Computer Journal,* Vol. 7, No. 1, pp. 42-43, 1973.

terms that are disadvantageous to persons on the other side. Among the more common examples of such concerted activity are price-fixing and boycotts among competing sellers; agreements to limit the supply, variety, or quality of goods; and allocations of customers or markets. Prohibitions against such concerted actions apply not only to competing entities but to agreements with and among customers of a seller that restrict the conditions and terms under which the customer can resell the product. Generally, such concerted actions are illegal without regard to their actual effects on competition or asserted economic justification.

2. Action against conduct by single enterprises by which opportunities available to their competitors are significantly reduced.

   Among the types of such conduct are: (1) arrangements by sellers or buyers to deal exclusively with important customers or suppliers; (2) requirements by sellers that buyers who wish to buy a particular commodity or service must also buy others from the same seller; (3) arrangements by which a buyer allocates his purchases from different suppliers in proportion to the relative amounts of products or services that these suppliers buy from him; and (4) discrimination by a supplier in the prices, terms, or promotional allowances that he affords to different buyers, or insistence by a buyer that his suppliers engage in such discriminations. In the language of antitrust, the first type of conduct is called exclusive dealing, the second tying or full-line, the third reciprocity, and the fourth discrimination. The illegality of such activity usually depends upon the relative market power and position of the transacting entities.

3. Action to prevent monopolization by a single enterprise or by a group of enterprises that act together.

   Monopoly that is unlawfully achieved or maintained by a single enterprise is itself unlawful. Monopolies that are collectively achieved or maintained through agreement or some form of concerted action are also unlawful, as are attempts to monopolize in order to achieve monopoly power. Recently some economists have argued that oligopolies* that collectively domi-

---

*In a monopoly situation, one firm dominates the market; in an oligopoly, a few firms dominate the market.

nate a market may have effects similar to those of concerted restriction or of monopoly; and some efforts have been made to apply antitrust sanctions to oligopolists that control significant segregable markets or parts of a market. Use of the antitrust laws to curb oligopoly, however, constitutes a comparatively new and unresolved area of legal interpretation.

4. Action to prevent mergers that substantially lessen competition or tend to monopolize.

   When merging enterprises are horizontally related,* concentration is treated as significant if it so reduces the number or so enhances the size of enterprises as to increase the probability that monopoly will develop or that competition will be significantly reduced. When the merging enterprises are vertically related† their union is treated as significant if it forecloses access by others to significant parts of the total supply or demand. When the merger unites unrelated enterprises (as conglomerates) it is treated as significant if it substantially reduces potential competition or entrenches the market control of the acquired company, or increases the probability of noncompetitive business conduct, such as use of reciprocity.

5. Action to prevent links among business enterprises that are equivalent to or facilitate concerted restrictions.

   The law contains specific prohibitions against interlocking directorates†† among competitors and against acquisition of significant stockholdings in related enterprises. The law has tended to deal with joint enterprises among competing or potentially competing entities in the same way as with mergers and acquisitions.

It is not possible to suggest all the situations in which antitrust problems could arise, but even a small company could become involved unintentionally. For example, a number of trade associa-

---

*Two companies in the same business are horizontally related, e.g. two software houses, but not a software house and a resort hotel.

†In vertical relationship, the various stages of production or distribution are related—for example, the making and showing of motion picture films.

††For example, when companies A and B are competitors and the chairman of A is on the board of directors of B, or even if the president of each of them is on the board of directors of Company C.

tions compile sales figures for statistical purposes. When this is done manually, the time lapse is so long that it is unlikely that the figures could be compiled and distributed in time for members of the association to change their prices to reflect what other companies are doing. But when these figures can be put in by remote terminal, messaged, and spewed out again within twenty-four hours, the capability exists of adjusting prices in ways that violate the antitrust laws.

As noted above, reciprocal buying agreements under which Company A buys Company B's products and Company B buys Company A's products, are now looked upon with great disfavor. If A and B arranged for their computerized inventory control system to enter automatic orders for each other's product, the trustbusters might claim a violation of the law, especially if either of the companies kept a running balance of sales in and sales out.

A third situation in which antitrust problems could arise is in the sale of a computerized data base to different customers at prices that are not related to the cost of sales. This could well be a violation of the Robinson-Patman Act, though this act usually has been applied to tangible products like bicycles. Whether the valuable information on a reel of tape is itself tangible has not yet been determined by courts. The same problem could arise if software was sold to people at different prices that did not reflect the cost of developing, maintaining, and marketing that software.

In a time-sharing environment, security considerations might suggest that only selected companies should be permitted to use the system. But antitrust law prohibits boycotts, and an excluded user might claim he had been unfairly treated.

While computer people confront legal problems in many areas, the antitrust area is one in which the need for competent legal advice is paramount. Any time an activity is contemplated that will include joint action with another company or person—particularly a competitor—that could possibly be considered by a third person as harmful to his interests, the proposal should be discussed with a lawyer. The objective can probably be achieved, but the way it is done can be as important as the end result.

part seven

Appendixes

APPENDIX A

Outline of the Court System

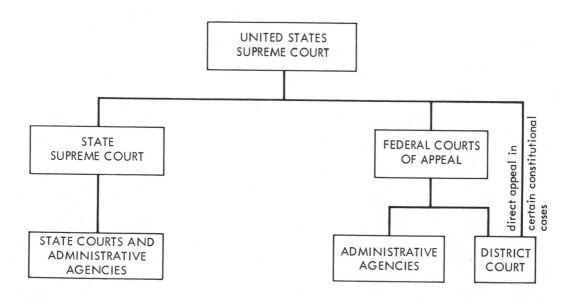

Rev. Rul. 71-20—What Are Records

26 CFR 1.6001–1: Records. (Code Sec 6001)

Rev. Rul. 71–20 [1]

Advice has been requested whether punched cards, magnetic tapes, disks, and other machine-sensible data media used in the automatic data processing of accounting transactions constitute records withing the meaning of section 6001 of the Internal Revenue Code of 1954 and section 1.6001–1 of the Income Tax Regulations.

In the typical situation the taxpayer maintains records within his automatic data processing (ADP) system. Daily transactions are recorded on punched cards and processed by the taxpayer's computer which prints daily listings and accumulates the individual transaction records for a month's business on magnetic tapes. At the month's end the tapes are used to print out monthly journals, registers, and subsidiary ledgers and to prepare account summary totals entered on punched cards. The summary data from these cards is posted to the general ledger and a monthly printout is generated to reflect opening balances, summary total postings, and closing balances. At the year's end several closing ledger runs are made to record adjusting entries. In other situations taxpayers use punched cards, disks, or

---

[1] Also released as Technical Information Release 1062, dated December 31, 1970.

other machine-sensible data media to store accounting information.

Section 6001 of the Code provides that every person liable for any tax imposed by the Code, or for the collection thereof, shall keep such records as the Secretary of the Treasury or his delegate may from time to time prescribe.

Section 1.6001–1(a) of the Income Tax Regulations provides that any person subject to income tax shall keep such permanent books of account of records, including inventories, as are sufficient to establish the amount of gross income, deductions, credits, or other matters required to be shown by such person in any return of such tax.

Section 1.6001–1(e) of the regulations provides that the books and records required by this section shall be retained so long as the contents thereof may become material in the administration of any internal revenue law.

It is held that punched cards, magnetic tapes, disks, and other machine-sensible data media used for recording, consolidating, and summarizing accounting transactions and records within a taxpayer's automatic data processing system are records within the meaning of section 6001 of the Code and section 1.6001–1 of the regulations and are required to be retained so long as the contents may become material in the administration of any internal revenue law.

However, where punched cards are used merely as a means of input to the system and the information is duplicated on magnetic tapes, disks, or other machine-sensible records, such punched cards need not be retained.

It is the desire of the Internal Revenue Service to provide fair and equitable treatment to all taxpayers using ADP accounting systems and to minimize undue hardships of ADP recordkeeping. It is recognized that ADP accounting systems will vary from taxpayer to taxpayer and, usually, will be designed to fit the specific needs of the taxpayer. Accordingly, taxpayers who are in doubt as to which records are to be retained or who desire further information should contact their District Director for assistance.

See Revenue Procedure 64–12, C.B. 1964–1 (Part 1), 672, which sets forth guidelines for keeping records within an ADP system.

An Interconnect Contract Checklist

Richard A. Kuehn* and Joseph Kalk**

Since the original Federal Communication Commission decision in the summer of 1968 to allow the interconnection of purchased equipment to the telephone network (Carterfone, 1 CLSR 1019), a new industry has been created. The interconnect or purchased telephone market has been estimated to reach $80 million in 1972. Simply checking any telephone directory under the heading "Telephone Apparatus" will uncover numerous suppliers of equipment in any major city. It has been estimated by some industry sources that up to 70 percent of the present suppliers of interconnect systems will no longer be in business in 1977. With this

Reprinted with permission from *Computer Law Service,* published by Callaghan & Company, 6141 N. Cicero Avenue, Chicago, Illinois 60646.

*Mr. Kuehn is president of RAK Associates in Cleveland, Ohio, a consultant on private telephone systems.

**Mr. Kalk is a member of the law firm of Kalk & Valore in Cleveland.

possibility and the long-term investment required in the purchase of telephone equipment, it is mandatory that the purchaser take steps, by contract, to protect himself.

Conversations with many of these suppliers indicate amazement on their part of the ease with which the interconnected system is sold. Normally, pay-out periods of well over five years are easily accepted by the purchaser with little analysis or investigation. At the same time such a decision involves the expenditure of considerable money. A system of only 30 lines can cost in excess of $50,000.

Ten-year lease or lease purchase contracts are not uncommon. This in turn increases system costs and commits the buyer to the supplier for the entire term of the lease or system pay-out in the case of a purchase. Too often this entire transaction is completed by signatures on a standard leasing company form provided by the seller.

This normally places the purchaser in the position of being obligated to make all payments while the seller's obligation is only to deliver the system. With the expenditure of many thousands of dollars and the requirement for a functioning communication system, so necessary in today's business environment, it is wise for the buyer to take some steps to protect himself contractually.

The interconnect supplier may argue that the telephone company will not sign any special contract with the purchaser when providing service. However, the telephone company is already obligated to provided service according to the rules of its publicly filed tariff and under the operating regulations prescribed by the regulatory bodies governing its action.

Using the following outline and commentary and some degree of common sense, it is possible for counsel to prepare a contract for the purchase of telephone equipment from an independent supplier. The points which should be included in every contract are as follows:

I. The System

    A. Switching Capability

        It is vital that the system be able to handle both present and anticipated telephone traffic with an acceptable rejection rate. Both the traffic handling requirements and rejection rates should be included, with specified present and anticipated future system size.

B. System Features

The systemwide features, such as switchboard capacity, station transfer, consultation hold, add-on conference, rotary hunting, line restriction, etc. should be enumerated.

C. Equipment Station Configuration

This is a complete detailed design of every telephone to be installed including its location, the lines to be answered on a key set, and other special features with unit prices. Since, in negotiating the price for additions or deletions from the contract the buyer is not in as strong a bargaining position as the seller, spelling these out in the seller's proposal will tend to equalize the parties.

D. Service Manuals and Parts Lists

Two complete sets of these should be delivered with the system. This will allow service by an outside source should the original supplier fail for any reason to be able to perform.

E. Acceptance Tests

Tests should be run on the system before it is accepted by the purchaser. This usually involves the testing or calling of all telephones, testing of system features and the artificial creation of anticipated peak traffic conditions.

F. System Reliability

The supplier should be willing to guarantee some reasonable criteria as to expected rate of service or downtime. This is applicable to both individual lines, trunks and total system. As a system owner, the telephone company neither charges for service nor wants excessive service calls, and therefore may decide to replace a system incurring excessive downtime. The system purchaser should obtain the same right from his supplier, if this should become necessary because of excessive service.

G. Compatibility with Exchange Network

The new state of the industry and the rapid changes being effected by electronics require a guarantee that the system be compatible with the Bell network for at least the term of the pay-out period. Since there is a distinct possibility that future systems will be "type certified" for use and not require the present "interface" units, an agreement that these additional cost units either can be removed or their cost paid by the supplier could save thousands of dollars over the system's life.

H. Changes and Attachments

If actual ownership of the system resides in a third-party leasing company, the buyer should have the ability to make system changes such as increased or decreased size and added special equipment, even when provided by other vendors.

I. Use and Function

If title is in the lessor, the user should be able to use the system as he wants.

J. Future Field Modifications

If the system is leased, it should be possible to incorporate new design changes in the existing switching or station equipment *if* technically feasible.

II. Delivery and Installation

A. What is the specific delivery date?

B. Buyer's Option To Obtain Early Delivery

If a new system is being installed in a new building, this clause could be of extreme importance if construction runs ahead of schedule.

C. Delays in Delivery

This is important to both the supplier and purchaser because of possible added costs that may be incurred by either party because of late delivery. For example, on a late delivery the supplier should be responsible for increased telephone company charges incurred by the buyer.

D. Freight Charges

These can be a sizable item for large systems and responsibility for their payment should be fixed.

E. Site Preparation

Many of today's telephone switching units carry very high floor-loading requirements (in the area of 200 pounds per square foot). The costs of this type construction or building reinforcement should be paid by the buyer with the seller responsible for furnishing adequate drawings of equipment areas indicating floor load and power requirements.

F. Location

This should provide the right to move the equipment to either a new location or other space within the existing location.

G. Method of Installation

Such items as whether the existing telephone company wire will be used or new cable will be installed should be covered. If new cable is used, will it be concealed or open wiring? If existing cable is used, will the organization be without telephone service for any period? What cabling will be used and how will it guarantee the future ability to expand the system? One of the first surprises for any system purchaser is the high cost of moving or installing interconnected telephones.

III. Supplier's Services

A. Response to Service Calls

It is best to receive guarantees as to how promptly the supplier will respond to service calls. This normally has two different time frames: (1) a rapid response for total system failure; and, (2) a somewhat longer guarantee for periods when only a telephone or other single component is malfunctioning.

B. Service Responsibility

Most telephone companies make a charge for service calls which turn out to be caused by interconnected equipment. The supplier should agree to pay any of these charges, if they occur.

C. Disaster Recovery

In the case of a complete disaster, such as fire or flood, what provisions can be made to assure rapid recovery of service?

D. Education and Training

The supplier should provide ongoing training of the system users and switchboard operators as employee turnover requires. The frequency and costs, if any, of this service should be enumerated.

E. Traffic and Usage Studies

Semiannually, studies should be taken of all system traffic to determine the adequacy of trunks, links and switchboard positions. Both the frequency, type of studies and any cost should be set forth.

F. Availability of Spare Parts

The supplier should guarantee the stocking of necessary spare parts for repair either in his office or preferably at the installation site.

G. Availability of Service

The supplier should guarantee the availability of service personnel trained by the system manufacturer.

IV. Payment Procedure and Price Protection

A. Before Delivery

It should not be possible to increase the price of system components prior to installation and acceptance.

B. What is the Term of the Lease?

C. During the Lease

The price should remain constant for the entire lease with

the exception of equipment additions or deletions from the system.

D. Method of Payment

This involves items such as required down payments, cash discounts allowed, and progress billing formulas.

E. Additional Equipment Units

Guaranteed prices for the duration of either the lease or payout period should be provided on items such as telephones, added lines, links or trunk equipment by the supplier. This usually takes the form of a present unit cost to be increased in the future by a percentage equal to either cost of living averages or average telephone company rate increases.

F. Component Cancellation

If purchased, the supplier should provide a schedule allowing the return of individual items (telephone sets, links, line modules, etc.) for credit, the amount depending upon their age. If the system is leased, a similar schedule should be incorporated for the term of the lease.

G. Maintenance, Supplies

Whether service is purchased under a maintenance contract or on a per call basis, the cost of these labor hours and parts should be guaranteed in the same manner as expansion units.

H. Support Services

If charges are to be made for support services such as training sessions or future traffic studies, these should be guaranteed in the same manner as previously used.

I. Buyer's Right To Withhold or Delay Payment

If the supplier does not complete the installation as scheduled or meet the acceptance tests as outlined, the purchaser's rights to delay or withhold payment and penalties incurred by the seller should be set out.

J. Tax Responsibility

The responsibility for sales, property, and use taxes should be specified, and the effect on the lease rate (if the rates on these taxes fluctuate) determined in advance.

K. Tax Credit

If the system is leased, will the lessor pass through any investment tax credit to the lessee?

L. Insurance Responsibility

If the system is leased, responsibility for payment of insurance premiums on the system, and allocation of claims' payments, should be fixed in advance.

V. Damages or Penalties

A. Breach Before Installation, After Installation
B. Liquidated Damages

Each individual installation is different and these provisions must be designed for the particular requirements of the user.

VI. Miscellaneous

A. Compliance with Law (particularly Building Codes)
B. Conformance to Standards
C. Protection from Patent Infringement
D. Who Has Title to the Equipment
E. Only Agreement, and Amendments in Writing
F. Assignment Rights
G. Favored Nation Clause
H. Notices to Other Parties
 I. Arbitration of Disputes

Since these last clauses are a normal part of most contracts, they have been included without comment.

The above contract outline can be used as a checklist when negotiating with interconnect suppliers. During the course of the negotiation, every one of the points or questions raised in the contract should be answered by each potential supplier.

Copyright Office Circulars 60 and 61
Library of Congress
Washington, D.C. 20559

COMPUTER PROGRAMS [Circular 61]

What Is a Computer Program?

In general, a computer program is either a set of operating instructions for a computer or a compilation of reference information to be drawn upon by the computer in solving problems. In most cases the preparation of computer programs involves substantial elements of gathering, choosing, rejecting, editing, and arranging material. Some programs also embody verbal material which is written by the programmer and can be considered literary expression.

Are Computer Programs Registrable for Copyright?

The registrability of computer programs involves two basic questions: (1) Is a program the "writing of an author" and thus copyrightable, and (2) Can a reproduction of the program in a form actually used to operate or be "read" by a machine be considered an acceptable "copy" for copyright registration?

Both of these are doubtful questions. However, in accordance with its policy of resolving doubtful issues in favor of registration whereever possible, the Copyright Office will consider registration for a computer proram if certain requirements have been met.

Registration Requirements for Computer Programs

Registration for a computer program will be considered if:

- The elements of assembling, selecting, arranging, editing, and literary expression that went into the compilation of the program are sufficient to constitute original authorship.
- The program has been published with the required copyright notice; that is, "copies" (i.e., reproductions of the program in a form perceptible or capable of being made perceptible to the human eye) bearing the notice have been distributed or made available to the public.
- The copies deposited for registration consist of two complete copies of the program in the form as first published. If the first publication was in a form (such as machine-readable tape) that cannot be perceived visually or read by humans, a visually perceptible reproduction or description (such as a print-out of the program) must also be deposited.
- An application for registration is submitted on Form A. Detailed instructions for registration are given on the application form.

- The applicant also submits a brief explanation of the way in which the program was first made available to the public, and the form in which the copies were published. This explanation is not essential in every case, but it will generally facilitate examination of the claim.

COPYRIGHT FOR BOOKS [Circular 60]

General Information

What Is a Book? The term "book" includes textual works, with or without illustrations. Common examples are fiction, nonfiction, poetry, compilations, directories, catalogs, and tables of information. Books may take the form of bound volumes, pamphlets, leaflets, cards, and single pages containing text.

Unpublished "Books" Not Registrable. The law does not provide for registration of "book" material in unpublished form. Therefore, unpublished manuscripts of novels, articles, stories, poems, words or songs without music, and similar material should not be sent to the Copyright Office. Unpublished books are protected by common law against unauthorized copying, publication, or use, without any action being required in this Office.

How to Copyright a Book

Three steps must be taken to comply with the law concerning copyright for books: (1) produce copies containing the copyright notice; (2) publish the book; and (3) register the copyright claim.

1. **Produce Copies Containing the Copyright Notice.** The copies may be reproduced by printing or other means of reproduction. To obtain a copyright, the person entitled to copyright protection must make sure that all copies bear a copyright notice in the required form and position. There is no need to get Copyright Office permission before using the copyright notice.

• ELEMENTS OF THE NOTICE. The notice must contain these three elements:

+ *The word "Copyright," or the abbreviation "Copr.," or the symbol* ©. Use of the symbol © may result in securing copyright in some countries outside the United States under the provisions of the Universal Copyright Convention.

+ *The name of the copyright owner.*

+ *The year date of publication.* This is the year in which copies of the work were first placed on sale, sold, or publicly distributed by the copyright proprietor or under his authority.

• FORM OF THE NOTICE. The three elements must appear together. Example:

© John Doe 1972

• POSITION OF THE NOTICE. The notice must appear on the title page or the page immediately following. The "page immediately following" usually means the reverse of the title page since a "page is regarded as one side of a leaf."

2. **Publish the Book Bearing the Copyright Notice.**   Copyright can be obtained only if the published copies bear the required notice.* "Publication," for copyright purposes, is generally regarded as the placing on sale, sale, or public distribution of copies.

3. **Register the Copyright Claim.** Promptly after publication, mail to the Register of Copyrights, The Library of Congress, Washington, D.C. 20540, two complete copies of the work as published with the notice, an application on Form A properly completed and notarized, and a fee of $6. Registration will usually be faster if you mail the application, copies, and fee together at the same time.

---

*NOTE: It is the act of publication with the notice that actually secures copyright protection. If copies are published without the required notice, the right to secure copyright is lost and cannot be restored.

Gottschalk v. Benson and Tabbot

Supreme Court of the United States, November 20, 1972
409 U.S. 63, 3 CLSR 256, 93 S Ct 253

[2 CLSR 1030 Reversed]

[4–2]   Patentability of algorithm

1. Phenomena of nature, though just discovered, mental processes, abstract intellectual concepts are not patentable, as they are the basic tools of scientific and technological work, regardless of whether a "product" claim or a "process" claim is sought.

2. Transformation and reduction of an article to a different state or thing is the clue to the patentability of a process claim that does not include particular machines.

3. One may not patent an idea.

4. Claims for a method of converting binary-coded-decimal (BCD) numerals into pure binary numerals, not limited to any particular art or technology, to any particular apparatus or machinery, or to any particular end use, were not patentable as a "process" under 35 USC 100(b). The mathematical formula involved had no substantial practical application except in connection with a digital computer, and thus the grant of a

patent would wholly preempt the mathematical formula and in practical effect would be a patent on the algorithm itself.

MR. JUSTICE DOUGLAS delivered the opinion of the Court.

Respondents filed in the Patent Office an application for an invention which was described as being related "to the processing of data by program and more particularly to the programmed conversion of numerical information" in general purpose digital computers. They claimed a method for converting binary-coded-decimal (BCD) numerals into pure binary numerals. The claims were not limited to any particular art or technology, to any particular apparatus or machinery, or to any particular end use. They purported to cover any use of the claimed method in a general purpose digital computer of any type. Claims 8 and 13 [1] were rejected by the Patent Office but sustained by the Court of Customs and Patent Appeals, 2 CLSR 1030, 441 F2d 682. The case is here on a petition for a writ of certiorari. 405 US 915.

The question is whether the method described and claimed is a "process" within the meaning of the Patent Act.[2]

A digital computer, as distinguished from an analogue computer, is that which operates on data expressed in digits, solving a problem by doing arithmetic as a person would do it by head and hand.[3] Some of the digits are stored as components of the computer. Others are introduced into the computer in a form which it is designed to recognize. The computer operates then upon both new and previously stored data. The general purpose computer is designed to perform operations under many different programs.

---

[1] They are set forth in the Appendix to this opinion.

[2] 35 USC § 100(b) provides:

The term "process" means process, art or method, and includes a new use of a known process, machine, manufacture, composition of matter, or material.

35 USC § 101 provides:

Whoever invents or discovers any new and useful process, machine, manufacture, or composition of matter, or any new and useful improvement thereof, may obtain a patent therefor, subject to the conditions and requirements of this title.

[3] See Benray, Understanding Digital Computers (1946), p 4.

The representation of numbers may be in the form of a time-series of electrical pulses, magnetized spots on the surface of tapes, drums, or discs, charged spots on cathode ray tube screens, or the presence or absence of punched holes on paper cards, or other devices. The method or program is a sequence of coded instructions for a digital computer.

The patent sought is on a method of programming a general purpose digital computer to convert signals from binary coded decimal form into pure binary form. A procedure for solving a given type of mathematical problem is known as an "algorithm." The procedures set forth in the present claims are of that kind; that is to say, they are a generalized formulation for programs to solve mathematical problems of converting one form of numerical representation to another. From the generic formulation, programs may be developed as specific applications.

The decimal system uses as digits the 10 symbols 0, 1, 2, 3, 4, 5, 6, 7, 8, and 9. The value represented by any digit depends, as it does in any positional system of notation, both on its individual value and on its relative position in the numeral. Decimal numerals are written by placing digits in the appropriate positions or columns of the numerical sequence, i. e., "unit" (10^0), "tens" (10^1), "hundreds" (10^2), "thousands" (10^3), etc. Accordingly, the numeral 1492 signifies (1×10^3) $+ (4 \times 10^2) + (9 \times 10^1) + (2 \times 10^0)$.

The pure binary system of positional notation uses two symbols as digits—0 and 1, placed in a numerical sequence with values based on consecutively ascending powers of 2. In pure binary notation, what would be the tens position is the two position; what would be hundreds position is the fours position; what would be the thousands position is the eights. Any decimal number from 0 to 10 can be represented in the binary system with four digits or positions as indicated in the following table.

Shown as the Sum of Powers of 2

Decimal		2^3 (8)		2^2 (4)		2^1 (2)		2^0 (1)		Pure Binary
0	=	0	+	0	+	0	+	0	=	0000
1	=	0	+	0	+	0	+	2^0	=	0001
2	=	0	+	0	+	2^1	+	0	=	0010
3	=	0	+	0^2	+	2^1	+	2^0	=	0011

Decimal		(8)		(4)		(2)		(1)		Pure Binary
4	=	0	+	2^2	+	0	+	0	=	0100
5	=	0	+	2^2	+	0	+	2^0	=	0101
6	=	0	+	2^2	+	2^1	+	0	=	0110
7	=	0	+	2^2	+	2^1	+	2^0	=	0111
8	=	2^3	+	0	+	0	+	0	=	1000
9	=	2^3	+	0	+	0	+	2^0	=	1001
10	=	2^3	+	0	+	2^1	+	0	=	1010

The BCD system using decimal numerals replaces the character for each component decimal digit in the decimal numeral with the corresponding four-digit binary numeral, shown in the righthand column of the table. Thus decimal 53 is represented as 0101 0011 in BCD, because decimal 5 is equal to binary 0101 and decimal 3 is equivalent to binary 0011. In pure binary notation, however, decimal 53 equals binary 110101. The conversion of BCD numerals to pure binary numerals can be done mentally through use of the foregoing table. The method sought to be patented varies the ordinary arithmetic steps a human would use by changing the order of the steps, changing the symbolism for writing the multiplier used in some steps, and by taking subtotals after each successive operation. The mathematical procedures can be carried out in existing computers long in use, no new machinery being necessary. And, as noted, they can also be performed without a computer.

[1] The Court stated in MacKay Co. v. Radio Corp., 306 US 86, 94, that "While a scientific truth, or the mathematical expression of it, is not a patentable invention, a novel and useful structure created with the aid of knowledge of scientific truth may be." That statement followed the long-standing rule that "An idea of itself is not patentable." Rubber-Tip Pencil Co. v. Howard, 20 Wall 498, 507. "A principle, in the abstract, is a fundamental truth; an original cause; a motive; and these cannot be patented, as no one can claim in either of them an exclusive right." LeRoy v. Tatham, 14 How 156, 175. Phenomena of nature, though just discovered, mental processes, abstract intellectual concepts are not patentable, as they are the basic tools of scientific and technological work. As we stated in Funk Bros. Seed Co. v. Kalo Co., 333 US 127, 130, "He who discovers a hitherto unknown phenomenon of nature has no claim to a monopoly of it which the law recognizes. If there is to be invention from such a discovery, it must come from

the application of the law of nature to a new and useful end." We dealt there with a "product" claim, while the present case deals only with a "process" claim. But we think the same principle applies.

Here the "process" claim is so abstract and sweeping as to cover both known and unknown uses of the BCD to pure-binary conversion. The end use may (1) vary from the operation of a train to verification of drivers' licenses to researching the law books for precedents and (2) be performed through any existing machinery or future-devised machinery or without any apparatus.

In O'Reilly v. Morse, 15 How 62, Morse was allowed a patent for a process of using electromagnetism to produce distinguishable signs for telegraphy. Id., at 111. But the Court denied the eighth claim in which Morse claimed the use of "electromagnetism, however, developed for marking or printing intelligible characters, signs, or letters, at any distance." The Court in disallowing that claim said, "If this claim can be maintained, it matters not by what process or machinery the result is accomplished. For aught that we now know some future inventor, in the onward march of science, may discover a mode of writing or printing at a distance by means of the electric or galvanic current, without using any part of the process or combination set forth in the plaintiff's specification. His invention may be less complicated—less liable to get out of order—less expensive in construction, and its operation. But yet if it is covered by this patent the inventor could not use it, nor the public have the benefit of it without the permission of this patentee." Id., at 113.

In The Telephone Cases, 126 US 1, 534, the Court explained the Morse case as follows: "The effect of that decision was, therefore, that the use of magnetism as a motive power, without regard to the particular process with which it was connected in the patent, could not be claimed, but that its use in that connection could." Bell's invention was the use of electric current to transmit vocal or other sounds. But the claim was not "for the use of a current of electricity in its natural state as it comes from the battery, but for putting a continuous current in a closed circuit into a certain specified condition suited to the transmission of vocal and other sounds, and using it in that condition for that purpose." 126 US at 534. The claim, in other words, was not "one for the use of electricity distinct from the particular process with which it is connected in his patent." Id., at 935. The patent was for that use of electricity "both for the magnetic and variable resistance methods." Id., at 538. Bell's claim in other words, was not one for all telephonic use of electricity.

In Corning v. Burden, 15 How 252, 267–268, the Court said "One may discover a new and useful improvement in the process of tanning, dyeing, etc. irrespective of any particular form or mechanical device." The examples given were the "arts of tanning, dyeing, making waterproof cloth, vulcanizing India rubber, smelting ores." Id., at 267. Those are instances, however, where the use of chemical substances or physical acts such as temperature control change articles or materials. The chemical process or the physical acts which transform the raw material are, however, sufficiently definite to confine the patent monopoly within rather definite bounds.

Cochran v. Deener, 94 US 780, involved a process for manufacturing flour so as to increase its quality. The process first separated the superfine flour and then removed impurities from the middling by blasts of air, reground the middlings, and then combined the product with the superfine. Id., at 785. The claim was not limited to any special arrangement of machinery. Ibid. The Court said:

> That a process may be patentable, irrespective of the particular form of the instrumentalities used, cannot be disputed. If one of the steps of a process be that a certain substance is to be reduced to a powder, it may not be at all material what instrument or machinery is used to effect that object, whether a hammer, a pestle and mortar, or a mill. Either may be pointed out; but if the patent is not confined to that particular tool or machine, the use of the others would be an infringement, the general process being the same. A process is a mode of treatment of certain materials to produce a given result. It is an act, or a series of acts, performed upon the subject-matter to be transformed and reduced to a different state or thing. Id., at 787–788.

[2] Transformation and reduction of an article "to a different state or thing" is the clue to the patentability of a process claim that does not include particular machines. So it is that a patent in the process of "manufacturing fat acids and glycerine

from fatty bodies by the action of water at a high temperature and pressure" was sustained in Tilghman v. Proctor, 102 US 707, 721. The Court said, "The chemical principle or scientific fact upon which it is founded is, that the elements of neutral fat require to be severally united with an atomic equivalent of water in order to separate from each other and become free. This chemical was not discovered by Tilghman. He only claims to have invented a particular mode of bringing about the desired chemical union between the fatty elements and water." Id., at 729.

Expanded Metal Co. v. Bradford, 214 US 366, sustained a patent on a "process" for expanding metal. A process "involving mechanical operations and producing a new and useful result." Id., at 385–386, was held to be a patentable process, process patents not being limited to chemical action.

Smith v. Snow, 294 US 1, and Waxham v. Smith, 204 US 20, involved a process for setting eggs in staged incubation and applying mechanically circulated currents of air to the eggs. The Court in sustaining the function performed (the hatching of eggs) and the means or process by which that is done, said:

> By the use of materials in a particular manner he secured the performance of the function by a means which had never occurred in nature, and had not been anticipated by the prior art; this is a patentable method or process. A method, which may be patented irrespective of the particular form of the mechanism which may be availed of for carrying it into operation, is not to be rejected as "functional," merely because the specifications show a machine capable of using it. 294 US at 22.

It is argued that a process patent must either be tied to a particular machine or apparatus or must operate to change articles or materials to a "different state or thing." We do not hold that no process patent could ever qualify if it did not meet the requirements of our prior precedents. It is said that the decision precludes a patent for any program servicing a computer. We do not so hold. It is said that we have before us a program for a digital computer but extend our holding to programs for analog computers. We have, however, made clear from the start that we deal with a program only for digital computers. It is said we freeze process patents to old technologies, leaving no room for the revelations of the new, onrushing technology. Such is not our purpose. What we come down to in a nutshell is the following.

[3, 4] It is conceded that one may not patent an idea. But in practical effect that would be the result if the formula for converting binary code to pure binary were patented in this case. The mathematical formula involved here has no substantial practical application except in connection with a digital computer, which means that if the judgment below is affirmed, the patent would wholly pre-empt the mathematical formula and *in practical effect would be a patent on the algorithm itself.*

It may be that the patent laws should be extended to cover these programs, a policy matter to which we are not competent to speak. The President's Commission on the Patent System [4] rejected the proposal that these programs be patentable: [5]

> Uncertainty now exists as to whether the statute permits a valid patent to be granted on programs. Direct attempts to patent programs have been rejected on the ground of nonstatutory subject matter. Indirect attempts to obtain patents and avoid the rejection, by drafting claims as a process, or a machine or components thereof programmed in a given manner, rather than as a program itself, have confused the issue further and should not be permitted.
>
> The Patent Office now cannot examine applications for programs because of a lack of a classification technique and the requisite search files. Even if these were available, reliable searches would not be feasible or economic because of the tremendous volume of prior art being generated. Without this search, the patenting of programs would be tantamount to mere registration and the presumption of validity would be all but nonexistent.
>
> It is noted that the creation of programs has undergone substantial and satisfactory growth in the absence of patent protection and that copyright protection for programs is presently available.

---

[4] To Promote the Progress of Useful Arts, Report of the President's Commission on the Patent System (1966).

[5] Id., at 13.

If these programs are to be patentable,[6] considerable problems are raised which only committees of Congress can manage, for broad powers of investigation are needed, including hearings which canvass the wide variety of views which those operating in this field entertain. The technological problems tendered in the many briefs before us[7] indicate to us that considered action by the Congress is needed.

Reversed.

MR. JUSTICE STEWART, MR. JUSTICE BLACKMUN, and MR. JUSTICE POWELL took no part in the consideration or decision of this case.

Appendix

Claim 8 reads:

The method of converting signals from binary coded decimal form into binary which comprises the steps of—

(1) storing the binary coded decimal signals in a re-entrant shiftregister,

(2) shifting the signals to the right by at least three places, until there is a binary "1" in the second position of said register.

(3) masking out said binary "1" in said second position of said register.

(4) adding a binary "1" to the first position of said register,

(5) shifting the signals to the left by two positions,

(6) adding a "1" to said first position, and

(7) shifting the signals to the right by at least three positions in preparation for a succeeding binary "1" in the second position of said register.

Claim 13 reads:

---

[6] See Wild, Computer Program Protection: The Need to Legislate a Solution, 54 Corn L Rev 586, 604–609 (1969); Bender, Computer Programs: Should They Be Patentable, 68 Col L Rev 241 (1968); Buckman, Protection of Proprietory Interest in Computer Programs, 51 J Pat Off Socy 135 (1969).

[7] Amicus briefs of 16 interested groups have been filed in this case.

A data processing method for converting binary coded decimal number representations into binary number representations comprising the steps of—

(1) testing each binary digit position i, beginning with the least significant binary digit position, of the most significant decimal digit representation for a binary "0" or a binary "1";

(2) if a binary "0" is detected, repeating step (1) for the next least significant binary digit position of said most significant decimal digit representation;

(3) if a binary "1" is detected, adding a binary "1" at the $(i + 1)$th and $(i + 3)$th least significant binary digit positions of the next lesser significant decimal digit representation, and repeating step (1) for the next least significant binary digit position of said most significant decimal digit representation;

(4) upon exhausting the binary digit positions of said most significant decimal digit representation, repeating steps (1) through (3) for the next lesser significant decimal digit representation as modified by the previous execution of steps (1) through (3) ; and

(5) repeating steps (1) through (4) until the second least significant decimal digit representation has been so processed.

IBM *Agreement for Machine Service (6399-19)*

International Business Machines Corporation

International Business Machines Corporation   *Armonk, New York 10504*

Agreement for IBM Machine Service
(Includes Systems Supplement)

To: International Business Machines Corporation   Agreement No.:

Branch Office Address: Br. Off. No.:

                                                                                              Customer No.:

Name and Address of Customer:

International Business Machines Corporation (IBM), by its acceptance hereof, agrees to furnish to the Customer, in accordance with this Agreement, its IBM machine service comprising the use of the below listed machines and features (called machine or machines) and machine maintenance service.

Type	Model/Special Feature	Description	Quantity	Monthly Availability Charge Each

Monthly Availability Charges invoiced will be as of the first of each month.
Payment shall be made in full within thirty days after the date of invoice.

Term of Agreement

    This Agreement is effective from the date it is accepted and shall remain in force, except as otherwise provided, for one year from the date the first machine is installed ready for use, and may be terminated by either party then, provided written notice is received three months prior, otherwise this Agreement shall remain in full force and effect. Thereafter it may be terminated or any of the machines may be discontinued by either party at the end of any calendar month provided three months' prior written notice is received.

Charges

    The charges shown on the face hereof are those currently in effect. All charges are subject to change upon three months' notice. If

Please send all communications to IBM at its branch office address listed above unless notified to the contrary.

Z120-6399-19
(U/M-025)   1   **CUSTOMER**

the Monthly Availability Charge is changed for any machine, the Customer may discontinue it or terminate this Agreement on the effective date of such change; otherwise, the new charge shall become effective.

There is a Monthly Availability Charge for each machine. In addition, there may be Additional Monthly Charges in accordance with the Rental Plan or Extra Shift Plan designated for each machine as follows:

RENTAL PLAN A

The Customer is entitled to accumulate up to 176 hours of billable time in any calendar month for the basic Monthly Availability Charge. IBM will install and maintain its meters for the purpose of recording billable time. In order to ensure timely meter readings, the Customer agrees to furnish a monthly report to IBM showing the meter readings for each machine as of the close of the last work day of each calendar month. The Customer agrees to use due care not to interfere with the proper operation of the meters. Additional monthly charges will be at IBM's established rates for billable time in excess of 176 hours in any calendar month. When a machine is installed for part of a calendar month, there are two alternative methods of prorating, and the hours of billable time for the partial month subject to the Additional Monthly Charges will be the lesser result of the two methods:

a) The 176 hours will be prorated on the basis of a 30-day month and the charge will be computed on the hours of billable time in excess thereof, or

b) When a machine has been installed for the three preceding calendar months, the average monthly hours of additional billable time for that period will be prorated on the basis of a 30-day month and the charges will be computed on the prorated portion.

RENTAL PLAN B

The Monthly Availability Charges for these machines are the entire charges for use in any calendar month. Charges for partial months will be prorated on the basis of a 30-day month.

EXTRA SHIFT PLAN

The Monthly Availability Charges include the use of machines by only one shift of machine operating personnel. When a machine is used by more than one shift of machine operating personnel, an extra charge for each hour of use by such extra shifts shall be made at the rate of 1/176th of 50% of the Monthly Availability Charges. Charges for partial months will be prorated on the basis of a 30-day month.

The Monthly Availability Charge for each machine commences on the day following that on which each machine is installed ready for use.

There shall be added to the above charges amounts equal to any taxes, however designated, levied or based on such charges or on this Agreement or the machines or their use, including state and local privilege or excise taxes based on gross revenue, and any taxes or amounts in lieu thereof paid or payable by IBM in respect of the foregoing, exclusive, however, of personal property taxes assessed on the machines and taxes based on net income.

Additional or Replacement Machines

Machines, in addition to the above or to replace any the Customer may have in use, will be furnished, if available, to the Customer under this Agreement, at the schedule of charges in effect on the date such machines are installed ready for use.

Cards and Tape

Cards, tape, other supplies, accessories and disk devices used to operate the machines are to meet the necessary IBM specifications.

Maintenance

IBM will keep the machines in good working order and will make all necessary adjustments and repairs. For this purpose IBM shall have full and free access to the machines. The required suitable electric current to operate the machines and a suitable place of installation with all facilities as specified in IBM's Installation Manual will be furnished by the Customer. IBM will not furnish maintenance service if the machines are located outside the United States, Puerto Rico or the Canal Zone.

Risk of Loss

During the period the machines are in transit or in the possession of the Customer, IBM and its insurers, if any, relieve the Customer of responsibility for all risks of loss or damage to the machines except for his responsibility for loss or damage caused by nuclear reaction, nuclear radiation or radioactive contamination.

Alterations and Attachments

Upon prior written notice to IBM, alterations in or attachments to the machines may be made. If the alteration or attachment interferes with the normal and satisfactory operation or maintenance of any of the machines in such manner as to increase substantially the cost of maintenance thereof, or create a safety hazard, the Customer will, upon notice from IBM to that effect, promptly remove the alteration or attachment and restore the machines to their normal condition.

Transportation and Traveling Expenses

All transportation, rigging and drayage charges upon the machines, both from and to the IBM plants, are to be paid by the Customer including those necessitated by capacity changes ordered by the Customer. Necessary packing cases for the return of the machines and a representative to supervise the packing will be furnished by IBM without charge. The cost of labor for crating and uncrating machines is a Customer expense except when it is performed at either an IBM plant or reconditioning location.

There will be no charge for travel expense associated with services under this Agreement except that actual travel expense shall be charged in those unusual instances where the site at which the machine is located is not normally accessible by private automobile or scheduled public transportation.

Warranty

IBM warrants that the above machines when installed will be in good working order and will conform to IBM's official published specifications. Without additional charge IBM will make all adjustments, repairs and parts replacements necessary to maintain the machines. All machines are supplied subject to these warranties, and IBM's obligation hereunder is limited to repair or replacement of any parts or machines when it determines that they do not conform to these warranties.

The foregoing Warranty is in lieu of all other warranties express or implied, including, but not limited to, the implied warranties of merchantability and fitness for a particular purpose.

Limitations

The use of the machines will be under Customer's exclusive management and control. The Customer will be responsible for assuring the proper use, management and supervision of the machines and programs, audit controls, operating methods and office procedures, for establishing the necessary control over access to data, and for establishing all proper check points and procedures necessary for the Customer's intended use of the machines and the security of the data stored therein.

IBM will not be liable for personal injury or property damage except personal injury or property damage caused by IBM's negligence.

IBM shall in no event have obligations or liabilities for consequential damages even if IBM has been advised of the possibility of such damages.

The Customer agrees that IBM will not be liable for any damages caused by Customer's failure to fulfill any Customer responsibilities as set forth above or for any lost profits or for any claim or demand by any other party.

CUSTOMER

General

The terms and conditions of this Agreement supersede those of all previous agreements between the parties with respect to IBM machine service, and such service hereafter is subject to the terms and conditions of this Agreement.

This Agreement is not assignable; none of the machines may be sublet, assigned or transferred by the Customer without the prior written consent of IBM. Any attempt to sublet, assign or transfer any of the rights, duties or obligations of this Agreement is void.

The Customer agrees to keep IBM informed of the location of all machines.

Either party may terminate this Agreement for failure of the other to comply with any of its terms and conditions.

All machines remain IBM's property and may be removed by IBM at any time after termination of this Agreement.

The Customer acknowledges that he has read this Agreement, understands it and agrees to be bound by its terms and further, agrees that it is the complete and exclusive statement of the agreement between the parties, which supersedes all proposals oral or written and all other communications between the parties relating to the subject matter of this Agreement.

This Agreement will be governed by the laws of the State of New York.

Received by IBM at _____
  DP Branch Office Name/Number

By_____
  Manager's Signature

_____
  Manager's Name (Type or Print)

On_____
  Date

Accepted by:
International Business Machines Corporation

By_____   By_____
  Authorized Signature   Authorized Signature

_____   _____
  Name (Type or Print)   Name (Type or Print)

_____   _____
  Title   Title

On_____   On_____
  Date   Date

PLEASE PRESS FIRMLY WITH BALL POINT PEN ON HARD SURFACE FOR MAXIMUM LEGIBILITY.

Z120-6399-19
(U/M-025)   3   **CUSTOMER**

References on Computer Contracts

1. Atkins, Robert J. and Roy J. Herrick, *ADAPSO Contract Analysis Survey.* Association of Data Processing Service Organizations, 1969.

2. "A Model Contract for Computer Equipment," *Data Processing Manual,* Parts 1-02-04, 1-02-05. Auerbach Publishers Inc.: Philadelphia, 1973.

3. Bernacchi, Richard L. and Gerald H. Larsen, *Data Processing Contracts and the Law.* Little, Brown & Co., 1974.

4. Brandon, Dick H. and Sidney Segelstein, *Data Processing Contracts,* Van Nostrand Reinhold Co., 1976.

5. Freed, Roy N., "Negotiating a Computer Contract Without Negotiating Trouble," *Innovation,* August 1969, reprinted in *Computer Law Service,* Volume 2, Section 3-2, Article 1.

6. Rowell, Harry B. Jr. and Carolyn Landis, *Contracting for Computing.* Princeton. N.J.: EDUCOM, 1973).

7. Scalletta, Philip J. Jr. and Joseph L. Walsh, *Syntax Legal Analysis of Standard Commercial Computer Purchase and Lease Agreements.* Data Processing Management Association, 1973.

Computer Contract Checklist

by Robert P. Bigelow

This is a checklist of items which the data processing manager and his attorney should consider from a contractual viewpoint when a system is installed or expanded.

1 SYSTEM DESIGN

Before you start contractual negotiations, a feasibility study should be made. The applications which the proposed system is to handle should be specified in as complete detail as possible both for

---

*Abridged and updated from Guide to Negotiating a Computer. Copyright © 1969, 1972, 1975 by Robert P. Bigelow.

internal use and for delivery to possible suppliers of hardware, software, and other services.

The critical factors in each application should be clearly identified. These include:

a. Accuracy standards—can any error be tolerated?
b. Permissible limits—e.g., manhours, dollars.
c. Job scheduling—how long until project completed?
d. Outside factors affecting the application. (One example might be a very complicated collective bargaining agreement specifying pay rates; this would have a considerable effect on a payroll application.)

The assumptions that are made should also be specified in detail. These might include:

a. The volume of input expected for each job (e.g., weekly payroll) both at normal levels and at peak load.
b. Personnel availability, including operators, programmers, and management.

2   RESPONSIBILITIES

Management should give detailed study to the various people whose work will need to be coordinated in preparing, installing, and operating the proposed data-processing system. These include:

a. The user.
b. The consultant, if any.
c. The hardware manufacturers, both of central processing units and of each peripheral unit.
d. The hardware owner, such as a leasing company.
e. The company(ies) that will supply communications (telephone, telegraph).
f. Suppliers of forms, furniture, etc.
g. Service bureaus for parts of the application, overflow, or backup.

     h. Designers of special software.

     i. Suppliers of prepared software packages.

     j. The contractor who will handle the construction work necessary for site preparation and all his sub-contractors, such as carpenters and electricians.

     k. The movers of equipment, both hardware and furniture.

     l. The landlord.

     m. Insurance agents.

The individual or individuals who are going to coordinate all of the above people, the individual who has the final decision in each area, and the individual who makes the final determination on any dispute should be decided upon at the very beginning.

3 BASIC SYSTEM SPECIFICATIONS

In designing the system, certain specifications should be nailed down completely and should be covered in proposals received by the company. These will include:

3.1. Hardware

     a. Performance specifications for each unit; for example 900 cards per minute. The greater the detail in specification the less likelihood of dispute at a later date. For example, even the address assignment methods in operating systems can differ and two systems which appear the same on the surface—but have different methods—may be incompatible.

     b. Manufacturers' specifications for accessories such as cards, ribbons, etc. should be determined in as complete detail as possible.

     c. Operating manuals should be specified.

     d. The communications equipment required should be clearly defined.

     e. Whenever it is possible, the system specification should call for standard items rather than for items particularly designed for the user. Not only do they cause less trouble, but they can be replaced more easily and are much less liable to be the cause of argument as to what is included within the description.

f. In secondhand sales, the equipment is usually FOB Seller. Title aspects and insurance coverages should be checked, see ¶8.3; a buyer should also be sure that the equipment has been properly maintained, and should obtain a written commitment for maintenance from the manufacturer or from a maintenance company before executing a purchase agreement. See ¶9.3.

3.2. Software

In specifying software, several matters should be considered, including:

a. Utility routines and diagnostics.

b. Assemblers, compilers, and generators.

c. Application packages, including (1) those developed by the manufacturer, (2) those developed by an independent programming service, and (3) those developed jointly by the manufacturer and the user, or by the programming house and the user.

d. For each type of program, the following items should be clearly determined: (1) the ownership rights in the program, (2) any limitations on use, such as the number of times the program can be run, whether it can be run at all installations the user has, whether the user has the right to copy for internal use, for external use, etc., (3) personalization costs of packages, (4) provision for updates, error corrections, and error reports, (5) where corrections will be made, vendor site or user's site, and (6) who pays for travel and personnel time for corrections.

e. Documentation requirements should be clearly set forth, including (1) by whom the documentation is to be done, (2) in what detail it is to be done, and (3) who is responsible for updating and modifying documentation when there are changes in the programs. The reference and operator manuals to be supplied should be listed.

f. The performance specifications in the software should be clearly detailed.

The system should specify that both hardware and software suppliers will indemnify the user against claims for infringement of patents, copyrights, or other proprietary legal protection.

The user's attorney should also review the software specifications to ensure that the programs proposed do not contemplate activities that would violate regulatory laws. A too obvious example is a program that would divide the market in violation of the laws; the documentation required to support the program could prove the opposition's case.

4 SITE PREPARATION

4.1. Suppliers, particularly hardware manufacturers, must supply specifications in sufficient time to permit the user to construct the necessary facilities. These time requirements must be clearly stated in the contract.

4.2. Operating and environmental requirements. Contractual documents should clearly specify site requirements for:

a. Air conditioning, both regular and emergency.
b. Power and light, both regular and emergency.
c. Floor-load limits.
d. Fire protection.
e. Communications wiring.

4.3. Space requirements. The following items should also be clearly spelled out:

a. Equipment layout, including (1) the air space around each hardware unit and (2) the maintenance access requirement for each unit.

    b. Service areas and storage.

    c. Libraries, including (1) vault space, (2), fire protection, and (3) temperature and humidity controls.

    d. Management and operations offices.

    e. Offices for the programming staff.

    f. Power rooms.

    g. User protection or pickup area.

4.4. Security Requirements

The user should also review its proposed security arrangements, including:

    a. Fire protection.

    b. Library check-in and check-out procedures.

    c. Limitations on access to the computer room.

    d. System security.

See generally Chapters 14 and 15.

5 PERSONNEL TRAINING

Considerable attention should be given to the problem of personnel training, including who gets the training, such as:

    a. Programmers.

    b. Systems analysts.

    c. Operators.

    d. Management.

What preliminary training do the students need before they attend the training courses? How long is each course? When are the courses given, such as:

    a. Pre-installation.

    b. During installation test periods.

    c. After acceptance.

    d. When modifications are made to the system.

Who gives each course:

    a. The supplier.
    b. The user.
    c. A consultant.

Who pays for instruction; travel and living expenses?

Where are the courses given?

    a. At supplier's facility.
    b. On site.
    c. At an educational institution.

6 DELIVERY AND ACCEPTANCE

6.1. Delivery dates should be specified in considerable detail.

    a. Software. Software should be delivered to the user before the hardware is delivered so that the user may train his personnel to become familiar with the software. The user should also be sure that the necessary equipment and the proper configuration is specified and will be available when the software is ready. One point should be clearly covered—who pays the cost involved in this training and familiarization period, including equipment rental and travel?

    b. Hardware. The contract should specify (1) in what order the units will arrive, and (2) who pays for storage if the equipment arrives before the site is ready. See ¶7.6.

    c. Remedies for supplier's failure to meet his delivery dates should be clearly set forth. See ¶7.7.

6.2. Installation

Certain problems can arise in the installation itself and should be considered well beforehand. They include:

    a. Getting the necessary permits to block the street if a crane is necessary to install the equipment.

b. Coordination of the transportation of equipment.
c. Determining who pays if the equipment is damaged in the course of transport. This usually depends on whose fault it is. See ¶8.3.
d. Investigating union requirements. In Honeywell, 1 CLSR 807, the manufacturer had to use union electricians, even though it ordinarily used its own personnel, and the government was not compelled to pay for the additional cost. See also ¶7.6d.

6.3. Testing

The testing stage is very important and should be considered in detail. Items to be considered and set forth in the contract include:

a. An initial checkout before beginning operating tests.
b. The test period schedule. This should cover all phases of the operation, including normal downtime. At least a month is needed to check on the time between failures and on the time needed to bring the system up to full operating speed again.
c. Benchmark tests, including (1) diagnostic routines, (2) tests using actual proven data, and (3) tests using specially prepared test data. The contract should specify who will prepare the tests, who will validate them, how long before the tests the software should be ready, and who will determine whether the tests have been met.
d. The performance levels required should be spelled out in detail, including (1) maximum downtime in a period (week, month), (2) maximum length of a continuous period of downtime, (3) maximum time allowed to get the system restarted and operating again, (4) the average downtime per month, or similar period, (5) the average time to restore failure (mean time to repair), and (6) mean time to failure.

6.4. The rent should not start, nor the first purchase or lease payment be due, until the system has met the tests. Some contracts provide that payment becomes due when the manufacturer certifies the equipment as ready, see National Cash Register Co. v. Marshall Savings and Loan Ass'n, 2 CLSR 332.

7   FINANCES

This paragraph covers quite a few items which might perhaps be expected to appear elsewhere, but since they all relate to money, they have been grouped here.

7.1.   Rental arrangements. All of the following items should be covered, or at least considered, in preparing a contract for rental of hardware or software:

    a. Is the equipment rental based on a specified number of hours per month? On shifts?

    b. How is the chargeable time defined? Does it include set-up time, reruns? Is it charged on the central processor only, or on each piece of equipment, including each peripheral individually?

    c. Are there shift differentials?

    d. What is the amount of up time which has been guaranteed by the supplier and what are the adjustments for failure to meet this guarantee.

    e. What credits are given for downtime? This can be particularly important when the computer system includes equipment from several companies, and other lessors' equipment is rendered inoperable by one lessor's failure. See ¶10.5d.

    f. Does the rent include maintenance?

    g. Does the rent include supplies?

    h. If software is rented, how are the charges determined—is there a rate per use, a rate per month, or what?

    i. What is the rental period?

    j. What records are to be maintained by the user, and what rights does the user have, if any, to inspect the supplier's records?

    k. What use discounts are available?

7.2.   Purchase of equipment and software. Among other points, the contract should cover:

    a. Options to buy, including (1) when the option may be exercised, and (2) whether the user can assign the option to a third party.

    b. Whether payments made as rent will be applied toward the purchase price?

    c. The payment arrangement upon exercise of an option and, specifically, whether the payments can be made in installments. Is there a "balloon" payment (big lump sum payment) at the end?

    d. The seller's security that installments will be made.

    e. The buyer's right to use the equipment when he is in default in his payment schedule.

    f. The time when the ownership and title to the property passes from the seller to the buyer.

    g. Particularly with respect to software, the buyer's right to resell or otherwise dispose of the property.

7.3. If the user is a nonprofit insitution, it may be able to get a special discount from the supplier.

7.4. If the buyer has sufficient muscle, it may be able to get a special discount from the supplier—or a "most favored supplier" clause—in which case the supplier agrees that if it later gives anyone else—including the government—a better deal, it will change the contract to give the same deal to this user.

7.5. The question of taxes should be discussed with the user's accountants before the contract is signed, and the contract should cover, to the extent possible, these items:

    a. Investment credit.

    b. Depreciation policy.

    c. Sales and use taxes.

    d. Personal and real property taxes; particularly with respect to equipment.

7.6. Site preparation, shipping, and installation charges should be covered contractually.

    a. The user usually pays site preparation costs, but the supplier may assist, particularly if the installation is an experimental one.

    b. In commercial situations, the cost of transporting both hardware and the media of software is usually paid by the supplier, but this should be clearly spelled out.

c. There should be agreement on who is paying the cost of the supplier's personnel during the installation and training period. Frequently these costs have been charged to the user, who has found to his regret that the individuals in question live in the best hotels and enjoy their creature comforts to the fullest.

d. If the people who do the installation, checkout, and other work prior to acceptance are not part of the user's staff, must they be union personnel? If this is not considered, the user may have labor-management problems. See ¶6.2d.

e. The cost of warehousing, if equipment is delivered before the site is ready, will probably depend upon why the site is not ready. The user should be sure that his construction contract includes these costs in the event that the delay is caused by the contractor.

7.7. Consideration should be given to the penalties for nonperformance or late performance. These are becoming much more frequent and, in some cases, up to one thousand dollars per day can be negotiated.

7.8. The person handling the contract should also review the paragraphs on:

a. When the liability for rent or purchase price commences ¶6.4.

b. Personnel training ¶5.

c. Maintenance ¶8.3.

d. Site preparation ¶4.

8 GENERAL OPERATIONS

Many items which will affect operations should be covered contractually when you deal with suppliers. Even if these items are not covered in the contract, they will affect the form it takes.

8.1. Environment Specifications

The user must know, and the supplier must tell him, the limits on:

 a. Permissible temperature and humidity, both high and and low for (1) hardware, unit by unit, and (2) the tape libary.
 b. Permissible power-range limits for (1) voltage, (2) frequency, and (3) waveform.

8.2. Personnel Problems

 a. The personnel requirements for (1) operators, (2) librarians, (3) programmers, and (4) management, should be determined as early as possible.
 b. The problem of unionization should be covered. There have recently been quite a few cases involving the unionization of console personnel as well as programmers. Collective bargaining agreements should be reviewed with counsel during the planning stage.
 c. The training of new personnel should be reviewed. See ¶5.
 d. User's counsel should review the provisions of manufacturers' contracts for support by systems and field engineering personnel and should discuss with management the problems likely to be encountered, for example, confidentiality of the user's data.

8.3. The Contract

The contract should cover loss of, or injury to, equipment or software and injury to personnel, and it should clearly set forth who pays for the injury in each possible case. The user should also examine his insurance coverages, not only those relating to the data-processing installation, but also to general liability and workmen's compensation. Reviewing insurance coverage is particularly important in the sale or purchase of used hardware, since the contractual documents may be minimal.

9 MAINTENANCE

The maintenance of the hardware and software is a very important aspect of any data-processing installation and should be given considerable attention not only in the planning stage, but throughout the life of the installation. The contractual aspects of this should be specified as clearly as possible and as far in advance as possible.

9.1. Particularly with equipment, the supplier should give guarantees of reliability, including:

  a. Minimum hours of usable time per day.
  b. Mean time between failures.
  c. Maximum time to repair.

9.2. Backup equipment. Management must consider where it can get backup equipment in a compatible configuration for use when there is a breakdown.

  a. This might be supplied by the manufacturer or might be an installation of another user.
  b. Management should arrange for continuing information on other installations that have compatible configurations.
  c. Consideration should be given to the cost of arranging for backup equipment on a standby basis, and also for the actual usage of it. The method of determining these costs should be specified. Management should also check insurance coverage on the data-processing installation to determine whether their policy covers all or part of these costs.

9.3. In routine maintenance there are several factors to be considered. These include:

  a. The source of supply, which can be either the supplier of the hardware or software, or an independent maintenance service.
  b. The costs of the various types of maintenance. These

include (1) a service contract or payment on a one-job basis, (2) travel and other expenses, and (3) how much notice does user get before rate change becomes effective. Upon occasion computer manufacturers have delayed maintenance costs because companies which had bought their equipment and leased it to users were frozen into their maintenance contracts.

c. What personnel will be supplied? Will they be full time or part time? Will they be regular supplier personnel or moonlighters? Should such personnel be unionized to avoid labor-management problems for the user?

d. What kinds of maintenance personnel are supplied: engineers, installers, programmers, mechanics?

e. When will in-house work be done—(1) during established downtimes, (2) maintenance during the operating cycle, (3) prime shift, (4) second or third shift?

f. What response time will be guaranteed by the supplier of maintenance, particularly as to (1) off-premises repairs, and (2) emergencies? This is particularly important, since even the standard computer system may have numerous unexpected interruptions, and suppliers of small peripheral equipment may not have large service forces.

g. What space requirements are needed for maintenance and maintenance personnel? Review ¶4.3.

h. Will maintenance personnel be on site or on call?

i. What is the effect of modifications of equipment or software on the maintenance problem? See ¶10.2.

10 MODIFICATION AND TERMINATION

No data-processing installation is static and modifications will take place in both hardware and software. It is also possible that the contract will be terminated with one supplier and a new system brought in or, in extreme cases, the data-processing department will be dispensed with entirely. This is particularly likely when the company is absorbed by a larger company which already has its own data-processing system. Management should consider the following, both from the management and contractual points of view.

10.1. Improvement by Suppliers

These can be both hardware and software, and consideration should be given to the following aspects:

a. If reliability is improved, the supplier should usually bear the cost.
b. If the capabilities of the equipment or the software package are improved or upgraded, the cost is usually borne by the user. However, under certain contracts the supplier will agree to furnish these improvements without additional charge.
c. The supplier should be required to inform the user of bugs discovered in hardware and software and of any changes or improvements which will assist the user in improving and operating his installation.
d. The user should be sure to get full documentation of any changes made in either hardware or software, to help him with later changes.
e. The user should have the option to refuse changes that he feels will not be useful to him.

10.2. Modifications by User

The user's rights to modify equipment or programs, particularly when rented, should be clearly spelled out. Among the items to be considered are:

a. What notice the user must give the supplier before the modification is started.
b. What effect these modifications may have on the maintenance contracts.
c. What ownership rights will the user and the supplier have in improvements? This can be particularly important in software changes.

10.3.   The Contract

The contract, particularly when equipment or software is rented, should clearly specify whether the lessee can rent out the equipment to other people or relocate it, and whether there are any limitations on the user acting as a service bureau for other people.

10.4.   Conversions

One major area where problems can occur is in converting from one system to another. The conversion should be regarded primarily as a new contract and a new installation, and all of the other items of this checklist should be reviewed. Contracts for equipment currently installed should be reviewed to determine the amount of time required for discontinuance notifications. However, the conversion also raises some special problems of its own such as:

a. When the system is being converted to a larger system from the same supplier, agreement should be reached on (1) how long both systems will be running parallel at a single rent, (2) the testing, (3) the systems audit, (4) the manufacturer's obligation to supply information and emulation programs, and (5) who pays for the programs needed to meet the user's requirements.

b. Another type of conversion occurs when the system as installed fails to meet the specifications—for example, by being down too often. The user should have the right to require replacement of the equipment or the software at the supplier's expense.

c. A third type of "conversion" might be the removal of certain support by a supplier. For example, when IBM unbundled, it discontinued support of some of its software. The notice which the user must receive before such a change can affect him should be clearly set forth.

10.5. Termination

This can be either the termination of an installation, or the conversion to another supplier. Among the things which should be considered and, when possible, covered in the contract are:

a. What notice is required from the party who is terminating the arrangement, which in some cases could be the supplier—for example, when the user hasn't paid his bill?

b. Who pays for removal? this usually depends on why equipment is being removed. Some possible reasons include (1) insolvency of the user, (2) nonpayment of the supplier's bills, (3) conversion to another manufacturer, (4) shift to time-sharing, (5) damage to the equipment, which could be caused by the supplier or by the user or by neither of them, and (6) failure of the equipment to meet test requirements.

c. The time requirements within which the equipment must be removed should be clearly specified.

d. To the extent that it is possible, the user should avoid dependence upon one supplier. Obviously this is rather difficult. It is unlikely that a single system will have more than one CPU. However, it is always well to have backup source of supply, even in such items as peripherals. Of course, if more than one company is a supplier for an installation, the maintenance people have a natural tendency to blame the other fellow for any breakdowns. While there may or may not be some truth in such allegations, they can cause some difficulties for management. A contractual clause on the question, perhaps with a provision for arbitration, may be helpful.

11   MISCELLANEOUS CONTRACT TERMS

Other items which should be carefully reviewed include:

11.1.   The Term of the Agreement

How long a period does the agreement between the parties cover, particularly if it is a rental agreement?

11.2.   Warranties

What warranties, representations, and guarantees does the supplier make to the user? This is an area which should be carefully detailed in the contract. The supplier will do his best to cut out every possible warranty, since failure to live up to these warranties provides a strong weapon for the user to get money from the supplier, or to terminate the contract for cause. The supplier will likely have a limitation of liability clause in the agreement; a common limit is the amount paid by the customer under the contract. Whether this is satisfactory is a matter that counsel for a user should carefully consider, and whether it protects the seller is a problem for the supplier's counsel, see Clements Auto Co. v. Service Bureau Corp., 2 CLSR 102, modified 2 CLSR 143.

11.3.   Assignment

The provision covering the assignment of the contract by the user should be clearly set forth.

11.4.   Notice

What notice is required if a specific notice is not required elsewhere?

11.5.   Governing Law

Since form contracts are usually written by lawyers for the supplier, this is usually the law of the supplier's home state. If the user has enough bargaining power, he may be able to get the law of his own state, which may be helpful in case of litigation.

11.6.   What Is the Contract?

The contract should clearly specify other documents which are incorporated by reference in the contract. These could include proposals made by the supplier or other contractual terms.

11.7.   Arbitration

A frequently useful clause is one calling for arbitration if there is a dispute between the supplier and the user.

Control Data Field Engineering E Service

CONTROL DATA

FIELD ENGINEERING
CONTROL DATA CORPORATION

CONTROL DATA CORPORATION

8100 34th Avenue South
Minneapolis, Minnesota 55440

AGREEMENT FOR FIELD ENGINEERING SERVICE

CUSTOMER NAME _____

STREET ADDRESS _____

CITY _____STATE_____

(hereinafter referred to as the Customer) agrees to purchase and Control Data Corporation (hereinafter referred to as Control Data) agrees to furnish at the place of installation indicated on Attachment A, maintenance service on the equipment listed on Attachment A (hereinafter referred to as the Equipment) in accordance with the terms and conditions contained in this Agreement, including specifically Article 8, Limitation of Remedy.

Commencement Date _____

1. **TERM OF AGREEMENT:**
This Agreement shall become effective upon the date accepted and signed by Control Data at Minneapolis, Minnesota. The Commencement Date of maintenance service is defined as the date noted above or, the day after completion of all initial repairs and adjustments provided pursuant to Article 2 below, and shall thereafter remain in effect until terminated as provided in Article 10, Termination.

2. **INSPECTION AND REPAIR:**
Prior to the Commencement Date of maintenance under this Agreement, the Equipment shall be subject to inspection, at no charge to the Customer, by Control Data to determine if it is in acceptable condition for maintenance under this Agreement. Any repairs of adjustments then deemed necessary by Control Data to bring the Equipment up to an acceptable condition shall be made prior to the commencement of maintenance service, and shall be the responsibility of the Customer.

3. **RESPONSIBILITIES OF CONTROL DATA:**
a. Control Data shall, for the total charges set forth on Attachment A, maintain the Equipment in good operating condition and furnish maintenance service during the Contracted Periods selected by the Customer on Attachment A. This maintenance service includes:
   (1) Scheduled Preventive Maintenance during the Contracted Periods of Maintenance Service.

(2) Unscheduled Remedial Maintenance Service during the Contracted Periods of Maintenance Service when notified that the Equipment is inoperative.

(3) All costs of labor and field installable parts for maintaining the Equipment; which costs are incurred as a result of normal usage and wear and tear of the Equipment.

(4) In the performance of maintenance, the use of new parts or parts equivalent to new in performance. Replaced parts shall become the property of Control Data.

(5) The installation of Engineering Changes released and sponsored by the Equipment manufacturer, at a rate equivalent to the Equipment manufacturer's charge for labor and materials, if any, and the monitoring of safety changes and changes necessary to insure the proper functioning of the Equipment which are controlled by the manufacturer to determine that such changes are installed on a timely basis.

(6) Maintenance of accurate and complete records of all Engineering Change Levels

CDC Contract No._____

and a history of maintenance activity for each unit of Equipment.

b. In the event the Customer terminates this Agreement in accordance with Article 10, Termination, Control Data at its option agrees to either:

(1) Reimburse the Customer, within thirty (30) days of cancellation, for those payments by the Customer to the Equipment manufacturer for the specific purpose of having such Equipment brought up to a condition so as to be acceptable to the manufacturer for maintenance service, based on the amount of the manufacturer's invoice and proof of payment, and a copy of the new Maintenance Service Agreement between the Customer and the Equipment manufacturer; or,

(2) Perform any maintenance services required by the Equipment manufacturer to put such Equipment into an acceptable condition for the manufacturer's maintenance service, at no charge to the Customer.

Control Data's obligation under sub-paragraph b above, includes only those adjustments or repairs resulting from normal usage, wear and tear, and does not cover charges for services excluded under Article 7, Excluded Services, nor does Control Data represent or warrant that the Equipment manufacturer will provide a contracted maintenance service agreement on the Equipment.

4. RESPONSIBILITIES OF THE CUSTOMER:

a. The Customer shall provide, free of charge and with ready access, storage space for spare parts, working space, heat, light, ventilation, electric current and outlets for the use of Control Data's maintenance personnel.

b. The Customer shall notify Control Data's maintenance personnel upon Equipment failure and shall allow Control Data full and free access to the Equipment subject to the Customer's industrial security rules.

c. The customer shall not authorize or cause maintenance or repairs to be made or attempted to Equipment during the term of this Agreement, except as specified and approved in advance by Control Data.

d. The Customer shall maintain site environmental conditions throughout the period of this Agreement in accordance with the specifications established by the Equipment manufacturer.

e. If the Customer causes modifications to be made, or accessories or devices not covered by this Agreement to be added to the Equipment, then maintenance service will be supplied unless such modifications or attachments make it impractical for Control Data to render maintenance service in which case Control Data shall be relieved of its responsibilities. If the modifications or additions increase maintenance costs, Control Data shall have the right to adjust accordingly the maintenance charges specified on Attachment A.

5. PERIODS OF MAINTENANCE SERVICE AVAILABILITY:

The Contracted Periods of Maintenance Service available to the Customer are as designated on Attachment A:

a. Principal Period of Maintenance - Any nine (9) consecutive hours per day between the hours of 7:00 a.m. to 6:00 p.m., Mondays through Fridays, excluding local holidays.

b. Option I — Extends maintenance service to sixteen (16) consecutive hours, Mondays through Fridays, excluding local holidays.

c. Option II — Extends maintenance service to twenty-four (24) hours per day, Mondays through Fridays, excluding local holidays.

d. Weekends — Extends maintenance service to Saturday and/or Sunday.

e. Modified Principal Period of Maintenance — Nine (9) consecutive hours daily, Mondays through Fridays, excluding local holidays, any part of which falls outside the hours of 7:00 a.m. to 6:00 p.m.

The Basic Monthly Maintenance Charge entitles the Customer to on-call maintenance service during the Principal Period of Maintenance. For the additional charges, indicated on Attachment A, the Customer is entitled to maintenance service during the optional extended Contracted Periods of Maintenance Service selected.

All equipment comprising a system shall, as a minimum, be covered during either the Principal or Modified Period of Maintenance. Additional coverage may be selected for individual Equipment. A system is defined as a combination of of equipments, which are interconnected by local signal and power cables. The Customer may change the periods of maintenance service by giving Control Data seven (7) days advance written notice. In the event of a change, the published rates then in effect for the newly selected periods of maintenance service shall apply.

6. INVOICES, PAYMENTS AND CHARGES:
    a. Monthly maintenance charges shall begin on the Commencement Date as specified in Article I and shall be invoiced monthly in advance. All other charges shall be invoiced after the month in which charges accrue. Invoices issued pursuant to this Agreement shall be due and payable thirty (30) days after date of invoice. Charges for maintenance services of less than one month duration shall be prorated at 1/30th of the monthly charges for each calendar day.

    b. Control Data may change the monthly rates specified herein by giving at least ninety (90) days written notice.

    c. In addition to the charges set forth on Attachment A of this Agreement, the Customer shall pay:

        (1) Labor and travel expenses for maintenance services performed outside the Contracted Periods of Maintenance at the request of the Customer provided, however, that when remedial maintenance is commenced during the Contracted Periods of Maintenance and Customer permits the work to continue beyond such periods, additional charges shall not be applicable until the hours of work performed outside the period exceed one (1) hour; and,

        (2) Labor, parts, and other expenses for Customer requested services outside the the scope of this Agreement.

    Charges for all labor and travel from the point of service shall be at Control Data's published rates in effect at the time that the services are furnished. Charges for labor shall include travel time to and from the installation site and be computed to the nearest one-quarter (1/4) hour.

7. EXCLUDED SERVICES:
    The following services are outside the scope of this Agreement:

    a. Electrical work external to the Customer's Equipment.

    b. Maintenance or repairs attributable to unauthorized attempts by or for the Customer to repair or maintain the Equipment, to catastrophe, fault or negligence of the Customer, its agents or employees, improper use or misuse of the Equipment, or causes external to the Equipment, such as but not limited to, power failure or air conditioning failure.

    c. Furnishing platens, supplies or accessories, or painting or refinishing Equipment.

    d. Making specification changes or performing services in connection with the relocation of Equipment or the addition or removal of attachments, features or other devices not classified as Engineering Changes.

8. LIMITATION OF REMEDY:
    CONTROL DATA SHALL NOT BE LIABLE FOR ANY DAMAGES CAUSED BY DELAY IN FURNISHING MAINTENANCE SERVICES OR ANY OTHER PERFORMANCE UNDER THIS AGREEMENT. THE SOLE AND EXCLUSIVE REMEDY FOR ANY BREACH OF WARRANTY, EXPRESS OR IMPLIED, INCLUDING WITHOUT LIMITATION ANY WARRANTIES OF MERCHANTABILITY OF FITNESS, AND THE SOLE REMEDY FOR CONTROL DATA'S LIABILITY OF ANY KIND INCLUDING LIABILITY FOR NEGLIGENCE WITH RESPECT TO MAINTENANCE SERVICES FURNISHED UNDER THIS AGREEMENT AND ALL OTHER PERFORMANCE BY CONTROL DATA UNDER OR PURSUANT TO THIS AGREEMENT SHALL BE LIMITED TO THE REPERFORMANCE OF ANY DEFECTIVE MAINTENANCE SERVICE PROVIDED BY CONTROL DATA, OR A REFUND NOT TO EXCEED THE AMOUNT CHARGED BY THE EQUIPMENT MANUFACTURER TO REPERFORM ANY DEFECTIVE MAINTENANCE SERVICE PERFORMED BY CONTROL DATA, AND SHALL IN NO EVENT INCLUDE ANY INCIDENTAL OR CONSEQUENTIAL DAMAGES.

9. TAXES:
    The Customer shall pay (or reimburse Control Data), in addition to any and all charges which may accrue pursuant to this Agreement, and as a separate item, all taxes (exclusive of taxes based on net income), however designated, including, but not limited to, Excise, Sales, Use, Privileges, Gross Receipts and Gross Income Taxes or amounts legally levied in lieu thereof, based upon or measured by the charges set forth in this Agreement, now or hereafter imposed under the authority of a federal, state, or local taxing jurisdiction.

10. TERMINATION:

    a. During the first year of this Agreement, either party may, at any time, terminate this Agreement by giving ninety (90) days prior written notice.

b. At the end of the first year, or any time thereafter, either party may terminate this Agreement by giving thirty (30) days prior written notice.

c. If the Customer petitions for reorganization under the Bankruptcy Act or is adjudicated a Bankrupt, or if a receiver is appointed for the Customer's business or if the Customer makes an assignment for the benefit of its creditors, or the Customer defaults in payment of any sum due hereunder, or otherwise fails to fulfill its obligations under this Agreement, then Control Data shall, without further notice, have the immediate right to terminate this Agreement. Control Data's termination shall be without prejudice to any other remedies Control Data may have.

11. GENERAL PROVISIONS:

a. Customer represents that he is the owner of the Equipment, or if not the owner that he has the authority to enter into this Agreement.

b. Control Data retains the right to subcontract any maintenance service described herein to subcontractor(s) of Control Data's choosing, including the Equipment manufacturer, provided that such subcontractor(s) shall possess qualifications equivalent to those of Control Data.

c. Except as provided in b, above, neither party shall have the right to assign or otherwise transfer its rights or obligations under this Agreement except with the written consent of the other party provided, however, that a successor in interest by merger, by operation of law, assignment, purchase or otherwise of the entire business of either party, shall acquire all interest of such party hereunder, and Control Data shall be entitled to assign all or part of the payments under this Agreement. Any prohibited assignment shall be null and void.

d. This Agreement shall be governed by the laws of the State of Minnesota. There are no understandings, agreements, or representations, express or implied, not specified in this Agreement.

e. The terms and conditions of this Agreement shall prevail notwithstanding any variance with the terms and conditions of any order submitted by the Customer. This Agreement shall not be deemed or construed to be modified, amended, rescinded, cancelled or waived in whole or in part, except by written amendment by the parties hereto.

f. No action, regardless of form, arising out of the transactions under this Agreement, may be brought by either party more than two (2) years after the cause of action has accrued.

AGREED TO:

ACCEPTED BY:

CONTROL DATA CORPORATION
8100 34th Avenue South
Minneapolis, Minnesota 55440

By _____

Title _____

Date _____

By _____

Title _____

Date _____

SERVICE BY
CONTROL DATA
CORPORATION
FIELD ENGINEERING

CONTROL DATA
CORPORATION

ATTACHMENT A

FIELD ENGINEERING

MAINTENANCE SERVICE AGREEMENT

CUSTOMER NAME _____

EQUIPMENT LOCATION _____

EQUIPMENT DESCRIPTION					EXTENDED SERVICE PERIODS									TOTAL MSA CHARGE
					MON - FRI		SATURDAY		SUNDAY					
TYPE (FEATURE)	SERIAL NO	MODEL	GROUP	BMM CHARGE	FROM / TO	OPT PCT	FROM / TO	OPT PCT	FROM / TO	OPT PCT	TOTAL OPT PCT	TOTAL EMSP		
SUBTOTAL											TOTAL			

NORMAL WORKING HOURS: FOR THE PURPOSE OF THIS AGREEMENT,
THE NORMAL WORKING HOURS OF CONTROL DATA CORPORATION ARE:
_____ TO _____ MONDAY THROUGH FRIDAY, EXCLUDING LOCAL HOLIDAYS.

AA5284

PAGE ____ OF ____

HRS.	MONDAY TO FRIDAY MACHINE GROUP			SATURDAY MACHINE GROUP			SUNDAY MACHINE GROUP		
	A	B	C	A	B	C	A	B	C
9	*10	*10	*10	4	5	8	15	6	9
15	18	22	28	7	8	11	9	10	14
24	26	34	46	9	11	15	12	14	18

*9 CONSECUTIVE HOURS, ANY PART OF WHICH IS OUTSIDE THE HOURS OF 7:00 AM TO 6:00 PM.

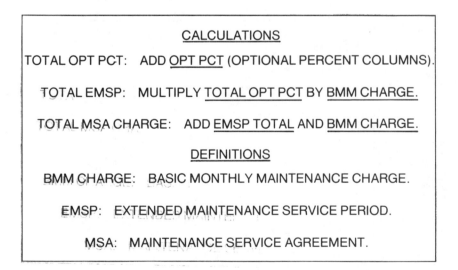

CALCULATIONS

TOTAL OPT PCT: ADD OPT PCT (OPTIONAL PERCENT COLUMNS).

TOTAL EMSP: MULTIPLY TOTAL OPT PCT BY BMM CHARGE.

TOTAL MSA CHARGE: ADD EMSP TOTAL AND BMM CHARGE.

DEFINITIONS

BMM CHARGE: BASIC MONTHLY MAINTENANCE CHARGE.

EMSP: EXTENDED MAINTENANCE SERVICE PERIOD.

MSA: MAINTENANCE SERVICE AGREEMENT.

Privacy Act of 1974

Public Law 93-579 / 93rd Congress, S. 3418 / December 31, 1974

An Act

To amend title 5, United States Code, by adding a section 552a to safeguard individual privacy from the misuse of Federal records, to provide that individuals be granted access to records concerning them which are maintained by Federal agencies, to establish a Privacy Protection Study Commission, and for other purposes.

Be it enacted by the Senate and House of Representatives of the United States of America in Congress assembled, That this Act may be cited as the "Privacy Act of 1974".

Privacy Act of 1974.
5 USC 552a note.

SEC. 2. (a) The Congress finds that—

(1) the privacy of an individual is directly affected by the collection, maintenance, use, and dissemination of personal information by Federal agencies;

Congressional findings.
5 USC 552a note.

(2) the increasing use of computers and sophisticated information technology, while essential to the efficient operations of the Government, has greatly magnified the harm to individual privacy that can occur from any collection, maintenance, use, or dissemination of personal information;

(3) the opportunities for an individual to secure employment, insurance, and credit, and his right to due process, and other legal protections are endangered by the misuse of certain information systems;

(4) the right to privacy is a personal and fundamental right protected by the Constitution of the United States; and

(5) in order to protect the privacy of individuals identified in information systems maintained by Federal agencies, it is necessary and proper for the Congress to regulate the collection, maintenance, use, and dissemination of information by such agencies.

(b) The purpose of this Act is to provide certain safeguards for an individual against an invasion of personal privacy by requiring Federal agencies, except as otherwise provided by law, to—

Statement of purpose.

(1) permit an individual to determine what records pertaining to him are collected, maintained, used, or disseminated by such agencies;

(2) permit an individual to prevent records pertaining to him obtained by such agencies for a particular purpose from being used or made available for another purpose without his consent;

(3) permit an individual to gain access to information pertaining to him in Federal agency records, to have a copy made of all or any portion thereof, and to correct or amend such records;

(4) collect, maintain, use, or disseminate any record of identifiable personal information in a manner that assures that such action is for a necessary and lawful purpose, that the information is current and accurate for its intended use, and that adequate safeguards are provided to prevent misuse of such information;

(5) permit exemptions from the requirements with respect to records provided in this Act only in those cases where there is an important public policy need for such exemption as has been determined by specific statutory authority; and

(6) be subject to civil suit for any damages which occur as a result of willful or intentional action which violates any individual's rights under this Act.

88 STAT. 1896
88 STAT. 1897

SEC. 3. Title 5, United States Code, is amended by adding after section 552 the following new section:

88 STAT. 1897

Pub. Law 93-579   - 2 -   December 31, 1974

5 USC 552a.

"§ 552a. Records maintained on individuals

"(a) DEFINITIONS.—For purposes of this section—

5 USC 552.

"(1) the term 'agency' means agency as defined in section 552(e) of this title;

"(2) the term 'individual' means a citizen of the United States or an alien lawfully admitted for permanent residence;

"(3) the term 'maintain' includes maintain, collect, use, or disseminate;

"(4) the term 'record' means any item, collection, or grouping of information about an individual that is maintained by an agency, including, but not limited to, his education, financial transactions, medical history, and criminal or employment history and that contains his name, or the identifying number, symbol, or other identifying particular assigned to the individual, such as a finger or voice print or a photograph;

"(5) the term 'system of records' means a group of any records under the control of any agency from which information is retrieved by the name of the individual or by some identifying number, symbol, or other identifying particular assigned to the individual;

"(6) the term 'statistical record' means a record in a system of records maintained for statistical research or reporting purposes only and not used in whole or in part in making any determination about an identifiable individual, except as provided by

13 USC 8.

section 8 of title 13; and

"(7) the term 'routine use' means, with respect to the disclosure of a record, the use of such record for a purpose which is compatible with the purpose for which it was collected.

"(b) CONDITIONS OF DISCLOSURE.—No agency shall disclose any record which is contained in a system of records by any means of communication to any person, or to another agency, except pursuant to a written request by, or with the prior written consent of, the individual to whom the record pertains, unless disclosure of the record would be—

"(1) to those officers and employees of the agency which maintains the record who have a need for the record in the performance of their duties;

"(2) required under section 552 of this title;

"(3) for a routine use as defined in subsection (a)(7) of this section and described under subsection (e)(4)(D) of this section;

"(4) to the Bureau of the Census for purposes of planning or carrying out a census or survey or related activity pursuant to the provisions of title 13;

"(5) to a recipient who has provided the agency with advance adequate written assurance that the record will be used solely as a statistical research or reporting record, and the record is to be transferred in a form that is not individually identifiable;

"(6) to the National Archives of the United States as a record which has sufficient historical or other value to warrant its continued preservation by the United States Government, or for evaluation by the Administrator of General Services or his designee to determine whether the record has such value;

"(7) to another agency or to an instrumentality of any governmental jurisdiction within or under the control of the United States for a civil or criminal law enforcement activity if the activity is authorized by law, and if the head of the agency or instrumentality has made a written request to the agency which

88 STAT. 1898

maintains the record specifying the particular portion desired and the law enforcement activity for which the record is sought;

"(8) to a person pursuant to a showing of compelling circumstances affecting the health or safety of an individual if upon such disclosure notification is transmitted to the last known address of such individual;

"(9) to either House of Congress, or, to the extent of matter within its jurisdiction, any committee or subcommittee thereof, any joint committee of Congress or subcommittee of any such joint committee;

"(10) to the Comptroller General, or any of his authorized representatives, in the course of the performance of the duties of the General Accounting Office; or

"(11) pursuant to the order of a court of competent jurisdiction.

"(c) ACCOUNTING OF CERTAIN DISCLOSURES.—Each agency, with respect to each system of records under its control, shall—

"(1) except for disclosures made under subsections (b)(1) or (b)(2) of this section, keep an accurate accounting of—

"(A) the date, nature, and purpose of each disclosure of a record to any person or to another agency made under subsection (b) of this section; and

"(B) the name and address of the person or agency to whom the disclosure is made;

"(2) retain the accounting made under paragraph (1) of this subsection for at least five years or the life of the record, whichever is longer, after the disclosure for which the accounting is made;

"(3) except for disclosures made under subsection (b)(7) of this section, make the accounting made under paragraph (1) of this subsection available to the individual named in the record at his request; and

"(4) inform any person or other agency about any correction or notation of dispute made by the agency in accordance with subsection (d) of this section of any record that has been disclosed to the person or agency if an accounting of the disclosure was made.

"(d) ACCESS TO RECORDS.—Each agency that maintains a system of records shall—

"(1) upon request by any individual to gain access to his record or to any information pertaining to him which is contained in the system, permit him and upon his request, a person of his own choosing to accompany him, to review the record and have a copy made of all or any portion thereof in a form comprehensible to him, except that the agency may require the individual to furnish a written statement authorizing discussion of that individual's record in the accompanying person's presence;   *Personal review.*

"(2) permit the individual to request amendment of a record pertaining to him and—   *Amendment request.*

"(A) not later than 10 days (excluding Saturdays, Sundays, and legal public holidays) after the date of receipt of such request, acknowledge in writing such receipt; and

"(B) promptly, either—

"(i) make any correction of any portion thereof which the individual believes is not accurate, relevant, timely, or complete; or

"(ii) inform the individual of its refusal to amend the record in accordance with his request, the reason

Pub. Law 93-579　　　- 4 -　　　December 31, 1974

88 STAT. 1899

for the refusal, the procedures established by the agency for the individual to request a review of that refusal by the head of the agency or an officer designated by the head of the agency, and the name and business address of that official;

Review.

"(3) permit the individual who disagrees with the refusal of the agency to amend his record to request a review of such refusal, and not later than 30 days (excluding Saturdays, Sundays, and legal public holidays) from the date on which the individual requests such review, complete such review and make a final determination unless, for good cause shown, the head of the agency extends such 30-day period; and if, after his review, the reviewing official also refuses to amend the record in accordance with the request, permit the individual to file with the agency a concise statement setting forth the reasons for his disagreement with the refusal of the agency, and notify the individual of the provisions for judicial review of the reviewing official's determination under subsection (g)(1)(A) of this section;

Notation of dispute.

"(4) in any disclosure, containing information about which the individual has filed a statement of disagreement, occurring after the filing of the statement under paragraph (3) of this subsection, clearly note any portion of the record which is disputed and provide copies of the statement and, if the agency deems it appropriate, copies of a concise statement of the reasons of the agency for not making the amendments requested, to persons or other agencies to whom the disputed record has been disclosed; and

"(5) nothing in this section shall allow an individual access to any information compiled in reasonable anticipation of a civil action or proceeding.

"(e) AGENCY REQUIREMENTS.—Each agency that maintains a system of records shall—

"(1) maintain in its records only such information about an individual as is relevant and necessary to accomplish a purpose of the agency required to be accomplished by statute or by executive order of the President;

"(2) collect information to the greatest extent practicable directly from the subject individual when the information may result in adverse determinations about an individual's rights, benefits, and privileges under Federal programs;

"(3) inform each individual whom it asks to supply information, on the form which it uses to collect the information or on a separate form that can be retained by the individual—

"(A) the authority (whether granted by statute, or by executive order of the President) which authorizes the solicitation of the information and whether disclosure of such information is mandatory or voluntary;

"(B) the principal purpose or purposes for which the information is intended to be used;

"(C) the routine uses which may be made of the information, as published pursuant to paragraph (4)(D) of this subsection; and

"(D) the effects on him, if any, of not providing all or any part of the requested information;

Publication in Federal Register.

"(4) subject to the provisions of paragraph (11) of this subsection, publish in the Federal Register at least annually a notice of the existence and character of the system of records, which notice shall include—

"(A) the name and location of the system;

December 31, 1974   - 5 -   Pub. Law 93-579
                                                              88 STAT. 1900

"(B) the categories of individuals on whom records are maintained in the system;

"(C) the categories of records maintained in the system;

"(D) each routine use of the records contained in the system, including the categories of users and the purpose of such use;

"(E) the policies and practices of the agency regarding storage, retrievability, access controls, retention, and disposal of the records;

"(F) the title and business address of the agency official who is responsible for the system of records;

"(G) the agency procedures whereby an individual can be notified at his request if the system of records contains a record pertaining to him;

"(H) the agency procedures whereby an individual can be notified at his request how he can gain access to any record pertaining to him contained in the system of records, and how he can contest its content; and

"(I) the categories of sources of records in the system;

"(5) maintain all records which are used by the agency in making any determination about any individual with such accuracy, relevance, timeliness, and completeness as is reasonably necessary to assure fairness to the individual in the determination;

"(6) prior to disseminating any record about an individual to any person other than an agency, unless the dissemination is made pursuant to subsection (b)(2) of this section, make reasonable efforts to assure that such records are accurate, complete, timely, and relevant for agency purposes;

"(7) maintain no record describing how any individual exercises rights guaranteed by the First Amendment unless expressly authorized by statute or by the individual about whom the record is maintained or unless pertinent to and within the scope of an authorized law enforcement activity;

"(8) make reasonable efforts to serve notice on an individual when any record on such individual is made available to any person under compulsory legal process when such process becomes a matter of public record;

"(9) establish rules of conduct for persons involved in the design, development, operation, or maintenance of any system of records, or in maintaining any record, and instruct each such person with respect to such rules and the requirements of this section, including any other rules and procedures adopted pursuant to this section and the penalties for noncompliance;

Rules of conduct.

"(10) establish appropriate administrative, technical, and physical safeguards to insure the security and confidentiality of records and to protect against any anticipated threats or hazards to their security or integrity which could result in substantial harm, embarrassment, inconvenience, or unfairness to any individual on whom information is maintained; and

Confidentiality of records.

"(11) at least 30 days prior to publication of information under paragraph (4)(D) of this subsection, publish in the Federal Register notice of any new use or intended use of the information in the system, and provide an opportunity for interested persons to submit written data, views, or arguments to the agency.

Publication in Federal Register.

"(f) AGENCY RULES.—In order to carry out the provisions of this section, each agency that maintains a system of records shall promulgate rules, in accordance with the requirements (including general notice) of section 553 of this title, which shall—

5 USC 553.

"(1) establish procedures whereby an individual can be notified in response to his request if any system of records named by the individual contains a record pertaining to him;

"(2) define reasonable times, places, and requirements for identifying an individual who requests his record or information pertaining to him before the agency shall make the record or information available to the individual;

"(3) establish procedures for the disclosure to an individual upon his request of his record or information pertaining to him, including special procedure, if deemed necessary, for the disclosure to an individual of medical records, including psychological records, pertaining to him;

"(4) establish procedures for reviewing a request from an individual concerning the amendment of any record or information pertaining to the individual, for making a determination on the request, for an appeal within the agency of an initial adverse agency determination, and for whatever additional means may be necessary for each individual to be able to exercise fully his rights under this section; and

Fees.

"(5) establish fees to be charged, if any, to any individual for making copies of his record, excluding the cost of any search for and review of the record.

Publication in Federal Register.

The Office of the Federal Register shall annually compile and publish the rules promulgated under this subsection and agency notices published under subsection (e)(4) of this section in a form available to the public at low cost.

"(g)(1) CIVIL REMEDIES.—Whenever any agency

"(A) makes a determination under subsection (d)(3) of this section not to amend an individual's record in accordance with his request, or fails to make such review in conformity with that subsection;

"(B) refuses to comply with an individual request under subsection (d)(1) of this section;

"(C) fails to maintain any record concerning any individual with such accuracy, relevance, timeliness, and completeness as is necessary to assure fairness in any determination relating to the qualifications, character, rights, or opportunities of, or benefits to the individual that may be made on the basis of such record, and consequently a determination is made which is adverse to the individual; or

"(D) fails to comply with any other provision of this section, or any rule promulgated thereunder, in such a way as to have an adverse effect on an individual,

Jurisdiction.

the individual may bring a civil action against the agency, and the district courts of the United States shall have jurisdiction in the matters under the provisions of this subsection.

Amendment of record.

"(2)(A) In any suit brought under the provisions of subsection (g)(1)(A) of this section, the court may order the agency to amend the individual's record in accordance with his request or in such other way as the court may direct. In such a case the court shall determine the matter de novo.

"(B) The court may assess against the United States reasonable attorney fees and other litigation costs reasonably incurred in any case under this paragraph in which the complainant has substantially prevailed.

Injunction.

"(3)(A) In any suit brought under the provisions of subsection (g)(1)(B) of this section, the court may enjoin the agency from withholding the records and order the production to the complainant of any agency records improperly withheld from him. In such a case the court shall determine the matter de novo, and may examine the contents of any agency records in camera to determine whether the records or any portion thereof may be withheld under any of the exemptions set forth in subsection (k) of this section, and the burden is on the agency to sustain its action.

"(B) The court may assess against the United States reasonable attorney fees and other litigation costs reasonably incurred in any case under this paragraph in which the complainant has substantially prevailed.

"(4) In any suit brought under the provisions of subsection (g)(1)(C) or (D) of this section in which the court determines that the agency acted in a manner which was intentional or willful, the United States shall be liable to the individual in an amount equal to the sum of— Damages.

"(A) actual damages sustained by the individual as a result of the refusal or failure, but in no case shall a person entitled to recovery receive less than the sum of $1,000; and

"(B) the costs of the action together with reasonable attorney fees as determined by the court.

"(5) An action to enforce any liability created under this section may be brought in the district court of the United States in the district in which the complainant resides, or has his principal place of business, or in which the agency records are situated, or in the District of Columbia, without regard to the amount in controversy, within two years from the date on which the cause of action arises, except that where an agency has materially and willfully misrepresented any information required under this section to be disclosed to an individual and the information so misrepresented is material to establishment of the liability of the agency to the individual under this section, the action may be brought at any time within two years after discovery by the individual of the misrepresentation. Nothing in this section shall be construed to authorize any civil action by reason of any injury sustained as the result of a disclosure of a record prior to the effective date of this section.

"(h) RIGHTS OF LEGAL GUARDIANS.—For the purposes of this section, the parent of any minor, or the legal guardian of any individual who has been declared to be incompetent due to physical or mental incapacity or age by a court of competent jurisdiction, may act on behalf of the individual.

"(i)(1) CRIMINAL PENALTIES.—Any officer or employee of an agency, who by virtue of his employment or official position, has possession of, or access to, agency records which contain individually identifiable information the disclosure of which is prohibited by this section or by rules or regulations established thereunder, and who knowing that disclosure of the specific material is so prohibited, willfully discloses the material in any manner to any person or agency not entitled to receive it, shall be guilty of a misdemeanor and fined not more than $5,000.

"(2) Any officer or employee of any agency who willfully maintains a system of records without meeting the notice requirements of subsection (e)(4) of this section shall be guilty of a misdemeanor and fined not more than $5,000.

"(3) Any person who knowingly and willfully requests or obtains any record concerning an individual from an agency under false pretenses shall be guilty of a misdemeanor and fined not more than $5,000.

"(j) GENERAL EXEMPTIONS.—The head of any agency may promulgate rules, in accordance with the requirements (including general notice) of sections 553 (b)(1), (2), and (3), (c), and (e) of this title, to exempt any system of records within the agency from any part of this section except subsections (b), (c)(1) and (2), (e)(4)(A) through 5 USC 553.

(F), (e) (6), (7), (9), (10), and (11), and (i) if the system of records is—

"(1) maintained by the Central Intelligence Agency; or

"(2) maintained by an agency or component thereof which performs as its principal function any activity pertaining to the enforcement of criminal laws, including police efforts to prevent, control, or reduce crime or to apprehend criminals, and the activities of prosecutors, courts, correctional, probation, pardon, or parole authorities, and which consists of (A) information compiled for the purpose of identifying individual criminal offenders and alleged offenders and consisting only of identifying data and notations of arrests, the nature and disposition of criminal charges, sentencing, confinement, release, and parole and probation status; (B) information compiled for the purpose of a criminal investigation, including reports of informants and investigators, and associated with an identifiable individual; or (C) reports identifiable to an individual compiled at any stage of the process of enforcement of the criminal laws from arrest or indictment through release from supervision.

5 USC 553.   At the time rules are adopted under this subsection, the agency shall include in the statement required under section 553(c) of this title, the reasons why the system of records is to be exempted from a provision of this section.

"(k) SPECIFIC EXEMPTIONS.—The head of any agency may promulgate rules, in accordance with the requirements (including general notice) of sections 553(b) (1), (2), and (3), (c), and (e) of this title, to exempt any system of records within the agency from subsections (c) (3), (d), (e) (1), (e) (4) (G), (H), and (I) and (f) of this section if the system of records is—

5 USC 552.   "(1) subject to the provisions of section 552(b) (1) of this title;

"(2) investigatory material compiled for law enforcement purposes, other than material within the scope of subsection (j) (2) of this section: *Provided, however,* That if any individual is denied any right, privilege, or benefit that he would otherwise be entitled by Federal law, or for which he would otherwise be eligible, as a result of the maintenance of such material, such material shall be provided to such individual, except to the extent that the disclosure of such material would reveal the identity of a source who furnished information to the Government under an express promise that the identity of the source would be held in confidence, or, prior to the effective date of this section, under an implied promise that the identity of the source would be held in confidence;

"(3) maintained in connection with providing protective services to the President of the United States or other individuals
18 USC 3056.   pursuant to section 3056 of title 18;

"(4) required by statute to be maintained and used solely as statistical records;

"(5) investigatory material compiled solely for the purpose of determining suitability, eligibility, or qualifications for Federal civilian employment, military service, Federal contracts, or access to classified information, but only to the extent that the disclosure of such material would reveal the identity of a source who furnished information to the Government under an express promise that the identity of the source would be held in confidence, or, prior to the effective date of this section, under an implied promise that the identity of the source would be held in confidence;

"(6) testing or examination material used solely to determine individual qualifications for appointment or promotion in the

December 31, 1974   - 9 -   Pub. Law 93-579
_____

Federal service the disclosure of which would compromise the objectivity or fairness of the testing or examination process; or

"(7) evaluation material used to determine potential for promotion in the armed services, but only to the extent that the disclosure of such material would reveal the identity of a source who furnished information to the Government under an express promise that the identity of the source would be held in confidence, or, prior to the effective date of this section, under an implied promise that the identity of the source would be held in confidence.

At the time rules are adopted under this subsection, the agency shall include in the statement required under section 553 (c) of this title, the reasons why the system of records is to be exempted from a provision of this section.   5 USC 553.

"(l)(1) ARCHIVAL RECORDS.—Each agency record which is accepted by the Administrator of General Services for storage, processing, and servicing in accordance with section 3103 of title 44 shall, for the purposes of this section, be considered to be maintained by the agency which deposited the record and shall be subject to the provisions of this section. The Administrator of General Services shall not disclose the record except to the agency which maintains the record, or under rules established by that agency which are not inconsistent with the provisions of this section.   44 USC 3103.

"(2) Each agency record pertaining to an identifiable individual which was transferred to the National Archives of the United States as a record which has sufficient historical or other value to warrant its continued preservation by the United States Government, prior to the effective date of this section, shall, for the purposes of this section, be considered to be maintained by the National Archives and shall not be subject to the provisions of this section, except that a statement generally describing such records (modeled after the requirements relating to records subject to subsections (e)(4)(A) through (G) of this section) shall be published in the Federal Register.   Publication in Federal Register.

"(3) Each agency record pertaining to an identifiable individual which is transferred to the National Archives of the United States as a record which has sufficient historical or other value to warrant its continued preservation by the United States Government, on or after the effective date of this section, shall, for the purposes of this section, be considered to be maintained by the National Archives and shall be exempt from the requirements of this section except subsections (e)(4) (A) through (G) and (e)(9) of this section.

"(m) GOVERNMENT CONTRACTORS.—When an agency provides by a contract for the operation by or on behalf of the agency of a system of records to accomplish an agency function, the agency shall, consistent with its authority, cause the requirements of this section to be applied to such system. For purposes of subsection (i) of this section any such contractor and any employee of such contractor, if such contract is agreed to on or after the effective date of this section, shall be considered to be an employee of an agency.

"(n) MAILING LISTS.—An individual's name and address may not be sold or rented by an agency unless such action is specifically authorized by law. This provision shall not be construed to require the withholding of names and addresses otherwise permitted to be made public.

"(o) REPORT ON NEW SYSTEMS.—Each agency shall provide adequate advance notice to Congress and the Office of Management and Budget of any proposal to establish or alter any system of records in order to permit an evaluation of the probable or potential effect of such   Notice to Congress and OMB.

Pub. Law 93-579   - 10 -   December 31, 1974

88 STAT. 1905

proposal on the privacy and other personal or property rights of individuals or the disclosure of information relating to such individuals, and its effect on the preservation of the constitutional principles of federalism and separation of powers.

Report to Speaker of the House and President of the Senate.

"(p) ANNUAL REPORT.—The President shall submit to the Speaker of the House and the President of the Senate, by June 30 of each calendar year, a consolidated report, separately listing for each Federal agency the number of records contained in any system of records which were exempted from the application of this section under the provisions of subsections (j) and (k) of this section during the preceding calendar year, and the reasons for the exemptions, and such other information as indicates efforts to administer fully this section.

5 USC 552.

(q) EFFECT OF OTHER LAWS.—No agency shall rely on any exemption contained in section 552 of this title to withhold from an individual any record which is otherwise accessible to such individual under the provisions of this section.".

5 USC prec. 500.

SEC. 4. The chapter analysis of chapter 5 of title 5, United States Code, is amended by inserting:

"552a. Records about individuals."

immediately below:

"552. Public information; agency rules, opinions, orders, and proceedings.".

Privacy Protection Study Commission. Establishment. 5 USC 552a note. Membership.

SEC. 5. (a)(1) There is established a Privacy Protection Study Commission (hereinafter referred to as the "Commission") which shall be composed of seven members as follows:

(A) three appointed by the President of the United States,

(B) two appointed by the President of the Senate, and

(C) two appointed by the Speaker of the House of Representatives.

Members of the Commission shall be chosen from among persons who, by reason of their knowledge and expertise in any of the following areas—civil rights and liberties, law, social sciences, computer technology, business, records management, and State and local government—are well qualified for service on the Commission.

(2) The members of the Commission shall elect a Chairman from among themselves.

Vacancies.

(3) Any vacancy in the membership of the Commission, as long as there are four members in office, shall not impair the power of the Commission but shall be filled in the same manner in which the original appointment was made.

(4) A quorum of the Commission shall consist of a majority of the members, except that the Commission may establish a lower number as a quorum for the purpose of taking testimony. The Commission is authorized to establish such committees and delegate such authority to them as may be necessary to carry out its functions. Each member of the Commission, including the Chairman, shall have equal responsibility and authority in all decisions and actions of the Commission, shall have full access to all information necessary to the performance of their functions, and shall have one vote. Action of the Commission shall be determined by a majority vote of the members present. The Chairman (or a member designated by the Chairman to be acting Chairman) shall be the official spokesman of the Commission in its relations with the Congress, Government agencies, other persons, and the public, and, on behalf of the Commission, shall see to the faithful execution of the administrative policies and decisions of the Commission, and shall report thereon to the Commission from time to time or as the Commission may direct.

December 31, 1974   - 11 -   Pub. Law 93-579
88 STAT. 1906

(5) (A) Whenever the Commission submits any budget estimate or request to the President or the Office of Management and Budget, it shall concurrently transmit a copy of that request to Congress.
Budget requests.

(B) Whenever the Commission submits any legislative recommendations, or testimony, or comments on legislation to the President or Office of Management and Budget, it shall concurrently transmit a copy thereof to the Congress. No officer or agency of the United States shall have any authority to require the Commission to submit its legislative recommendations, or testimony, or comments on legislation, to any officer or agency of the United States for approval, comments, or review, prior to the submission of such recommendations, testimony, or comments to the Congress.
Legislative recommendations.

(b) The Commission shall—

(1) make a study of the data banks, automated data processing programs, and information systems of governmental, regional, and private organizations, in order to determine the standards and procedures in force for the protection of personal information; and
Study.

(2) recommend to the President and the Congress the extent, if any, to which the requirements and principles of section 552a of title 5, United States Code, should be applied to the information practices of those organizations by legislation, administrative action, or voluntary adoption of such requirements and principles, and report on such other legislative recommendations as it may determine to be necessary to protect the privacy of individuals while meeting the legitimate needs of government and society for information.
Ante, p. 1897.

(c) (1) In the course of conducting the study required under subsection (b) (1) of this section, and in its reports thereon, the Commission may research, examine, and analyze—

(A) interstate transfer of information about individuals that is undertaken through manual files or by computer or other electronic or telecommunications means;

(B) data banks and information programs and systems the operation of which significantly or substantially affect the enjoyment of the privacy and other personal and property rights of individuals;

(C) the use of social security numbers, license plate numbers, universal identifiers, and other symbols to identify individuals in data banks and to gain access to, integrate, or centralize information systems and files; and

(D) the matching and analysis of statistical data, such as Federal census data, with other sources of personal data, such as automobile registries and telephone directories, in order to reconstruct individual responses to statistical questionnaires for commercial or other purposes, in a way which results in a violation of the implied or explicitly recognized confidentiality of such information.

(2) (A) The Commission may include in its examination personal information activities in the following areas: medical; insurance; education; employment and personnel; credit, banking and financial institutions; credit bureaus; the commercial reporting industry; cable television and other telecommunications media; travel, hotel and entertainment reservations; and electronic check processing.

(B) The Commission shall include in its examination a study of—

(i) whether a person engaged in interstate commerce who maintains a mailing list should be required to remove an individual's name and address from such list upon request of that individual;

88 STAT. 1907

(ii) whether the Internal Revenue Service should be prohibited from transfering individually indentifiable data to other agencies and to agencies of State governments;

(iii) whether the Federal Government should be liable for general damages incurred by an individual as the result of a willful or intentional violation of the provisions of sections 552a (g)

Ante, p. 1897.

(1) (C) or (D) of title 5, United States Code; and

(iv) whether and how the standards for security and confidentiality of records required under section 552a (e) (10) of such title should be applied when a record is disclosed to a person other than an agency.

Religious organizations, exception.

(C) The Commission may study such other personal information activities necessary to carry out the congressional policy embodied in this Act, except that the Commission shall not investigate information systems maintained by religious organizations.

Guidelines for study.

(3) In conducting such study, the Commission shall—

(A) determine what laws, Executive orders, regulations, directives, and judicial decisions govern the activities under study and the extent to which they are consistent with the rights of privacy, due process of law, and other guarantees in the Constitution;

(B) determine to what extent governmental and private information systems affect Federal-State relations or the principle of separation of powers;

(C) examine the standards and criteria governing programs, policies, and practices relating to the collection, soliciting, processing, use, access, integration, dissemination, and transmission of personal information; and

(D) to the maximum extent practicable, collect and utilize findings, reports, studies, hearing transcripts, and recommendations of governmental, legislative and private bodies, institutions, organizations, and individuals which pertain to the problems under study by the Commission.

(d) In addition to its other functions the Commission may—

(1) request assistance of the heads of appropriate departments, agencies, and instrumentalities of the Federal Government, of State and local governments, and other persons in carrying out its functions under this Act;

(2) upon request, assist Federal agencies in complying with the requirements of section 552a of title 5, United States Code;

(3) determine what specific categories of information, the collection of which would violate an individual's right of privacy, should be prohibited by statute from collection by Federal agencies; and

(4) upon request, prepare model legislation for use by State and local governments in establishing procedures for handling, maintaining, and disseminating personal information at the State and local level and provide such technical assistance to State and local governments as they may require in the preparation and implementation of such legislation.

(e) (1) The Commission may, in carrying out its functions under this section, conduct such inspections, sit and act at such times and places, hold such hearings, take such testimony, require by subpena the attendance of such witnesses and the production of such books, records, papers, correspondence, and documents, administer such oaths, have such printing and binding done, and make such expenditures as the Commission deems advisable. A subpena shall be issued only upon an affirmative vote of a majority of all members of the Com-

December 31, 1974   - 13 -   Pub. Law 93-579
_____
                                              88 STAT. 1908

mission. Subpenas shall be issued under the signature of the Chairman or any member of the Commission designated by the Chairman and shall be served by any person designated by the Chairman or any such member. Any member of the Commission may administer oaths or affirmations to witnesses appearing before the Commission.

(2) (A) Each department, agency, and instrumentality of the executive branch of the Government is authorized to furnish to the Commission, upon request made by the Chairman, such information, data, reports and such other assistance as the Commission deems necessary to carry out its functions under this section. Whenever the head of any such department, agency, or instrumentality submits a report pursuant to section 552a (o) of title 5, United States Code, a copy of such report shall be transmitted to the Commission.

Reports, transmittal to Commission. Ante, p. 1897.

(B) In carrying out its functions and exercising its powers under this section, the Commission may accept from any such department, agency, independent instrumentality, or other person any individually indentifiable data if such data is necessary to carry out such powers and functions. In any case in which the Commission accepts any such information, it shall assure that the information is used only for the purpose for which it is provided, and upon completion of that purpose such information shall be destroyed or returned to such department, agency, independent instrumentality, or person from which it is obtained, as appropriate.

(3) The Commission shall have the power to——

(A) appoint and fix the compensation of an executive director, and such additional staff personnel as may be necessary, without regard to the provisions of title 5, United States Code, governing appointments in the competitive service, and without regard to chapter 51 and subchapter III of chapter 53 of such title relating to classification and General Schedule pay rates, but at rates not in excess of the maximum rate for GS-18 of the General Schedule under section 5332 of such title; and

5 USC 5101, 5331.

(B) procure temporary and intermittent services to the same extent as is authorized by section 3109 of title 5, United States Code.

5 USC 5332 note.

The Commission may delegate any of its functions to such personnel of the Commission as the Commission may designate and may authorize such successive redelegations of such functions as it may deem desirable.

(4) The Commission is authorized—

(A) to adopt, amend, and repeal rules and regulations governing the manner of its operations, organization, and personnel;

Rules and regulations.

(B) to enter into contracts or other arrangements or modifications thereof, with any government, any department, agency, or independent instrumentality of the United States, or with any person, firm, association, or corporation, and such contracts or other arrangements, or modifications thereof, may be entered into without legal consideration, without performance or other bonds, and without regard to section 3709 of the Revised Statutes, as amended (41 U.S.C. 5);

(C) to make advance, progress, and other payments which the Commission deems necessary under this Act without regard to the provisions of section 3648 of the Revised Statutes, as amended (31 U.S.C. 529); and

(D) to take such other action as may be necessary to carry out its functions under this section.

88 STAT. 1909

Compensation.

(f) (1) Each [the] member of the Commission who is an officer or employee of the United States shall serve without additional compensation, but shall continue to receive the salary of his regular position when engaged in the performance of the duties vested in the Commission.

Per diem.

5 USC 5332 note.

(2) A member of the Commission other than one to whom paragraph (1) applies shall receive per diem at the maximum daily rate for GS-18 of the General Schedule when engaged in the actual performance of the duties vested in the Commission.

Travel expenses.

(3) All members of the Commission shall be reimbursed for travel, subsistence, and other necessary expenses incurred by them in the performance of the duties vested in the Commission.

Report to President and Congress.

(g) The Commission shall, from time to time, and in an annual report, report to the President and the Congress on its activities in carrying out the provisions of this section. The Commission shall make a final report to the President and to the Congress on its findings pursuant to the study required to be made under subsection (b)(1) of this section not later than two years from the date on which all of the members of the Commission are appointed. The Commission shall cease to exist thirty days after the date on which its final report is submitted to the President and the Congress.

Penalties.

(h) (1) Any member, officer, or employee of the Commission, who by virtue of his employment or official position, has possession of, or access to, agency records which contain individually identifiable information the disclosure of which is prohibited by this section, and who knowing that disclosure of the specific material is so prohibited, willfully discloses the material in any manner to any person or agency not entitled to receive it, shall be guilty of a misdemeanor and fined not more than $5,000.

(2) Any person who knowingly and willfully requests or obtains any record concerning an individual from the Commission under false pretenses shall be guilty of a misdemeanor and fined not more than $5,000.

5 USC 552a note.

Sec. 6. The Office of Management and Budget shall—

(1) develop guidelines and regulations for the use of agencies in implementing the provisions of section 552a of title 5, United States Code, as added by section 3 of this Act; and

Ante, p. 1897.

(2) provide continuing assistance to and oversight of the implementation of the provisions of such section by agencies.

5 USC 552a note.

Sec. 7. (a) (1) It shall be unlawful for any Federal, State or local government agency to deny to any individual any right, benefit, or privilege provided by law because of such individual's refusal to disclose his social security account number.

(2) the provisions of paragraph (1) of this subsection shall not apply with respect to—

(A) any disclosure which is required by Federal statute, or

(B) the disclosure of a social security number to any Federal, State, or local agency maintaining a system of records in existence and operating before January 1, 1975, if such disclosure was required under statute or regulation adopted prior to such date to verify the identity of an individual.

(b) Any Federal, State, or local government agency which requests an individual to disclose his social security account number shall inform that individual whether that disclosure is mandatory or voluntary, by what statutory or other authority such number is solicited, and what uses will be made of it.

December 31, 1974   - 15 -   Pub. Law 93-579

88 STAT. 1910

SEC. 8. The provisions of this Act shall be effective on and after the date of enactment, except that the amendments made by sections 3 and 4 shall become effective 270 days following the day on which this Act is enacted.

Effective date.
5 USC 552a
note.

SEC. 9. There is authorized to be appropriated to carry out the provisions of section 5 of this Act for fiscal years 1975, 1976, and 1977 the sum of $1,500,000, except that not more than $750,000 may be expended during any such fiscal year.

Appropriation.
5 USC 552a
note.

Approved December 31, 1974.

LEGISLATIVE HISTORY:

HOUSE REPORT No. 93-1416 accompanying H.R. 16373 (Comm. on Government
         Operations).
SENATE REPORT No. 93-1183 (Comm. on Government Operations).
CONGRESSIONAL RECORD, Vol. 120 (1974):
      Nov. 21, considered and passed Senate.
      Dec. 11, considered and passed House, amended, in lieu of
            H.R. 16373.
      Dec. 17, Senate concurred in House amendment with amendments.
      Deo. 18, House concurred in Senate amendments.
WEEKLY COMPILATION OF PRESIDENTIAL DOCUMENTS, Vol. 11, No. 1:
      Jan. 1, Presidential statement.

O

APPENDIX K

Source Materials on Security

1. Donn B. Parker, Susan Nycum and S. Stephen Oura, *Computer Abuse,* Stanford Research Institute. Available from National Technical Information Service. $4.75.

2. *Security Review Manual,* American Federation of Information Processing Societies, Montvale, New Jersey. $10.00.

3. William F. Brown, *Computer and Software Security.* Advanced Management Research, New York. $29.50.

4. James Martin, *Security, Accuracy and Privacy in Computer Systems.* Prentice-Hall, Englewood Cliffs, New Jersey. $22.50.

5. Robert H. Courtney, Jr., "Commonly Found Deficiencies in the Security of Data Processing Activities". 2 Computer Law Service, Section 2-2, Article 1.

6. Carol Estin, "System and Software Controls for On-Line Systems". 2 Computer Law Service, Section 2-2, Article 6.

7. Donn B. Parker and Susan Nycum, "The New Criminal". Datamation, Vol. 20, p. 56 (January, 1974).

8. National Bureau of Standards, *Privacy and Security in Computer Systems.* U.S. Department of Commerce, Special Publication 404 (September, 1974).

9. National Bureau of Standards, *Guidelines for Automatic Data Processing Physical Security and Risk Management.* U.S. Department of Commerce, FIPS Publication 31 (June, 1974).

10. Susan H. Nycum, "Computer Abuses Raise New Legal Problems." American Bar Association Journal Vol. 61, p. 444 (April, 1975); reprinted 3 CLSA, Section 5-1.

11. Robert P. Abbott, Liena M. Boone, Ivan M. Morvay, and Shigeru Tokubo, *A Bibliography on Computer Operating System Security,* Lawrence Livermore Laboratory, University of California, Livermore (1974).

12. Robert Patrick, "Computer Security—A Review of Recent Publications" Datamation, Vol. 20, p. 205 (April, 1974).

13. M.K. Hunt, R. Turn, *Privacy and Security in Databank Systems: An Annotated Bibliography, 1970-1973.* The Rand Corporation #R-1361-NSF.

14. Peter S. Browne, Ed., *Computer Security Manual,* Computer Security Institute, Northboro, Mass.

The Insurance of Electronic Data Processing Operations

*by H.A. Chadwick**

SOME STANDARD PROPERTY INSURANCE FORMS

When one contemplates the insurance of property, the exposure must be defined in terms of the item to be protected and the perils (that cause the damage) from which the item must be protected. *Property Insurance* includes at least Fire Insurance, which includes the perils of fire and lightning. A Fire Insurance policy's perils may be broadened by the attachment of the Extended Coverage Endorsement. Insurance men remember the perils included in the Extended Coverage Endorsement by use of the name "W. Shaver,"

---

*Mr. Chadwick is associated with a major underwriter of EDP coverages. Abridged from *Computer Law Service*, Section 2-5 Article 1. Copyright 1972 by H.A. Chadwick.

the letters in the name standing for Wind, Smoke, Hail, Aircraft, Vehicle, Explosion, Riot. Riot in this case does not include Vandalism and Malicious Mischief which must be purchased as an addition to the Extended Coverage Endorsement.

Since it is obvious that these perils do not catalog the total sources of injury to property, a number of other broadening coverages, bearing titles such as *Optional Perils* or *Broad Form* are available as "proprietary" offerings by some insurance companies. They specifically add certain other perils such as *Water Damage* (not *Flood*, but damage arising from such things as ruptures in domestic water sources and piping), collapse through weight of ice and snow, and similar selected causes. These forms by their specification of peril are known to the insurance industry as *Named Peril* forms. While frequently adequate to a given situation they share a common fault: the need to select the right peril or combination of perils. If the company has not selected a form providing protection against the peril which causes loss, the insurance might as well not have been purchased.

A community of forms known categorically as *All Risk* is becoming increasingly common. All-Risk forms, as opposed to Named-Peril forms, remove the burden of perils selection from the insured and his broker, or at least lessen it. The forms are not, of course, truly all risk in their nature since they have an insuring agreement that reads ". . . insures against all risks of direct physical loss or damage except as hereinafter provided." It is the "except" that determines the worth of the form to the client and an All Risk property form ought to exclude only those losses which are not in themselves insurable by their very nature such as wear and tear, or which are more adequately and correctly insured in a specialized form or market.

While "the-fewer-the-exclusions-the-better" is a useful rule for measuring the worth of a form, care must be taken not to overbuy. Except in specialized situations, the two most important coverage differences (and ones for which a charge will be made), are *Earthquake* and *Flood*. Earthquake may be written as a separate coverage or included within an All Risk form. The separate form may be subject to higher rates and more restrictive underwriting than the coverage would receive with an All-Risk form (no sensible reason for this—just the nature of underwriters), but even in an All-Risk form, earthquake coverage will increase the cost. Unless a client is in a known active earthquake area (seismologists tell us that every part of the country has a "quake potential," but the West Coast seems to be the only place where underwriters are loath to sell the coverage, and that is a pretty good indication that that is where it is really needed), or is locked into a lease requiring the coverage, cost comparisons for coverage with and without Earthquake should be obtained.

Flood insurance is purchased less for the occurrence of "flood" as the layman uses this term, than as a means of obtaining adequate water damage protection. Insurance policies either provide (at additional cost) remarkably broad coverage in this area, by "not excluding," or are so limited as to be inadequate for anyone except the occupant of a one-story building in the desert. If forms restrict water damage, the coverage is usually restricted only to damage arising out of domestic appliances and piping. Between this limited protection and the total coverage provided by full Flood insurance is a wide area of exposure. The failure of standing surface water to run off quickly enough after a heavy rain can cause entry of water (and damage) into a premises, as can the backing up of sewers and drains; neither of these things can be called a flood yet neither is included as Water Damage Coverage.

Unless a company is situated in an area known to suffer true flood damage, buying Flood Insurance is an unnecessarily expensive way of countering the common water exposures. A policy which excludes flood but does not otherwise exclude water damage is adequate if it can be agreed with the underwriters just what the word "flood" means.

EDP EQUIPMENT INSURANCE

The fragility (real or supposed) of electronic data processing equipment has engendered broadened variations of All Risk coverage. Beyond the treatment of exposures of Earthquake and Water Damage, inclusion of coverage for damage from electric power surges, referred to in the form as ". . . artificially generated electric power . . ." is the most notable feature. The forms (and underwriters) are silent on damage from "lack of power," i.e., the "brown outs" caused by power shortages, but since any such damage is preventable by shutting down the equipment, and the insured has a duty to prevent loss if possible, and to minimize it if not, claim for coverage of such a loss would be resisted, probably successfully.

Each category should be looked at from the standpoint of "What can happen? What is likely to happen? What can be protected at what cost?" and bought accordingly within the budget.

The survey of insurance needs must examine each category or property separately: the coverage needed to insure an IBM "main frame" properly will differ from that needed for the IBM typewriters in the steno pool. Electronic data processing equipment should not be lumped with the client's other property and protected as part of a general property form. To use one set of terms to protect all is either to over-protect the general property or to under-protect the EDP equipment.

The insurance coverage of a client's owned EDP equipment must be All Risk, with exclusions limited to only those situations and perils not likely to occur, or better covered under some other form. Ideally, a form for a company not located on the West Coast or in a river bottom or at the foot of a dam will exclude wear-and-tear (phrased more elegantly); damage to the machine from its own operation; damage caused by a dishonest employee (a very real source of damage but more adequately dealt with by a coverage known as Employee Dishonesty); and damage by flood (if the form or underwriters confirm that a "flood" means only rising waters or regularly existing bodies of water operating beyond their usual boundaries), earthquake, war (this exclusion lists civil wars and rebellions among the kinds of conflicts for whose damage the underwriters will not be responsible. None of the Detroit, Newark, or Watts-type riots of the 1960s was considered to be within this exclusion, and damage caused by them was paid under forms containing such language), and nuclear reaction (important only to a client who actually handles radioactive materials. When a client is in such a business, protection is available from a syndicate known as the Nuclear Energy Property Insurance Association which specializes in this peril. An affiliate, Nuclear Energy Liability

Insurance Association, provides comparable "third-party" coverage).

LEASED EQUIPMENT

If a client is leasing EDP equipment and the lease is silent on responsibility for insurance or fixes the responsibility of the client, coverage at least equal to the amount that would be provided for owned property is the prudent purchase; "at least equal to" because leases which hold the lessee responsible tend to do so in general terms, and include dangers against which insurance cannot be purchased. At least two EDP leasing companies offered machines under leases which required the lessee to provide insurance against "all risks" with no further ameliorating terms or exclusion. In theory the lessee would have been responsible (and uninsured) for war damage or radiation damage, even if the lessee had bought the broadest coverage available.

The original theory of net leasing sought to place the lessee in the position of owner in every way possible and this included risks of damage. The theory has been reformed by the pressures of actual practice and is now more livable. A user need not lease from a lessor whose insurance requirements are more stringent than would be satisfied by an All Risk insurance policy, properly modified to reflect the user's risk circumstances. Competition in this field has brought some sense. Competition has, in fact, brought more than sense: definite bargains in insurance are available.

Leasing companies have used their buying power, based upon the many millions of dollars of desirable property they have to insure, to obtain excellent terms and the lowest possible rates from insurance carriers, and will often quote leases including all necessary insurance. Whenever this option is offered, a comparison of costs with the client providing his own insurance should be made; it will be a rare situation where the "including insurance" quote is not the lower cost.

Some leasing firms, in buying coverage on all of their equipment under lease, have arranged a form of rental-income protection to protect their rents if a "rent-abatement-through-equipment-damage" option is exercised. The offer of lessor-arranged coverage is at least an indication that such rental income coverage may have been purchased and, because of it, more liberal abatement-through-damage terms may be available to the client.

HOW MUCH INSURANCE?

Regardless of the perils against which insurance is bought or whether property is owned or leased, the amount of insurance needed requires study. This is true whether one is discussing an electronic data processing machine, a structure or any other tangible property. In times of inflation, tax incentives for quick write-off of equipment and planned generational obsolescence make determination of the insurable value of property most difficult.

Until recently, property insurance policies presumed that property had only one value, its "actual cash value." In the eyes of insurers, property was purchased for its cost new and, as it was gradually "used up," was depreciated until it was eventually worn out and without value. At any given point the amount of "wear and tear" could be evaluated, and the residual value of the property represented its actual cash value. A basic premise of insurance is that an insured ought not to make a profit from an insured loss; insurers saw any attempt to pay losses on any other valuation basis than actual cash value as a means of giving the insured a profit; he was being paid for the used-up portion of his property. Happily this idea has largely passed from the scene and valuations other than actual cash value are obtainable, although vestiges of the old concept remain in insurance lore, producing occasional remarkable, and ineffective, compromises.

Replacement Cost valuation is offered as a standard condition by almost all insurance carriers today, but, like the term All Risk, not all Replacement Cost valuations are of equal value. If actual cash value is considered to be cost new on date of loss, less depreciation, then Replacement Cost ought to be, simply, cost new on date of loss. Almost all insurance companies modify this definition by adding "if actually replaced" reflecting their desire not to allow the insured to make a profit by using a piece of property and, by its fortuitous destruction, receiving its current new value without spending the money to replace it. This modifying condition is acceptable but it is frequently limited further. Insurers vary the amount of time allowed for such replacement from a liberal "within a reasonable time" to specified periods of as little as 90 days. Further limitations imposed by some insurers require reconstruction on the same site if a structure, or, if equipment, require that while the equipment may be new rather than used, it must be identical equipment to that lost or damaged, and not upgraded in any way. As a practical matter, limitations such as these force insureds into unwise situations if they wish to obtain full payment of the insurance purchased. Replacement Cost Valuation clauses must be examined to be certain that they allow for functional replacement and allow the client as great a freedom of action as possible.

Companies with equipment located in California must consider a new definition of actual cash value. A recent court decision held that actual cash value does not mean replacement cost less depreciation, but "fair market value"—what a willing buyer not under compulsion to buy would pay a willing seller not under compulsion to sell. It seems especially important for companies located in the state of California to purchase replacement cost insurance and avoid this muddle.

COINSURANCE

Deciding upon a method of valuation and then, in accordance with that method, arriving at an adequate insurable value is important for two reasons. Obviously an incorrect basis for valuation or an inadequate valuation will result in under-insurance at the time of loss; further, at time of loss the basis of valuation and the amount of insurance bought will figure in the application of the *Coinsurance Clause.*

The Coinsurance Clause is designed to make all insureds carry "enough" insurance so that the rates, which are based upon "enough" insurance, may properly work and yield a profit to the insurance carrier. A Coinsurance Clause or its equivalent is in almost all property insurance, or the effect of a Coinsurance Clause is obtained by some other means. The Coinsurance Clause says that an insured will carry insurance equal to a specified percentage (often 80%) of the *insurable value* of the property being insured. In consideration of this, the insured is granted a lower rate than if the clause were not included. If the clause is included and the insured does not carry insurance equal to the specified percentage, a penalty is figured by reducing any loss payment in proportion to the lack of insurance.

For example, a piece of equipment has an insurable value of $10,000, and the contract under which it is insured contains a Coinsurance Clause specifying that the insured will maintain insurance equal to at least 80 percent of that value, in this case $8,000. The insured through neglect or avarice actually buys only $6,000 of insurance. In the event of a loss the insured will receive three-fourths of his loss payment ($6,000/$8,000 equals 3/4) up to the limit of the insurance policy. This happens not only in the case of total loss but in the event of partial loss: theoretically, in the example given, if the insured equipment were to be damaged enough to require $1,000 of repair work, the insurance company would pay only $750, even though there was much more insurance in force than the needed $1,000.

The Coinsurance Clause problem is dealt with by deciding upon a means of valuation, either actual cash value, replacement cost, or some other "tailored" values, whichever suits the company's circumstances, by making certain that the customer and his insurance broker's understanding of that valuation agrees with the underwriters, and then by valuing or appraising the property against that valuation standard to establish the needed amount of insurance. The appraisal may be made by one of the several firms specializing in such appraisal work, or by dealers in new and used equipment who will often quote prices for new and used equipment in the hope of obtaining orders when additional purchases are made, or by the insurance broker's own staff as one of the services that may be offered by the broker to obtain the business.

To express the agreement of the underwriters and the insured once the valuation method and insurable value have been established, insurers have developed several forms of terminology. Policy endorsements entitled "Agreed Amount," "Stated Amount," or "Stipulated Amount" are available. These forms impose certain minor duties upon the insured in terms of maintaining adequate appraisals and records but do clear up doubt as to whether or not the requirements of the Coinsurance Clause have been met. A less formal but equally effective technique is the practice of supplying the insurer, through the client's broker, at regular intervals with updated statements of the values that have been established.

GENERAL OFFICE EQUIPMENT

A data processing operation's activities may center about the computer but other equipment cannot be ignored for it is vital to the client's operation. General equipment insurance needs are determined by the same method as is applied to the electronic data processing equipment itself. The tests of adequacy of perils and correctness of evaluation must be met. All Risk terms are advisable although the supposedly more durable nature of such equipment would allow more exclusions in the form, limiting the protection without unduly increasing the hazard. Such decrease in protection ought to cause the rate to be charged for All Risk on general office equipment to be less than the rate charged for All Risk on the electronic data processing machine. Office equipment is not readily traced and is very easily disposed of by the amateur thief. The recent boom in such thefts shows that this is becoming increasingly known. Since All Risk insurance includes Burglary and Theft, the protection against these perils is reason enough to buy the coverage.

Deciding upon the correct valuation method for general office equipment and setting the insurable value in terms of that valuation is as important as the valuation and determination of insurable value of the client's EDP equipment, but is a good deal easier, as there is a ready market in both new and used office equipment of all types and the prices charged will be available to set the value of the inventory of equipment.

EDP BUILDING MODIFICATIONS

Electronic data processing installations frequently require extensive modification of that portion of the building in which they are housed. Pedestal floors in the EDP machine area, walls and partitions that isolate the area, separate specialized temperature and humidity controls, as well as the duct work and climate-control machinery, all represent considerable expenditures. If the user owns the building, the insurance broker must be reminded that the insurable value of the Improvements and Betterments are to be included in the insurable value set upon the building and documented (appraisal or letter of intent to the underwriters) in such a way that there will be no question if loss or damage should occur. The same need exists of the user as a tenant, but the complicating factor of lease requirements is present. If the tenant must insure the Improvements and Betterments they may be included in the policy dealing with general office contents. It is possible for the insurance broker to apply a separate rate made on just the Improvements and Betterments and if they are extensive enough ($25,000 or more in value would be a reasonable starting point) this should be suggested to the broker, as specific rates on Improvements and Betterments are lower than the General Contents and Equipment rate. (A separate rate will not be needed if the client is the building owner and has the Improvements and Betterments added to his building's insurable value, as building rates will be lower than either Improvement and Betterment rates or Contents rates.)

MEMORY DEVICES AND SOFTWARE

The raw material feeding, and end product of, the electronic data processing machinery is referred to in general as *media*. Data processors themselves are more specific and tend to refer to the type of media they mean as cards, tapes, disc packs, or drums, but the term *media* is inclusive and understandable enough in dealing with the company's insurance broker.

If the user processes media only for its own purposes there will be no question as to responsibility to insure, but if the computer organization uses slack time on its installation, or is primarily engaged in processing for others, this responsibility must also be dealt with. The work order agreement under which such processing is done should deal with the responsibility for obtaining insurance (if the data processor is not to obtain the insurance his customer should waive subrogation rights against the processor to avoid having the customer's insurance company attempt recovery, from the processor, of a loss payment made to the customer); if the agreement requires the processor to maintain coverage it must also set forth the value of the media or, if that is not possible, how value may be determined in the event it is lost or damaged.

Valuation, this problem of setting a value to a media, also faces the user who processes its own media exclusively. Traditional valuation techniques can be summarized as "cost of media blank, (e.g.. a new disc pack) plus cost of reproduction." Too often "reproduction" is considered to be "transcription," that is, the cost of reconstructing from easily available sources, little more than copying. In a catastrophe, reproduction may well require the development of the original, raw, source material and the total rerunning of all programs to refine that raw data to the point where it is a replacement for the lost media. Such total reconstruction costs considerably more than transcription from easily available documents. In some situations it has been necessary to compute the actual cost of producing a tape or disc by estimating the clerical time needed to produce the cards that were later converted to the tape, the salary cost of that clerical time including all assigned expenses and overhead and, using that estimate as a basis, to project the probable percentage of unidentified cost by increasing that base by some arbitrary factor such as 25 percent or 50 percent to arrive at an adequate limit. The EDP supervisor and the controller should be available to the insurance broker to help him construct the owned-media valuation. If the broker does not use this help, the valuation method developed by the broker should be explained to the EDP supervisor and controller for their reaction.

INTERRUPTION OF OPERATIONS

In spite of adequate valuations and purchase of sufficiently high limits of insurance on electronic data processing equipment or other property, no business endures a catastrophe unscathed. Operating, even a losing business earns a part of its expenses and carries the hope of improving its results. Shut down by a disaster such as a fire, a prosperous business may not reopen its doors. Expenses that continue in spite of the shutdown, loss of customers to competitors, as well as loss of key men to those same competitors, can turn even a relatively short shutdown into a permanent one.

A number of ways are open to a company to be sure that damage to property will not wipe it out. Insurance men refer to this area of protection as *Time Element* since it revolves around the expected length of time needed to restore business to its prior level of operation. Perhaps the most familiar of these coverages is *Business Interruption*, which attempts to restore to a shutdown business its lost profits, if any, and expenses. The most common of such forms is referred to as *Gross Earnings*. This is a Coinsurance form; the coinsurance percentage would be applied against the gross earnings (defined as sales less cost of materials sold) at the date of loss, not the date on which the insurance was purchased. The broker must be adequately advised on the company's expected growth rate, and the adequacy of the amount of insurance purchases should be reviewed at least annually to avoid application of a coinsurance penalty if loss occurs. It is possible to reduce this amount of insurance required to be bought by limiting ordinary payroll or eliminating it entirely from the definition of gross earnings thereby reducing the amount of insurance needed to satisfy the computation of the Coinsurance Clause. This stipulation raises the rate and, considering the importance to a client of his data processing staff, seems a false economy in most situations. The minimum coinsurance allowed with the Gross Earnings form is 50 percent, requiring the coverage to be bought for one half of the year's gross earnings. If replacement equipment and facilities are available in a lesser period of time, this will force an overbuying of limit and may make other seemingly more expensive forms (more expensive because of certain more attractive features) competitive. When a decision is made that a business can be restored in a shorter time period than that indicated by the Coinsurance Clause, it must be remembered that the clause specifies a percentage of gross earnings and an expression of those dollar gross earnings in "time" is rendered invalid by seasonal variations in operation.

The client's broker has available as an alternate form or protection *Earnings* insurance which, for a slightly higher rate, will provide a monthly limitation of payment in lieu of a Coinsurance Clause and a more bearable definition of what is insured. (Earnings is net profit plus continuing expenses as determined by the client.)

Available in the insurance marketplace, but not known to many insurance men, is a variety of per diem coverage forms. These forms provide a total limit of insurance and specify an amount-per-day-of-downtime that will be paid. They do not contain a Coinsurance Clause nor do they require that the insured define the usages to which the loss payment will be applied. In the broadest form in which these coverages are written, the cessation of operations must be proved (by previously defined measure) but an actual loss need not be proved. Just as all All Risk is not the same, so all per diem forms are not of equal value. Lessor forms that may be offered limit the per diem loss by tying it to "actual loss sustained" which may be infinitely more difficult to prove on a per diem basis than under a Gross Earnings, and include as part of the policy an application and worksheet; the user warrants the accuracy of his preparation as a condition of the coverage. The more limited forms do not carry lower rates and the effect of their limitations must be considered before they are accepted.

Not a form condition, but a practice of underwriters must also be guarded against: in writing coverage for as specialized an operation as electronic data processing, underwriters will occasionally attempt to limit per diem forms to loss arising out of damage to the machines they insure for physical damage, justifying their action by the complementary nature of the loss payments. A client may depend heavily for his operation on machines leased from others and insured by the lessor. Damage to such a machine would halt the client's operation without providing him with a "valid" claim under his per diem form.

A major carrier in this field denied liability for a claim on these grounds. Fire for which the insured was not responsible damaged climate-conditioning equipment owned by the building owner and needed in the data processing operation but not under the control of the data processing tenant. To avoid injuring his insured equipment the data processor ceased operations and presented a claim for the downtime which was denied on the grounds that damage had not occurred to "insured" property. The data processor brought suit against the carrier and established liability. Datatab, Inc. v. St. Paul Fire & Marine Ins. Co., 3 CLSR 238.

Ideally, the best interruption is no interruption at all. Given enough funds and some foresight, you can lessen any downtime, and in some cases eliminate it entirely. Foresight is the key: before a catastrophe strikes, alternate facilities may be arranged (and guaranteed by contract) with a competitor having a compatible configuration of equipment. Compatibility of facilities is a relative thing and no EDP room supervisor will ever be entirely happy with substitute facilities, but his objections will be less, and more meaningful, if they are heard and answered in advance. The "extra" costs incurred in operating in substitute facilities will include such things as payment to the substitute facility operator, cost of transporting the EDP staff and media to the temporary site, cost of additional staff to accommodate the problems inherent in using a makeshift system, and a myriad of unforeseeable but very real expenses. Business Interruption forms provide some payment for such temporary costs if they are incurred in maintaining operations and will reduce or prevent a Business Interruption claim; such payments, however, are limited to the amount that the insurance carrier saves and no more. This amount saved is a difficult thing to prove and unless the user is prepared to stand the expense out of its own pocket if the expense is disallowed, a dangerous one to attempt to predict.

Coverages titled *Extra Expense* or *Additional Expense* are available. The intent of these forms is to provide the "Extra Expense necessarily incurred in continuing normal business activities"; they do meet the need. In an attempt to make insureds buy enough coverage, most such forms provide that no more than a specified percent of the amount purchased is payable in any one 30 day period. The function of this limitation is akin to the Coinsurance Clause in property insurance. The maximum rate of payment is 40 percent in the first month. In recent years this need to "overbuy" has been removed as some carriers now offer Extra Expense with a full limit available in the first month. The user needs as much freedom of action as possible and the adequacy of limited forms offered by the insurance broker must be weighed before they are accepted.

It is possible to buy all of the *Time Element* forms on the same All Risk terms as are available for direct property damage. It makes little sense to insure this important field of protection for fewer or more limited perils than is provided in the machinery forms.

INTERNAL DISHONESTY

A major exclusion in the All Risk forms and one against which protection must be bought is the area of *Employee Dishonesty* commonly referred to as *Fidelity* or simply *Bonding*. A typical clause says that the carrier will "pay and make good to the insured . . . losses . . . sustained . . . of money, securities, and other property through any fraudulent or dishonest act . . . committed by . . . employees of . . . insured." Other insuring clauses will go on to protect, specifically, money and securities (excluded by general property forms) from destruction, disappearance or "wrongful extraction" on or off the premises, or acceptance of counterfeit money orders or forgery or alteration of checks and drafts issued by the insured.

While it is possible to limit the cost of such protection by naming the employees to which it applies (by job or by name), prudence dictates that all employees be covered. Electronic data processing machines, with their lack of readily-available-to-auditors written records, provide unique "hiding places" for embezzlements. Enterprising though dishonest employees have used computers to maintain fictitious payrolls, to round-off a few cents from each coworker's paycheck to credit to their own, or to commit more traditional acts of embezzlement through bypassing audit checks. The "mystique" of the computer room provides an especially good cloak for such activities and an Employee Dishonesty bond with a sufficiently high limit applying to all employees, coupled with effective internal audit controls, is the best defense. An additional benefit from such a bond will be the recommendations to improve the internal audits and controls that the insurance carrier may make.

Of special importance to the electronic data processing field is the problem of theft of information contained in the media, since the computer area represents a centralizing of the informational life-blood of any firm. While such acts, when discovered, provide grounds for criminal prosecution and perhaps civil damage suits against beneficiaries of those thefts, the Fidelity bond does not provide for restitution of the financial loss suffered. This nonpayment is not based upon a policy exclusion but rather upon a valuation clause which under the heading *Other Property* states "in no event shall the Company be liable . . . for more than the actual cost of . . . replacing any such other property with property of like quality and value." The words "like quality and value" refer to the material value of the records and not the information contained therein. Insurance companies have begun to update their forms to give clearer statements of coverage. A 1970 edition of a major carrier's bond says, "This bond does not cover . . . the cost of reproducing any information contained in any lost or damaged books of account or other records."

If the EDP organization is engaged in the processing of media for others the problem is still more acute, since the internal auditing controls that client's customers have in effect will not be applied to the client's own employees. The Public Liability Insurance available to the user will exclude property in its "care, custody and control" and will not provide for defending the user against a suit based upon the theft of information from its customer's records. Protection against this exposure requires consideration of several areas: the user's own internal audit procedures, the contractual definition of responsibility (or lack of it) designed by counsel, and some limited and expensive specialized insurance. While there is no "standard" form of coverage available in this area, underwriters can be approached and occasionally will attempt the necessary protection. Recently, a life insurance company "rented" its culled mailing list to a processor, but, before releasing the list to the processor, insisted upon some guarantee that an illicit copy of the list would not be developed. A solution offered by the underwriter was a tailor-made form covering the information contained on the tapes, valuing it at so much per name (apparently a readily identifiable value and upon which rental fees of such lists are based). The rate quoted by the underwriter for the coverage was one percent of the agreed-upon valuation.

ERRORS AND OMISSIONS

The entrusting of vital information and information services by one firm to another, occasioned by the growth of the electronic data processing service industry, has created new areas of potential liability for a data processor. Error in processing the data of others has provided successful grounds for damage actions. The need for protection against such damage actions has caused the development of *Data Processing Errors and Omissions* coverages. The company's Public Liability policy provides coverage for damages arising out of Personal Injury (or Bodily Injury) and Property Damage. But damages arising out of data processing errors and omissions are based upon neither and are therefore not covered by "standard" Comprehensive General Liability forms. There is no "standard" form of Electronic Data Processing Errors and Omissions coverage but the language used by several insurance companies is quite similar, and will begin with an insuring clause that reads, "to pay on behalf of the insured sums which the insured shall become legally obligated to pay as damages by reason of claim against the insured arising out of negligent act," making no reference to bodily injury or to property damage.

The "insuring agreement" will state the activity from which errors or omissions may arise and in so doing may so limit the coverage as to render it useless for the client's purpose. A typical form will say, "in the processing of data or records of others in the insured's business as a data processor." But other forms say such things as, "in the processing of financial data or financial records of others."

Insurance underwriters are loath to define the boundaries of "data processing" but at least one prominent company in the field admits that it will include the necessary systems design and programming inherent in a processing system; that is, software errors in processing a customer's data are covered. This insurer, however, attempts to "underwrite out" those insureds who are primarily software designers. Before the data processor accepts the term "processing," an agreement that the term includes the necessary support programming should be obtained from the insurance company.

Major exclusions from this coverage are: liability to others assumed by the client under contract; libel; invasion of privacy; dishonest, fraudulent or criminal act; and liability for punitive damages.

By its use of the term "processing" and the exclusions, the typical Data Processing Error and Omission coverage resists attempts to expand it to a policy covering general business error.

Recently, an underwriter was asked if a salesman's error in promising delivery date could be construed as a "data processing error." He replied that the policy was an honest attempt to provide coverage for errors arising in the performance of work for others and was not a general business guarantee policy. Thus, prices quoted by salesmen, incorrect delivery dates, promises of internal savings which mislead a customer, and the like, may result in claims entirely outside of any data processing policy purchased by the client.

Not all errors in data processing are discovered immediately and the effects of an error may continue to be felt long after the original error has been corrected. If a company is to receive maximum value for its protection, any policy it accepts must contain provisions allowing for reporting of claims after the policy expires or is cancelled, based upon errors occurring before the termination date. If a policy does not contain such language providing for a "discovery period" of adequate time (except in special situations six-to-twelve-month discovery periods are granted with regularity), an otherwise insured claim may be disallowed only because it was reported after the termination date.

An EDP manager will occasionally find that his company has in force a policy without an adequate discovery period. The company is not thereby "married" to its existing insurance company in fear of termination and loss of protection. It is possible to obtain from some underwriters coverage for acts prior to the inception date of their policy. Stated generally, the intent of the extension granted by these companies is that they will pay for acts prior to their policy's inception, if valid insurance was in force on the date of the act (even though not discovered within the valid policy period) and such valid insurance is no longer collectable. They will grant no more coverage than would have been available under the replaced form but will in effect provide the missing, and needed, discovery period.

Data processors traditionally process a customer's data on an individual basis with the result that a single error will cause a single claim. An increasing number of processors, however, are dealing in "package programs" which enable them to apply a single program to many separate customers. Such package programs can cause many claims from a single error. If a data processor uses package programs, the limit of liability in the Data Processing Errors and Omissions form must apply per *claim*, that is, the amount of the policy is available for a payment of damages to each of the multiple claimants, rather than applying per *occurrence*, which would provide the limit of the policy for all claims arising out of the error.

Claims in the data processing field are often avoided by the correct rerunning of erroneously run programs, thereby satisfying the customer. While such a rerunning is in effect a claim-avoiding technique, it is a "cost of doing business expense" akin to the "damaged during manufacturing" problems that arise in any other industry and for this reason insurance men are opposed to paying such claims. They feel, correctly, that a large number of such claims would tend to result in a spiraling "dollar swapping" situation with their insureds. Since such claims are within the language of the policy, although not the intent, the traditional elimination device has been a form of deductible set high enough to avoid the average "rerun" cost of the data processor. Assuming that the company's form has deductible to reduce its cost, the terminology of the deductible, that is "per claim" or "per occurrence" must be reformed to match its operation, as was the case with its limit of insurance. The application of a deductible to *each claim* arising out of a *single error* in a *package* program might, however, cost the insured 30 or 40 times the amount it expected to absorb in the event of a claim. For this reason, a package program user should consider requiring its deductible to be applied *per occurrence* (that is, for each error) even though its limit is to apply per claim. Conversely, a processor not using package programs may want its deductible to be applied per claim.

FINDING THE RIGHT BROKER

The right broker is the one who can successfully identify all the company's exposures to loss or claim, and obtain coverage at a reasonable cost. As a minimum, the company has a right to expect that insurance be purchased on its behalf in the amounts and for the purposes specified, and that its broker will maintain close enough contact, and deep enough interest, to keep coverages up-to-date. An annual review of the program by the broker is to be expected.

Considering the highly sophisticated nature of the insurance requirements of electronic data processing machine ownership and use, the personal-service oriented generalists should be avoided. The "hometown" real estate, insurance, notary public, and travel agency, while a valuable member of the community and providing very necessary services, hardly represents the skills required by the user of EDP equipment.

Many of the extremely large brokerage houses offer a battery of services such as staff appraisers, staff adjusters, and surveyors to detect hazard and prevent loss (and reduce rates) as well as a structured organization to manage the account executives and their subordinates who service the insured. As an additional benefit such a "Super Broker" has the ability to exert leverage on an insurance company to extract underwriting concessions and have doubts resolved in favor of the insured. Obviously, such an organization as described is capable of fully meeting the insured's needs. It is possible, however, in dealing with a Super Broker, to receive second-class treatment. It is not unusual to hear of cases where companies had been given expert handling by an account team of first quality only to find their annual reviews conducted by a disinterested clerk via telephone. The danger of becoming a small fish in a big pond is present.

Between the extremes of the Super Broker and the small town agency are a vast number of insurance organizations of varying quality. Among these are many brokers capable of satisfying the needs of any insured. They may not maintain a full range of staff adjusters, appraisers, and surveyors but the brokers are often capable of performing these services themselves in a highly interested fashion. What is a relatively small account to a Super Broker can be the mainstay of a medium-sized agency. Consider an agency of two or three principals with some spread in age indicating infusion from time to time of new blood and ideas, as well as stability and continuity. Attractive, well-organized premises with an able clerical staff and an air of quiet efficiency in the office will often be the first sign of such an organization. Agency representation (or a strong brokerage affiliation) with perhaps a half-dozen of the major insurance companies is a further indication. The major companies are extremely selective in the agency appointments they make and keep, and the representation of such companies by the agent is an indication of his worth. Questions concerning staff services may reveal that the agent has, in addition to his own ability to perform in these areas, the support of specialists from some of his insurance companies in providing such services and in many cases such talent may well exceed that available through the Super Broker's staff. An agressive, skilled medium-sized agency can often out-perform the Super Broker both in initial insurance counseling and in long-range servicing.

Once selected, the broker of record ought not to be replaced without good cause. It is always possible for a broker to find an underwriter willing to shave a few mils off the rate being charged a profitable account by a competitor in the hope of switching the business, but such shaving may well be at the expense of some of the finer points of coverage or liberality of interpretation.

Index

279

Privacy Act (1974), 139*fn*
    facsmiile, 239-53
    provisions of, 142-43
Privilege, in regard to defamation, 133-34
Privity, definition, 8
Process control, as cause of labor-management
    problems, 159-60
Products liability, 131-32
Program products-licenses, as contracts, 117-18
Property insurance forms, 257-58
Proprietary legal rights:
    hardware and software, 61-63
    protection:
    competition, 161
    two party programs, 63-64
Protection of Electronic Computer/Data Processing
    Equipment standard, 170
Publication, definition, 196

"Rateable amortization," 52-53
Records:
    corporate requirements, 16-18
    improper reliance on, 18
    Internal Revenue definition, 183-184
    Internal Revenue definition, 183-84
    retention facilities required, 19-20
    tax, 19-20
Regulatory forces, 23-38
Replacement cost valuation, 262-63
Reports, definition, 6
Report system, and poor design of, 15
Request for Proposals (RFP), as procurement activity
Request for Proposals (RFP), as procurement
    activity, 113
Res Ipsa Loquitur, 129, 136
Robinson-Patman Act, 93, 175
Rostow Report, 25*fn*, 38
Routine decisions, 15

Satellites (*see* Communications, COMSAT)
Securities and Exchange Commission (SEC), 41, 149
Security:
    bibliographical sources, 255-56
    internal risks, 165
    legal aspects, 166-67
    people, planning for, 165
    physical, planning for, 165
    as responsibility, 163
    and risk assessment, 164-65
    and value analysis, 163-64
Service bureaus, roles of, 119-20
Sherman Antitrust Act (1890), 42, 93, 95, 174, 175
Site preparation, space and security checklist, 217-18
Slander, 133
Software:
    basic system specifications, 216-17
    contracts for, 117-19
    definition, 52-53
    difficulties, 53-55
    expensing and amortizing, 47-49
    federal taxation, 51-52
    insurance on, 267-68
    proprietary legal rights in, 61-63
    protection:
        antitrust considerations, 93-95
        common law methods, 65-71
        federal preemption, 91-93
        statutory methods, 74-95
    state taxation, 55
Standard damages, 107
Standards, 20-22

Stanford Research Institute, 42, 122, 165
Statute of Frauds, 103
Straight-line method, 47, 48 (*T*)
Strict liability, 131
Sum of the year's digits method, 49
System design, checklist of critical factors, 213-15

Tariffs, 39-40
Taxation:
    cash flow, 46-49
    of computer services, 56-57
    customs duties, 55-56
    federal hardware, 49-50
    federal softwae, 51-55
    state and local hardware, 50-51
    state software, 55
Tax legislation, 8
Tax records, 19-20
Telpak, problems with, 31-32
Tie-in, definition, 93-94
Time Element insurance forms, 268, 271
Time-sharing and networks, 39-41, 120-21
Tort-feasor, definition, 127
Torts, 127-37
Trademarks, 90
Trade secrets:
    definition, 67
    liability for misuse, 67-68
    as protective method, 62-63
TRW Credit Data Corp., 146, 147

Unfair competition, 132-33
    as common-law doctrine, 68-69
    and federal preemption, 91-93
Unfair price discrimination, 175
Uniform Commercial Code (UCC), 69, 70, 102, 105,
    112, 113, 117, 120
Unions:
    automation and process control, 158-60
    and data processing department, 157-58
U.S. Patent Office, 81, 84, 87, 88, 89
    position of with respect to software patents, 82-83

Value analysis, and computer security, 163-64
Vendor contracts, analysis of, 111
Vendor leasing, 115-16
Vendors, problems with multiple, 123-24
Vicarious liability, 131

"Warm-body"contracts, 118
Warranties, 105-106
Western Electric Co., 43, 44, 90
Western Union, 32, 34
Wide Area Telephone Service (WATS), 32
Wire communications, regulatory problems with,
    31-32

CASE TABLE

Accountant's Computer Services v. Kosydar, 57
Arnold D. Kamen & Co. v. Young, 17
ADAPSO v. data-processing by banks, 16, 43
Baker v. Selden, 76
Bernhart and Fetter, 85, 87
Boeing Co. v. Seattle Professional Engineering
    Employees Ass'n., 159
Bunker-Ramo Corp. v. Porterfield, 57
Carterfone, 28-29, 185